Sport and National Identity in Post-War World

What is the relationship between sport and national identity? What can sport tell us about changing perceptions of national identity?

Bringing together the work of established historians and younger commentators, this illuminating text surveys the last half-century, giving due attention to the place of sport in our social and political history.

It includes studies of:

- English football and British decline
- Englishness and sport
- Ethnicity and nationalism in Scotland
- Social change and national pride in Wales
- Irish international football and Irishness
- Sport and identity in South Africa
- Cricket and identity crisis in the Caribbean
- Baseball, exceptionalism and American sport
- Popular mythology surrounding the sporting rivalry between New Zealand and Australia.

Sport and National Identity in the Post-War World presents a wealth of original research into contemporary social history and provides illuminating material for historians and sociologists alike.

Adrian Smith is a Senior Lecturer in History at the University of Southampton, and has published widely in modern British and Commonwealth history.

Dilwyn Porter is a Reader in History at University College Worcester, and has published widely in modern British social and political history and the history of sport.

Sport and National Identity in the Post-War World

Edited by Adrian Smith and Dilwyn Porter

LONDON AND NEW YORK

First published 2004
by Routledge
11 New Fetter Lane, London EC4P 4EE

Simultaneously published in the USA and Canada
by Taylor & Francis Inc
29 West 35th Street, New York, NY 10001

Routledge is an imprint of the Taylor & Francis Group

Typeset in Times by Wearset Ltd, Boldon, Tyne and Wear
Printed and bound in Great Britain by MPG Books Ltd, Bodmin

Every effort has been made to ensure that the advice and
information in this book is true and accurate at the time of going to
press. However, neither the publisher nor the authors can accept any
legal responsibility or liability for any errors or omissions that may
be made. In the case of drug administration, any medical procedure
or the use of technical equipment mentioned within this book, you
are strongly advised to consult the manufacturer's guidelines.

British Library Cataloguing in Publication Data
A catalogue record for this book is available from the British Library

Library of Congress Cataloging in Publication Data
A catalog record for this book has been requested

ISBN 0–415–28300–0 (hbk)
ISBN 0–415–28301–9 (pbk)

Contents

Contributors

Francis D. Cogliano is Reader in American History at the University of Edinburgh and is the author of *Revolutionary America 1763–1815: A Political History* (Routledge, 2000). He has published on the subject of American national identity in the *Journal of American Studies* and is presently writing a book on Thomas Jefferson's reputation.

Michael Holmes is Director of European Studies at Liverpool Hope University College. He has researched and written on various aspects of Irish foreign policy and the role of Ireland in Europe. He is co-author of *The Poor Relation: Irish Foreign Policy and the Third World* (Trocaire, 1993) and co-editor of *Ireland and India: Connections, Comparisons, Contrasts* (Folens, 1997).

Martin Johnes is Senior Lecturer in Sports Studies at St Martin's College, Lancaster. His publications include *Soccer and Society: South Wales 1900–39* (University of Wales Press, 2002) and *Sport in Wales, 1800–2000* (St. David's Press, 2003). He is an executive member of the British Society of Sports History.

Marc Keech is Senior Lecturer in Sports Studies at the Chelsea School, University of Brighton. He has written a number of articles on sport in South Africa and is the co-editor of *Issues and Values in Sport and Leisure Cultures* (Meyer and Meyer, 2000). As well as teaching and researching in domestic and international sport policy, Marc has also undertaken client-based research for Sport England and the South East Regional Sports Board.

Ronald Kowalski is Senior Lecturer in Russian/Soviet History at University College Worcester. His previous publications have focused on the Russian Revolution, in particular on the ideologies of the revolutionary movements. More recently, he has begun to research and write on the history of British–East European sports relations since 1945, co-authoring 'Political Football: Moscow Dynamo in Britain, 1945' in the *International Journal of the History of Sport* (1997).

Martin Polley is Senior Lecturer in Sport Studies at the University of Southampton. He is the author of *Moving the Goalposts: A History of Sport and Society since 1945* (Routledge, 1998), *A–Z of Modern Europe since 1789* (Routledge, 2000) and various articles on sports history in the *Sports Historian*, the *International Journal of the History of Sport* and *Contemporary British History*. His five-volume collection of edited primary sources, *The History of Sport in Britain, 1880–1914*, was published by Routledge in 2003.

Dilwyn Porter is Reader in History at University College Worcester. He has contributed articles on the social history of football in post-war England to the *International Journal of the History of Sport* and *Contemporary British History* and reviews regularly for *Soccer and Society*. He co-edited, with Adrian Smith, *Amateurs and Professionals in Post-War British Sport* (Frank Cass, 2000). Among other interests he is currently researching the history of financial journalism and the history of mail order retailing.

Keith A.P. Sandiford has long been recognised as a major authority on the history of West Indies cricket, and is Emeritus Professor in History at the University of Manitoba.

Adrian Smith is Senior Lecturer in History at the University of Southampton and has published widely in modern British and Commonwealth history. Previous books include *The New Statesman: Portrait of a Political Weekly* (Frank Cass, 1996) and *Mick Mannock, Fighter Pilot: Myth Life and Politics* (Palgrave, 2001). Recent articles on the history of rugby union have appeared in *Contemporary British History* and the *International Journal of the History of Sport*.

David Storey is Senior Lecturer in Geography at University College Worcester. He has research interests in national identity, territoriality, migration and rural social change. He is the author of *Territory: The Claiming of Space* (Prentice Hall, 2001) and *Citizen, State and Nation* (Geographical Association, 2003).

Introduction

Adrian Smith and Dilwyn Porter

The relationship between sport and national identity is complex and multi-faceted. Arguably it has become more so since the end of the Second World War as the far-flung empires established by Britain and other European powers in the nineteenth century disintegrated and independent states legitimised by the principle of national self-determination were created. These developments tended to raise levels of national consciousness across the globe. Nationalist ideologies remain an important factor in determining the course of world politics, not least when they are frustrated or otherwise unfulfilled. While this has been happening, however, various countervailing developments have become apparent. In many parts of the globe, for example in Western Europe, regional co-operation between groups of nation states for economic, military and political purposes has been a major feature of the post-war experience. More generally, the emergence of a powerful corporate multinationalism, along with the increasing tendency for media output to transcend territorial boundaries, threatens to submerge individual awareness of national identity in an ocean of globalised consumerism. In addition, people of almost all nationalities have become more mobile. Mass migration, in pursuit of freedom from danger or economic self-advancement, has become commonplace.

These changes have provided the context in which sport, both within and between nations, has developed across the second half of the twentieth century and into the twenty-first. Nation states, multinational corporations and diasporas have proliferated simultaneously. It is a confusing and complex backdrop, ever shifting at someone else's behest, like the electronic advertising boards that now routinely surround the field of play when nation meets nation at football. In these circumstances, the relationship between sport and national identity surfaces in a variety of forms and it is the intention to explore some of the most important of these in the chapters that follow.

The idea, for example, that sport in general, or one sport in particular, creates or fosters a sense of nationhood is important, not least because international competition generates a seemingly endless number of occasions when nations are embodied in something manifestly real and visible.

Having once made the requisite imaginative leap and accepted that the eleven men who appear in white shirts at Wembley, or the fifteen at Twickenham, are 'England', the possibilities for defining or redefining what it means to be 'English' are inextricably linked to what happens on the field of play. And the English are not unique in this respect. The success enjoyed by the Irish Republic's soccer team in the late 1980s and early 1990s, according to Michael Holmes and David Storey, 'made Ireland exist'.[1] It might also be argued that the astute exploitation of FIFA's qualification rules, enabling the sons and grandsons of exiled Irishmen and women to wear the green shirt, conferred a kind of cultural legitimacy on the Irish diaspora. It certainly made it more visible.

But if sport supplies a mirror that a people holds up to itself we have to accept that the reflected image is often clouded with confusion. Indeed, how, given the competing tendencies evident in the global economy and world politics, could it be otherwise? Ethnic minorities submerged within a majority national culture, for example, may identify more strongly in some circumstances with representatives of the nation state that they or their parents have left rather than with the one they actually inhabit. A tour of England by an Indian, Pakistani or West Indian test cricket side finds Edgbaston or the Oval crowded with people born in England who would cheerfully fail Lord Tebbit's famous 'cricket test'.[2] This reminds us that sporting occasions may provide as many opportunities not to belong as to belong and that a sense of what we are not may be as important as a sense of what we are in determining national identity. The traditional indifference of nationalists in Northern Ireland to the fortunes of the team that plays its home internationals at Belfast's Windsor Park contrasts starkly with their enthusiasm for and interest in the Irish Republic's recent performances in international competition. It betokens a whole set of attitudes derived from their view of the legitimacy of the state they inhabit and their place in it.

There are other ways in which the image in the mirror might confuse. Given the global movements of population in the post-war era, it is increasingly likely that those who wear a nation's sporting colours may have a rather complicated relationship with the country they represent. 'Fate had decreed that he should marry and settle in South Africa', it has been observed of 'Sandy' Greig, father of Tony, England's cricket captain in the 1970s, 'but he still had the right to feel that his sons were eligible to play for England, even though he was a Scotsman'.[3] 'English' cricketers, born in South Africa or Zimbabwe, (not to mention Scotland and Wales), spring to mind here, along with New Zealand-born rugby union players appearing for the home team at Edinburgh or Cardiff. It seems important to ask if this development weakens links between sport and national identity that have previously been taken for granted or if it might, in some circumstances, break them altogether. It might be recalled that the British public never took Zola Budd, the South African-born distance runner granted a passport to enable her to compete in the Los Angeles Olympics, to its collective heart. But, again, the picture is more complicated than this might suggest. Jack Charlton, manager of the Irish Republic's most successful international soccer team, achieved folk hero status in his adopted land, despite being English born and bred. He recalled that this was subsequently acknowledged more formally when the Irish Prime Minister, Charles Haughey, 'made me an honorary Irishman, in a little function over a few drinks in his office'.[4]

Other complications arise when national identity is traditionally associated with a particular sport, not least when changing political, economic and social conditions erode the connection. The legend that rugby union coaches in South Wales simply have to whistle down a convenient coal mine to find an outside-half of international quality dies hard but seems increasingly fanciful in a largely post-industrial landscape. Moreover, the capacity of rugby union to represent the Welsh nation is diminished as alternative leisure opportunities multiply and the ethnic composition of those living within its borders becomes more varied. Cardiff's Millennium Stadium may well be a source of justifiable pride as, indeed, occasionally, are the red-shirted team that plays rugby there. At a time, however, when even Plaid Cymru ('The Party for Wales') has adopted an English-language subtitle, it may be that the capacity of the Welsh side to embody modern Wales and all its inhabitants, by taking on the English in the time-honoured fashion at rugby, has been reduced. Caribbean cricket supplies another example. Now that the various islands have achieved independent political status the very idea of 'the West Indies' seems a relic of British rule. Increasingly young men look to American basketball, beamed in via satellite television, for their sporting role models. In these changed circumstances, cricket has lost the unique capacity it once had to embody the aspirations of black Afro-Caribbeans in that region and elsewhere. West Indian fast bowlers rattling the ribs of hapless English batsmen was a defining motif of the immediate post-colonial era, but that era has now passed.

Some sports, it seems, are more effective than others in serving as cultural signifiers of national identity. Followers of English football, reeling from the shock of their team's 6–3 defeat by Hungary in November 1953, would hardly have been consoled by the news that Britain's table tennis players had been rather more successful. 'At least we beat them at ping-pong!': the headline writer neatly put the two events into perspective.[5] Apart from the relative capacities of football and table tennis to attract spectators and public interest generally there is a question of ownership at issue here. Association football was one of those games that the British, and especially the English, like to think that they 'gave to the world'; table tennis did not fit into this category and victory, therefore, could be discounted. Even when a particular sport has not spread widely across the globe it might still retain the capacity to encapsulate a nation's idealised image of itself. As Frank Cogliano indicates in his contribution to this collection, this has been especially evident in relation to baseball in the United States though, ironically, when it was taken up in Cuba, baseball supplied a focus for nationalist sentiment that took delight in beating the Americans at their own game. Moreover, it seems likely that the assertion, in a cultural sense, of exclusive ownership rights in relation to a particular sport or sports, along with American 'exceptionalism' generally, is open to negative interpretation elsewhere. One recent letter to an English newspaper criticising United States foreign policy concluded defiantly: 'Anyway, any country that plays incomprehensible versions of rounders, rugby and netball and calls them World Championships leaves a lot to be desired'.[6]

Most mainstream commentators on nationalism pay remarkably little attention to sport. Thus Anthony D. Smith clearly sees sporting competition as peripheral to the 'paradigm debates' that define our understanding of the nation and nationalism. Admittedly Smith's principal concern is with social theory, but not even his most empirical study makes explicit mention of sport; and this despite insisting that 'common myths and memories' and 'a mass, public culture' are crucial to national consciousness.[7] Several of the contributors to this volume draw heavily upon Benedict Anderson's persuasive theory of 'imagined communities' and Eric Hobsbawm's concept of 'invented tradition'.[8] The latter assumes that if no suitable past exists then one can readily be invented. This is explored, for example, in Adrian Smith's chapter on sporting rivalry across the Tasman where satellite television has demanded a much keener sense of competition between Australia and New Zealand, ignoring the fact that historically neither country considered the other its principal opponent.

Both Hobsbawm and Anderson share a common discourse whereby nations are engaged in an evolutionary process of reinvention, often gradual, but on occasions urgent and comprehensive. Thus the national identity assumed by an 'imagined community' is moulded by specific historical circumstances at a particular point in time. Refreshingly, Hobsbawm uses sport to make precisely this point, drawing upon personal experience to illustrate what has proved to be a permanent fusion of nationalist aspiration and sporting ambition. Like George Orwell, he first became conscious of this fresh phase of 'national struggle' in the late 1920s, with the 1936 Berlin Olympics evidently a defining moment for 'competitive national self-assertion'.[9] Marc Keech's chapter highlights how the sheer spectacle of a major sporting occasion renders it a convenient and impressive means of displaying a collective national identity. The 1995 final of rugby union's World Cup undoubtedly marked a pivotal moment in the emergence of a 'new' South Africa, and yet Keech doubts if sport will fulfil the same role of underpinning and projecting national identity as was the case under apartheid. Football's place and function within the 'Rainbow Nation' is fundamentally different to rugby's former status as a pillar of Afrikan hegemony. There are, in fact, remarkably few examples where the overwhelming majority of the population identifies wholeheartedly with a particular sport and/or national team, notwithstanding television's potential to generate a mass audience, for example, through BBC coverage of rower Steve Redgrave's last appearance in an Olympic final. Moreover, when the bulk of the nation clearly has rallied behind a team then the potential for disappointment is that much greater. In his chapter, Adrian Smith highlights the furore in New Zealand over the 'betrayal' by its all-conquering America's Cup crew – not only were these heroes swayed by commercial rather than patriotic considerations, but they went on to secure the trophy in a singularly humiliating fashion.

Hobsbawm readily applies to sport Anderson's argument that all nations are imagined or constructed, not least in the degree to which each community's common identity is rooted in a potent mix of popular mythology, invented tradition, and particular cultural artefacts. Sport, he argues, at least for males, has proved 'uniquely effective' in generating a sense of belonging to a nation. He accounts for this by recalling 'the ease with which even the least political or public individuals can identify with the nations as symbolised by young persons excelling at what practically every man wants, or at one time in his life, has wanted, to be good at'. The national team thus become a focus for these powerful, if unrealisable, fantasies:

> The imagined community of millions seems more real as a team of eleven named people. The individual, even the one who only cheers, becomes a symbol of his nation himself.[10]

Note, by the way, the dual assumption that such feelings are essentially a male preserve, and that most (English) men dream of being David Beckham or Nasser Hussain.

Both Eric Dunning and Lincoln Allison have urged caution when linking sport and national sentiment in such an unequivocal fashion. Though sport is clearly important to any understanding of political nationalism, the 'civilising process' dictates that support for the national side may often be a neutral or even potentially defusing experience.[11] This has long been the assumption in the United States, though, as Frank Cogliano's chapter makes clear, the increasingly cosmopolitan nature of baseball renders the argument for American 'exceptionalism' largely obsolete. Similarly, Martin Polley and Dilwyn Porter, in their contributions to this collection, signal how devolution, multi-culturalism, and perceived national decline together prompted the question, 'What does it mean to be English?'

Until the late twentieth century communal soul-searching over national identity was deemed to be the preserve of the Celtic nations, nowhere more so than in Wales and Scotland, as confirmed by both Martin Johnes and Ronald Kowalski. Here are what Tom Nairn would label 'old nations', both with a keen sense of perceived oppression (at the hands of the English), and both generating in the past an almost tribal sense of loyalty. Sport, or more specifically rugby union and football, provided the most visible and the most populist 'cultural marker of nationalism'.[12] But how valid is such a description today? The repeated failure of the Welsh rugby team to recall the glory days of the 1970s reflects the demise of a sophisticated working-class, nonconformist culture embracing both industrial and rural Wales. Yet Johnes sees recent phenomena such as the popularity of Welsh rock bands and, more significantly, the recent success of the football team in international competition, as confirming the emergence of a new post-industrial, post-devolution Wales unencumbered by tradition and national stereotypes.

Kowalski similarly posits a positive, if qualified, scenario for Scotland, echoing Nairn's insistence that 'old nations' can enjoy certain clear advantages when belatedly empowered to establish their proto-state global credentials. Rather than stifle national sporting cultures, globalisation can in fact act as a challenge – albeit in Scotland's case a formidable one given that by current international standards both its football and rugby teams appear chronically under-resourced. Yet the global market places great store on repackaging and repositioning, and nowhere more so than in sport. Emulating the success of Irish fans over the past two decades, the 'Tartan Army' consciously endeavours to project a positive image of Scotland on the world stage, despite lingering problems associated with sectarianism and racism at home.

It is the differences rather than the divisions that Martin Polley explores in his postmodernist scenario of contemporary English sport. Aside from perhaps athletics, which major sport can boast a national side that accurately reflects English multicultural society at the start of the twenty-first century? The class-less, racially mixed football team might be seen to fulfil such a role, but how can this be the case when its individual players are paid more per week than most workers earn in a year? Notwithstanding the presence of Jason Robinson, the England rugby team remains remarkably homogenous: white, educated, middle-class – and attractive to a wider social base only because it wins matches, not because it constitutes a cross-section of society. The cricket team, still largely indifferent to the obvious pool of Asian and Afro-Caribbean talent despite the family history of its captain, remains both remote *and* relatively unsuccessful. The *Daily Mail* is of course by no means unique in interpreting yet another England defeat as indicative of the state of the nation, and football has often prompted just such a debate. Dilwyn Porter returns to this theme in his chapter on the 'condition of England' during three unusually eventful decades: at least cricket had Headingley 1981, but was the crisis in football – both on and off the pitch at that time – symptomatic of national decline? Clearly Mrs Thatcher thought so, and her bizarre intervention in the debate over hooliganism reflected the neo-conservative view that a revival in England's sporting fortunes demanded both the heavy hand of the state *and* a healthy injection of free market economics.

Marc Keech's chapter reminds us how an individual sport can come to be seen as embodying and exemplifying the spirit of the nation, or in this case the 'white tribe' of Afrikanerdom. At the World Cup final in 1995 Nelson Mandela had no need for words – simply wearing a Springbok shirt sent out such a powerful appeal for *all* South Africans to cheer on their team and for the rugby establishment to make that final break with white exclusivity. In fact, few if any countries in the English-speaking world remain synonymous with a single sport, not least because television has a vested interest in promoting rivals to the 'national game'. As in South Africa, rugby in Wales and even in New Zealand no longer enjoys its one-time hegemonic position; although Martin Johnes would question whether enthusiasm in the Valleys for the oval ball was ever as universal as popular legend suggests. David Storey and Michael Holmes together address the issue of competing sports *and* competing conceptions of national identity. With Gaelic football and hurling restricted to the 'island of Ireland', and rugby union embracing all 32 counties, only the football team can claim to be an unambiguous representative of the Irish Republic on the world sporting stage. But just how unambiguous given that Ireland's impressive achievements over the past two decades are largely attributable to coaches and players born and/or based in England? This is a team of the Irish diaspora, at home in secular, cosmopolitan Dublin but scarcely aware of another, much older but now passing Ireland: Catholic, rural, inward-looking. The men in green shirts are as much talismans of the 'Celtic Tiger' as U2 or Mary Robinson, their exploits in three World Cups drawing attention to the self-confidence of a nation that was now both more at ease with itself and with its role in the modern world.

Irish rugby aptly illustrates how national sporting representation need not be determined by state boundaries: indifferent to partition, each province has made its own distinctive contribution to the resurgence of the national side. Both codes of rugby field 'British' multi-state sides, although only union claims to represent the whole of the archipelago. Furthermore, the subsuming of Home Nations loyalties in to a single cause is deemed only possible on tour, hence the Barbarians providing a convenient badge on those very rare occasions when a *de facto* British and Irish Lions side play in their own back yard. However, another composite international side does play regularly 'at home', and that is, of course, the West Indies cricket team. Keith Sandiford's chapter asks how deep-rooted is the crisis in Caribbean cricket, and what the wider implications of that crisis are for the region as a whole. Prior to 1995 the all-conquering 'Windies' triumphed in 27 consecutive test series, but since then they have played 80 matches and won only 23. An irresistible force of brutal pace bowling and swashbuckling batting has been tamed, with decline blamed on complacency, indiscipline, lack of leadership, weak administration, and an absence of raw young talent. The latter signals the arrival from America of basketball – high energy, easy to play, and potentially far more lucrative than representative cricket. Can the game survive as a bonding and unifying force cutting across historic differences and divisions within the English-speaking islands of the Caribbean (plus Guyana)? Indeed, is there an argument that, ironically, cricket is now potentially a divisive force, with traditional island rivalries becoming increasingly intense and anatagonistic?

It is easy to depict cricket in the West Indies as a victim of globalisation, aggressive free market economics, an all-pervasive drug culture, and an atlanticist hegemony. Sandiford questions whether trans-national economic and social changes are so profound that the current run of poor results, culminating in February 2003 with yet another early exit from the World Cup, marks the end of cricket as a key cultural phenomenon in underpinning the Anglophone islands' collective post-colonial identity. Surprisingly perhaps, Sandiford finds grounds for optimism, and further evidence of a future revival in Caribbean cricket is the imaginative appointment of the Australian Cricket Academy's head coach. As Adrian Smith observes, the Australians are remarkably generous in exporting their expertise – but then they can afford to be. Australia, dubbed the 'lucky country', remains the paradigm whereby a nation defines itself in terms of its sporting success, taking aggressive remedial action at the moment when elite performance across the board clearly no longer matches the very highest expectations.

Notes

1 M. Holmes and D. Storey, 'Football and national identity: the case of the Republic of Ireland', paper delivered at the Textports Conference, Liverpool, 2001.
2 In 1990 the Conservative politician, Lord Tebbit, proposed that one way to test the loyalty of Britain's Asian and Afro-Caribbean people was to ask whether they supported England rather than India, Pakistan or the West Indies at cricket. See M. Phillips and T. Phillips, *Windrush: the Irresistible Rise of Multi-Racial Britain*, London: HarperCollins, 1999, pp. 389–90; also M. Polley, *Moving the Goalposts: A History of Sport and Society since 1945*, London: Routledge, 1998, p. 135.
3 D. Lemmon, *Changing Seasons: A History of Cricket in England, 1945–1996*, London: Andre Deutsch, 1997, pp. 278–9.
4 J. Charlton (with Peter Byrne), *The Autobiography*, London: Partridge, 1996, p. 360.
5 *Daily Mirror*, 25 November 1953.
6 Letter from D. Gordon of Leeds, *Metro*, 17 April 2001.
7 A.D. Smith, *National Identity*, London: Harmondsworth, 1991, and *The Nation in History: Historiographical Debates About Ethnicity and Nationalism*, London: Polity Press, 2000, p. 3.
8 B. Anderson, *Imagined Communities: Reflections on the Origins and Spread of Nationalism*, revised edition, London: Verso, 1983; E.J. Hobsbawm, 'Introduc-

tion' and 'Mass-producing traditions: Europe 1870–1914', in E.J. Hobsbawm and T. Ranger (eds) *The Invention of Tradition*, Cambridge: Cambridge University Press, 1983, pp. 1–14; 263–307.

9 E.J. Hobsbawm, *Nations and Nationalism since 1780: Propaganda, Myth, Reality*, second edition, Cambridge: Cambridge University Press, 1992, pp. 142–3.

10 Hobsbawm, *Nations and Nationalism*, p. 143.

11 E. Dunning, 'Figurational sociology and the sociology of sport', in E. Dunning and C. Rojek (eds) *Sport and Leisure in the Civilising Process: Critique and Counter-critique*, Toronto: University of Toronto Press, 1992, pp. 221–84; L. Allison, 'Introduction', in L. Allison (ed.) *The Changing Politics of Sport*, Manchester: Manchester University Press, 1993, pp. 1–26.

12 T. Nairn, *The Break-Up of Britain*, London: Verso, 1981. On how rugby in pre-devolution Scotland temporarily supplanted football as a vehicle of nationalist sentiment, see G. Jarvie, 'Sport, nationalism and cultural identity', in Allison (ed.) *Changing Politics of Sport*, pp. 58–79.

1 Sport and national identity in contemporary England

Martin Polley

Britannia, she's half English, she speaks Latin at home
St George was born in the Lebanon, how he got here I don't know
And those three lions on your shirt,
They never sprang from England's dirt
Them lions are half English and I'm half English too.
Billy Bragg, 'England, Half English'[1]

In 2002, the England men's football team qualified for the World Cup finals. The manner of their qualification, which included a spectacular 5–1 defeat of Germany in Munich and a late equaliser against Greece, raised popular expectations about England's chances of winning the trophy for the first time since 1966. As the tournament started in Japan and South Korea, the popular mood surrounding the team manifested itself through the widespread flying of the England flag on a scale not seen during previous sports tournaments. 2002 saw a move away from the Union flag and towards the flag of St George as a symbol of English sport and, by extension, English identity. During May and June, it was easy to see where the celebrations for Queen Elizabeth II's golden jubilee were being marked with the red, white, and blue, and where St George was being mobilised for the England team. People flew the England flag from homes, pubs, shops, and vehicles; some people even painted the outside of their houses with the design. Most of these flags disappeared soon after England's disappointing quarter-final defeat by Brazil. A few remained into the winter, hanging worn and neglected from car radio aerials.

The significance of this public show of identity was not purely sporting. The choice of the St George cross over the Union flag suggested that many English people were waking up from history, and were recognising that the unquestioning use of the United Kingdom's flag to stand for England was no longer viable. Nationalism in Northern Ireland, Scotland, and Wales had provided models for a more overtly English sense of identity. While there was little explicit overlap between the football fans and those calling for other forms of English separateness, we must note the timing of

2002's flag-waving in the context of the Labour government's policy of devolution within the UK. Moreover, this trend was taking place in a European setting in which nation states were being reshaped by federalism from above and regionalism from below. In such times, an England football team wrapped in a historical symbol of Englishness was an attractive way for many people to express their own sense of belonging. For a month, the everyday flag flying of Michael Billig's 'banal nationalism'[2] was replaced by a more active nationalism of flag waving. What was also noticeable was that it was not only white supporters who were flying the flag. Despite the flag's strong association in the 1970s and the 1980s with the far right, 2002 saw many England fans of Afro-Caribbean and Asian backgrounds sharing in the celebrations. This mood was captured by Ravi Deepres, a photographer whose Patriots exhibition of 2003 was based on the newly-visible diversity of England football followers: 'I saw Sikh men wearing turbans decorated with St George's crosses ... St George's crosses were much in evidence outside Indian restaurants and corner shops'. When he asked white English fans about their attitudes towards black and Asian English fans displaying the flag, 'Most of them had no problem at all ... In fact, they seemed surprised that we'd asked the question'.[3]

This cameo is a useful introduction to the problematic subject of sport and national identity in contemporary England. The ambiguities and multiple possibilities involved in being 'English', and the sometimes conflicting pulls of localism, nationalism, and globalism, found focus for many in the apparently simple act of flying a particular flag for a football team. It was one of Tim Edensor's 'quotidian, unreflexive acts by which people inscribe themselves in place'.[4] This chapter aims to explore some of the issues that this cameo highlights, and to outline and analyse some of the notable trends that have been occurring in the relationship between sport and national identity in England in the recent past. It will do this through two themes. First, attention will be given to the ways in which traditional models of sporting Englishness have become more diverse and flexible in line with cultural and demographic change. Second, it will examine some of the ways in which trends associated with globalisation in sport have posed challenges to the traditional model. Diversification, challenge, and adaptation thus form the chapter's central threads.

Sport and national identity

Keith Cameron stated a commonplace when he claimed that national identity is 'one of those terms which is used frequently but which often beggars definition'.[5] Globalisation, the decline of European empires, and political and cultural separatist movements throughout the world have created the climate within which we often know who we are, but find it hard to explain it. Common sense definitions of identity – those which have currency, for example, in the London-based popular press during debates over the UK's involvement in European federalisation, or in controversies over asylum seekers – are based on orthodox, tangible criteria such as place of birth, language, parents' nationality, and race. However, the lived experience of thousands of people who do not comfortably fit into such a conservative definition throws up alternatives. Here, each individual's autobiography is crucial, with national identity based more on such subjective criteria as perception, image, ethnicity, and sense of belonging. This reading allows for the possibility of dual or multiple identities. In England, the complexities of these subjective criteria have been particularly obvious since the imperial period as military, economic, religious, and cultural links created networks over which family histories from both imperial power and colonies diversified. Since the 1940s, the migration and settlement in England of significant numbers of Asian and Caribbean families has become an obvious symbol of these longstanding networks.[6] For the white English person given to reflection rather than reflex, national identity is further complicated by a long-term history of conquest, migration, and colonisation that has left Roman, Scandinavian, and Norman influences within the apparently simple identity of white Englishness. These influences are still evident in place names, surnames, and genes.[7] From the 1990s, such influences became increasingly accessible through popular archaeology television programmes such as *Meet the Ancestors*, as the search for roots and identity in an apparently fragmenting world spread further.

For the purposes of this chapter, national identity is being treated in a subjective sense, concentrating on ways in which people feel English or not-English, however they may be defining what Englishness actually is. Indeed, sport is an excellent subject for such a study. People's national sporting affiliations are among the most public statements that they make about their identities. This is because one of the dominant features of modern sport has been its links with the geopolitical ideology of nationalism. The emergence of most team sports – cricket is the main exception – in their recognisable modern forms during the second half of the nineteenth century and the connections they quickly made with the simultaneously emerging model of the nation state was not coincidental. By 1908, the twelve-year old Olympic Games had informally taken on the role of a multinational sporting event at which nations represented themselves with their best athletes. Media coverage of the Olympics from this time, and the political patronage that surrounded them, certainly fed into a discourse in which nations were deemed to be representing themselves through their sportsmen and women. The Olympics have remained the epitome of this relationship which grew throughout the twentieth century. Most team sports – elite motor racing being the most significant exception – and many individual ones, developed organisational structures and elite competitions that were based on the model of national representation. In some cases, national sports teams existed before the nation did in any clear political sense. An Australian cricket XI in 1876, 24 years before the creation of Australia, and a Hungarian Olympic team from 1896, 22 years before Hungary's full independence from the Habsburg Empire, testify to sport's appeal as an entity which 'sometimes channels, sometimes releases, sometimes even creates complex and powerful nationalist sentiments'.[8] Closer to home, the history of Irish, Northern Irish, Scottish, and Welsh sport since the late nineteenth century tells the same story. The reasons for these links need not detain us here: they underpin the whole collection. Briefly, the physical, competitive, supra-linguistic, and populist nature of most sports have made them perfect media for the expression of group identities. Sports are places in which groups can find peaceful physical fora for the beliefs they hold about themselves as entities, a feature that much sports historiography has linked to Benedict Anderson's model of the 'imagined community'.[9]

British sports teams and organisations played important parts in the development of the links between the nation state and the structure and form that sport took. It is impossible to overlook the role of British teams, associations, and models in the formal development of the Olympic Games, test cricket, representative football, rugby union, rugby league, international lawn tennis, competitive winter sports, and many other activities. Even in developments in which the British took little interest at first, such as FIFA's World Cup from 1930 until after the Second World War, the British role as the apparent originator and homeland of modern sport created a legacy out of proportion to British achievements.

Tradition and new political developments throughout the post-1945 period ensured that the national units from the British Isles being represented varied from sport to sport and from time to time. In the Olympic Games, the United Kingdom continued to be represented by a team called Great Britain. British Olympic competitors could also compete for their smaller national units of England, Northern Ireland, Scotland and Wales in the Empire Games, established in 1930 (and subsequently renamed the British Empire and Commonwealth Games in 1950, the British Commonwealth Games in 1966, and the Commonwealth Games in 1978). The four nations have separate football associations and thus separate representative teams. In rugby union, England, Scotland, and Wales continued to be run alongside a united Ireland team and, in the British Lions, an all-British Isles team. The England cricket team has included Welshman such as Robert Croft, Simon Jones, and Tony Lewis, while golfers in the representative Ryder Cup found the unit they were representing moving from Great Britain (1927–71) to the British Isles (1973–77) to Europe (since 1979). Despite this confusion, which even many English people have trouble keeping up with, British international teams took a full part in most international sport, with varying degrees of success.

Where success has been specifically English, as in the 1966 football World Cup, the 1981 Ashes victory over Australia in cricket, and the 2002 rugby union demolitions of Australia, New Zealand, and South Africa, triumph was widely linked in popular discourse to characteristically English attributes. This is, as Joseph Maguire has observed, a very particular form of Englishness, one 'dominated by male upper class values'.[10] Courage, determination, a historical right to do well, loyalty, strong team spirit, and the solid leadership or heroic examples of individuals have all been applied to these successes.[11] Indeed, even sporting failures have become linked to supposedly core markers of this narrow Englishness. The ski-jumper Eddie 'the Eagle' Edwards, who finished fifty-fifth out of 56 entrants in the 1988 Winter Olympic competition in Calgary – the fifty-sixth entrant was disqualified – was constructed in the media as a specifically English eccentric demonstrating courage and indifference to failure. Similarly, defeated teams who had played well – especially if the opposition was German – have been presented as sporting embodiments of the Dunkirk spirit. Indeed, it has been in relation to Anglo-German footballing contacts that the common sense association between Englishness and sport has been most evident. Maguire quotes an editorial from the day before the 1966 World Cup final between England and West Germany: 'if, perchance, on the morrow Germany [*sic*] should beat us at our national game, let us take comfort from the fact that twice we have beaten them at theirs'.[12] As each new match since that English World Cup victory occurred, the replaying of wartime motifs became more noticeable. In 1996, for example, one popular newspaper attempted to fly a Second World War Spitfire over the German team's training ground; while the fans' taunt of 'Two world wars and one world cup' kept the relationship in all its chauvinism visible.[13]

However, despite the proliferation of England flags in 2002 mentioned in the introduction to this chapter, the common sense links between the English nation and sport are no longer stable. The apparently straightforward tradition that linked sportsmen and women, nation and population, has been challenged. In Gramscian terms, this orthodoxy has long held sway as the hegemonic norm. It is a view that drew from the specific class basis of modern sports as they emerged in the nineteenth century, and one that has informed the bulk of popular discourse on sport and national identity. A critical reading of the apparent traditions of Englishness in sport suggests that the versions of England they have represented have always been limited and selective. Popular discourses may use the label 'we' to link a team to the English population: 'we won', 'we were cheated', 'we have much to be ashamed of', and so on. The reality is more complicated. Thus, while an England success in one sport may be deeply meaningful for many in the country, it can also be irrelevant for others. A straw poll of undergraduate Sport Studies students suggests that this is the case even for young, well-educated, sports enthusiasts. Impressionistic though these exercises are, they suggest that the bulk of the male students but only a minority of females feel included by a newspaper's 'we' applied to the England men's football team. The gender positions reversed when dealing with the national women's team, but none of the English students felt a natural affinity with the all-Scottish women's curling team of the 2002 Winter Olympics. Very few felt that the 'we' of a story about English teams in bowling or equestrianism applied to them. Even the supposed 'national' sports of association football and cricket have traditional constituencies that are in no way truly national.[14] Identities linked to social class, region, gender, and age have undercut the apparent national community throughout English history, and the 'we' to which much media sports coverage is addressed has always been limited.

Diversifying and alternative identities

The common sense links between nation and sport have not been able to remain stable in the post-war period, particularly since the 1960s. The growth of an equal opportunities culture, and the continued ethnic diversification of England's population, have been the contexts for the development of a variety of national identities which go beyond an unreflective Englishness. Sport, along with literature and popular music, has been one of the cultural fora in which these identities have been played out. The growth of a multiethnic population has been the prime reason for the diffusion of English identities in the post-war period. The diversity of this population is suggested by the Office of National Statistics' figures for 2001, which show that for Great Britain as a whole, 7.1 per cent of the population was non-white, a heading which includes the following ethnic groupings: black Caribbean, black African, black other, black mixed, Indian, Pakistani, Bangladeshi, and Chinese. This heterogeneous group of non-whites totalled approximately 4,000,000 people.[15] These figures do not show the ethnic diversity within the white population, which includes long-term English as well as twentieth century migrants from other parts of the British Isles, the former dominions, and continental Europe. They alert us, however, to the scale of diversity.

English people in earlier periods clearly experienced Englishness in various ways, with north/south and urban/rural varieties evident throughout the early modern and modern periods. Linda Colley's description of Great Britain in the early eighteenth century is a good rejoinder to mythical readings of a homogenous English culture 'before we had ethnic minorities', as one of the Parkeh Report's focus group's members put it.[16] Colley writes of Great Britain at the time of the 1707 Act of Union as being:

> much less a trinity of self-contained and self-conscious nations than a patchwork in which uncertain areas of Welshness, Scottishness and Englishness were cut across by strong regional attachments, and scored over again by loyalties to village, town, family and landscape.[17]

Although economic and political change ameliorated some of these differences, they have remained evident into the twenty-first century. These differences have always been evident in sport. Pre-modern variations between regions may have been diluted, but regional identities have remained strong. FA Cup finals between northern and southern teams regularly showed up different cultures, as did the development of rugby league and league cricket in northern counties.[18] These differences remained evident in the economic climate of the late 1980s, when fans of London football clubs would wave banknotes at fans from northern clubs with the taunt of 'Sign on with no hope in your heart / For you'll never get a job'. However, the demographic consequences of post-war Caribbean, African, and Asian immigration – the 4,000,000 non-whites of 2001 – multiplied Colley's older 'attachments'. The relatively straightforward sense of belonging experienced by earlier generations had new layers added to them as thousands of people had to learn to live with at least two identities: an English one, and one linking them to their own place of birth. The confusions that this could raise for those experiencing this situation were legion, particularly when religious and linguistic differences made the difference between domestic and external cultures so pronounced. For children born to migrant families, the situation was more complex. This is what Massive Attack sang of in 'Blue Lines' in 1991: 'English upbringing, background Caribbean'[19]; and it is what Zadie Smith picked up on in her novel *White Teeth* when she gave Millat, a London-born teenager who resented his Bengali family heritage, the following reflections:

> He knew that he ... was a Paki no matter where he came from; that he smelt of curry; had no sexual identity; took other people's jobs; or had no job and bummed off the state; or gave all the jobs to his relatives; that he could be a dentist or a shop-owner or a curry-shifter, but not a footballer or a film-maker; ... that no one who looked like Millat, or spoke like Millat, or felt like Millat, was ever on the news unless they had recently been murdered. In short, he knew he had no face in this country, no voice in the country.[20]

To many, this development has been problematic, as the blending of identities has been perceived to mean a dilution of Englishness and a division of loyalties. The growth of far right political parties such as the National Front, the British Movement, and the British National Party is evidence of a backlash. Mainstream politics, particularly under the influence of post-war welfarism and a liberalism informed by an equal opportunities culture, has been more accommodating, although immigration laws have become increasingly stringent since the early 1960s. Beyond legislation, cultural and educational projects aimed at raising awareness of multiculturalism have helped to create recognition of the diversities of Englishness. We can see the results of this diversity in drama, when black actors have been given roles other than Othello, and in the success of post-colonial fine artists such as Chris Ofili. The presence of ethnic minority characters in television and radio dramas and soap operas, and the success of programmes that have grown from black British and Anglo-Asian culture, such as *Desmond's* and *Goodness Gracious Me*, is further evidence of this. Popular music has also played its part: the huge black influence on popular music through soul, reggae, ska, and dance forms, and the critical and commercial success of bands with Anglo-Asian roots such as Cornershop and Asian Dub Foundation, have helped to create a diverse and diffuse English culture. The face of England presented to the rest of the world, and the activities and achievements held up as something for the English to be proud of, have become more than merely white. What role has sport played in this development?

The most obvious way in which sport has been involved in this cultural change has been in the increasing diversity of the ethnic background of English representative sportsmen and women. Imperial connections meant that a small number of black and Asian sportsmen played in England from the eighteenth century onwards. Some, such as the cricketer Kumar Shri Ranjitsinhji ('Ranji') and the Great Britain Olympic sprinters Jack London and MacDonald Bailey, competed at representative level.[21] However, it was not until the 1960s and 1970s that we saw significant numbers of elite-level sportsmen and women from migrant and settler families. Given its traditions of accessibility to migrant communities, boxing was one of the first sports to see this diversity. There are long traditions of fighters from Jewish families, such as Daniel Mendoza in the eighteenth century, and the inter-war Londoners Jack 'Kid' Berg and Gershon Medeloff who fought as Ted 'Kid' Lewis. In the post-war period, many of England's leading boxers have been black, starting with Randolph Turpin, the son of a white mother and a black British Guianese father who had settled in England after the First World War, who won the European and World middleweight titles in 1951. Although some black English boxers continued to be discriminated against by the boxing authorities, since the 1970s boxers such as John Conteh, Maurice Hope, Frank Bruno, and Lennox Lewis have continued in Turpin's footsteps. Naseem Hamid, the Sheffield-born son of a Yemeni family, has further diversified the ethnic profile of elite boxing. English representative athletics saw a major influx of black talent from the late 1970s onwards, including decathlete Daley Thompson, javelin thrower Tessa Sanderson, and runners Linford Christie, John Regis, Sonia Lannaman, and Kelly Holmes. The England football team fielded its first black player, Viv Anderson, in 1978, and by the end of the century was regularly fielding mixed teams. Rugby league's first black Great Britain player was the Welshman Clive Sullivan, but the England team has built on this diversity through players such as Martin Offiah and Ikram Butt. Cricket and rugby union were a little slower, but representative teams in these sports by the end of the century had included players of various ethnic backgrounds. In rugby union, Jeremy Guscott, and in cricket, Roland Butcher and Nasser Hussain are examples. Hussain's captaincy of the England team at the time of writing suggests a high degree of acceptance by the sports establishment of the country's ethnic diversity.

Taken together, these examples suggest one of the most positive signs of how English national identity in sport has been shifted to be more inclusive. On the face of it, sport should be the dream cultural activity of the equal opportunities lobby. Indeed, many of the sportsmen and women named have done more than simply play for England: they have openly embraced Englishness through displaying both orthodox and original acts of allegiance. The more orthodox include flag-waving and flag-wearing in moments of triumph, and acceptance of establishment patronage through the Queen's honours lists. One example, whose own history illustrates the complexities of sporting nationality and belonging, can suffice to illustrate these tendencies. Ashia Hansen was born to an American Afro-Caribbean mother in Indiana, and adopted as a baby by an English woman and her Ghanaian husband. She spent her childhood in Ghana and London. An elite triple jumper, she represented Great Britain in the 2000 Olympic Games and England in the 2002 Commonwealth Games. After winning the gold medal in the latter competition, she did a lap of honour wrapped in an England flag. She was awarded an MBE in the 2003 New Year's Honours list. Many sportsmen and women drawing on other cultural traditions to display their allegiance have supplemented such orthodox displays of Englishness. Returning to popular music, a good example comes from 'World in Motion', the England football team's official record for the 1990 World Cup. Recorded with the band New Order, the song included a rap section, which was delivered by Jamaican-born England player, John Barnes.[22]

The family connection from George Cohen, a defender in the victorious England football team of 1966, to his rugby union-playing nephew Ben, an England winger at the time of writing, is an example of Jewish assimilation within the scope of English identity, following a tradition made famous by the boxers mentioned above, and by the athlete Harold Abrahams in the 1920s. Indeed, the fictionalised version of Abrahams represented in the Oscar-winning film *Chariots of Fire* (1980) scorned the white upper class English establishment for their doubts about his loyalty to England. His impassioned speech to his anti-semitic college dons that he was a Cambridge man and an Englishman above all else was a perfect text for the early 1980s, as England became used to people of various ethnic and racial backgrounds representing it at sport. This fictionalised form found a real echo from Jamaican-born England and Great Britain sprinter Linford Christie in 1995: 'By representing my country, I'm trying to show that there is really no need for the problems we have ... [B]lack sportsmen are uniting the country'.[23]

However, it would be naïve in the extreme to allow this positive account of assimilation, acceptance, and integration to stand on its own. Despite the successes of an elite, the lived experiences of many people from ethnic minorities in English sport remain influenced by explicit racism or simple everyday stereotyping. Some parts of the sporting establishment have been overtly racist in their attitudes on people from various ethnic groups. This has had a significant impact at grassroots and club levels, where many clubs in areas with ethnically-mixed populations have failed to fully enfranchise those potential supporters: Yorkshire County Cricket Club and West Ham United Football Club are famous examples of clubs with relatively untapped Asian populations to draw on. At the national level, stereotyping has persisted in some areas. Such attitudes must be held responsible for the low profile of Asian sportsmen and women in representative teams. Since the late 1990s, a number of sports have attempted to deal with racism at club and community level, based on the assumption that educating the young about racism through the cultural sphere will help to change attitudes. The most famous scheme, the joint Commission for Racial Equality/Professional Footballers' Association 1993 scheme Let's Kick Racism Out Of Football, has been supported by clubs and by the England team. Other schemes, such as rugby league's Rugby Exchange in Bradford (run by former England international Ikram Butt), have also used sport as a means of promoting tolerance. However, as the controversy surrounding Leeds United footballers' 2001 trial for assaulting an Asian youth showed, cultures of racism and indifference still persist in sport.

These attitudes have, on occasion, been stated bluntly in ways that have started debates about ethnicity, identity, and loyalty. The most famous examples have come in relation to cricket. In 1990, the Conservative politician Norman Tebbit famously posited the 'test match test'. He argued that second and third generation black and Asian English people's choice of international cricket teams indicated how far they had integrated with 'English' society: 'If someone is looking back to the country from where their family came instead of to the country where they live and make their home, you say are they really integrated or are they just living here?'[24] Made at a time of high racial tension in England, this was a controversial and provocative statement, which Marqusee has expertly analysed. Marqusee has also provided a detailed account of another race-based debate that erupted in cricket in 1995 when the influential *Wisden* ran an article called 'Is it in the blood?' which, among other things, questioned the loyalty of black and Asian players in the England team. He asked if 'the coloured England-qualified player feels satisfaction (perhaps subconsciously) at seeing England humiliated', and asserted that 'the interlopers' would damage the team spirit that would naturally form amongst '11 unequivocal Englishmen'.[25]

What Tebbit famously missed, of course, and what he was criticised for, was a basic racist double standard: he did not ask the question of English migrants and settlers in other countries, or of white migrants and settlers in England. Many black and Asian English people welcomed the chance to watch and support visiting teams from the West Indies, India, Pakistan, or Sri Lanka, and welcomed the opportunity such events gave for expressions of communal identity and heritage. The famous carnival atmosphere at test matches between England and the West Indies, for example, were a highlight for Anglo-Caribbean communities. Such celebrations help us to see that, despite the large amount of assimilation that has taken place, migrants and their children have not used sport solely as a means of buying into a traditional English identity. Beyond behaving in certain ways on the Oval or at Edgbaston, a number of sports, particularly team games, have been played by members of migrant communities as a way of maintaining older loyalties and identities.

This is not a new phenomenon, and it has, of course, been perpetuated by British migrants: imperial and, latterly, expatriate communities maintaining English sports clubs, and Gaelic football clubs being established throughout the Irish diaspora are examples of this trend. As one of Tebbit's critics, Tara Mukherjee, put it, 'ask the English settlers in Australia which side they support when a Test is played in Australia against Australians'.[26] This trend gave rise, before our period, to some clubs in England that were based on non-English national affiliations. The most famous examples come from rugby union, with London Scottish (formed in 1878), London Welsh (1885), and London Irish (1898), all acting as exiles' clubs for members of metropolitan-based migrant communities. As London Welsh still proclaim on their official website, the club was established for 'London Welshmen exiled in a foreign field'.[27] The Welsh and Irish in particular have embraced the professional culture of contemporary rugby union, and no longer exclusively serve their original communities. London Welsh, for example, include Frenchman Florent Rossigneux and Englishman Greg Botterman in their 2002–03 squad. The more successful London Irish field players of various nationalities, one of whom, Jeffrey Fahrensohn, is a perfect example of contemporary sports' global nature. Born in New Zealand, Fahrensohn plays his rugby for London Irish, a club set up by Irish migrants to the English capital but now based in Berkshire, and plays his international rugby for Germany thanks to his family heritage. Despite their acceptance of professionalism and its effects on team identity, London Irish and London Welsh retain strong links with their original constituencies, particularly through commercial and business links, and both continue to use symbols of their non-English identity in colours, badges, and vocabulary, all of which show a certain resilience to the hegemony of their host nation. For example, alongside the resolute professionalism that has made them one of the most successful clubs in Europe, London Irish continue to promote an older, more community-based Irishness:

Wherever you are in rugby circles worldwide, mention London Irish and you are greeted with a smile. Such is the club's reputation for the warm welcome and hospitality it dispenses so generously. There is a great sense of fun about the club and its match day '*Craic*' is legendary.[28]

More recently, clubs using the same model but drawing on more diverse ethnic and national communities have joined these Celtic clubs. Most successful have been London Nigerians RFC, formed 1992 by 'a group of Nigerian friends who had learned their rugby mainly in English public schools'.[29] The Nigerians form part of a rich exiles' rugby club culture that also includes London Kiwis, formed in 1998 as 'a place for kiwi rugby-lovers to feel at home away from home',[30] and London Springboks, formed in 1996 with the aim of developing a 'rugby team that carries the fine traditions found in South African rugby union'.[31] All of these clubs cater for the same impulse felt by residents – in many cases British nationals – of England who have family histories overseas. The rugby club acts as a link with the traditions and cultures of home, and their membership of it acts as a public sign that each individual involved has a sense of identity that is not purely 'English'. Gaelic sports have also maintained these cultures, with many English-based clubs currently working within the Gaelic Athletic Association's structures, such as Bristol's Western Gaels, the Parnells of London, and the Brothers Pearse in Huddersfield.

This trend has not been limited to rugby union or only to migrant communities linked to celtic or white commonwealth migration. A famous example is the growth of hockey clubs and leagues based on Anglo-Asian communities. Workplaces, schools, neighbourhoods, and places of worship have all been the basis for clubs in areas of high Asian population, such as the cities in the Midlands. In 2001, for example, the Coventry-based hockey club Sikh Union initiated a national event which attracted South Asian community clubs from Nottingham, Wolverhampton, Birmingham, and London.[32] Afro-Caribbean cricket and football teams in London and other cities, and Jewish teams in a variety of sports based on synagogues, schools, and on the Maccabi movement, are also abundant. English Jews also compete in the international Jewish sports festival, the Maccabiah Games, thereby stressing the importance of their ethnic identity as well as their national one.[33]

What this shows is that, far from the narrow-minded assumptions behind the Tebbit test, it is possible for people to maintain parallel identities. The boxer Naseem Hamid has outlined the complexities here when speaking of his own identity:

I see myself as a British Arab – born and bred in Britain and I am proud to be British, proud to be Arab, I'm proud to be black and I'm proud to be from Sheffield. I think Britain is one of the best countries in the world to live and I'd never live anywhere else – not even for tax purposes.

Hamid's biographer refers to the boxer's 'multi-layered identity', in which 'each aspect [has] been absorbed with obvious pride and without prejudice against the others'.[34] Clearly, many players and followers have happily combined dual identities in sport. Many white English sports followers are adept at this, too, as when they support a Scottish athlete in the Great Britain Olympic team but revert to a traditional anti-Scottish stance when national teams meet in football or rugby. The London-based media is also experienced in this kind of support. When an England team fails to qualify for a major tournament, the media quickly appropriates other British or Irish teams as 'ours'. However, in the realm of individuals and communities choosing to prioritise one identity over another, the Tebbit debate has highlighted the controversies that can surround such a choice. Sport's public and emotive aspects, and its strong links with family and community history, make it an easy target for those wishing to impose a standard English identity.

At the start of the twenty-first century, then, the face of English identity in sport was no longer exclusively white. A number of individuals who are not white have become broadly accepted as national representatives and, indeed, heroes and heroines. To the earlier chronicles of white English sporting greats who have embodied such values as courage, strength, determination, and excellence, we must add Frank Bruno, Linford Christie, Jeremy Guscott, Naseem Hamid, Ashia Hansen, Nasser Hussain, Paul Ince, Denise Lewis, and Tessa Sanderson. However, it has not just been in ethnic terms that we have seen a diversification in who the England label has been representing.

Since the Second World War, and particularly since the social and cultural changes of the 1960s, English national identity in sport has evolved in interesting ways. First, we must note the establishment of national teams and international competition in high profile women's sports. In some sports this has been a question of continuity, notably in hockey, netball, lacrosse, athletics, and cricket. Here, the post-war period has seen more opportunities for the various England teams, and these opportunities have received marginally more attention than in previous decades. In sports where early women's traditions were effectively suppressed by male establishments, such as football and both rugby codes, the 1970s and 1980s saw a restarting from scratch in which representative England teams quickly joined in with international competition. This is, of course, not to suggest that national male teams (particularly in cricket, rugby union, and football) do not have strong traditions of female support: but recent changes have given more opportunities for women to express their sporting Englishness on their own terms. Cricket was the first in the field – indeed, the women's world cup was set up in 1973, two years before the equivalent men's competition. England won it in 1973, and again in 1993. The women's world cups in football and rugby union both began in 1991. In the former, England qualified in 1995 and reached the quarter-finals. In the latter, the English women's team have achieved much, being winners in 1994, beaten finalists in 1991 and 2002, and semi-finalists in 1998. As with the growth of multiethnic England teams in these sports, the growth of separate women's teams effectively enfranchised many who had not felt included in the 'we' of popular discourse and helped to challenge Maguire's 'male, upper class Englishness'. The traditional model included a sexual politics in which women were not supposed to participate in demanding sports involving bodily contact; the emerging one is far more progressive. Individual sportswomen in physically extreme sports, such as yachtswomen Ellen MacArthur, have also pushed the traditional definitions.

In terms of sexuality, recent developments have also added a layer to the varieties of sporting Englishness as the loosening of taboos surrounding homosexuality has given rise to a vibrant gay sports culture. While parts of the USA and Australia have led the way here, particularly through the establishment of the Gay Games as an inclusive Olympic alternative, English men and women have participated and succeeded.[35] The English non-specialist media may ignore the Gay Games, but this competition has given the chance for English people who would not be represented in mainstream sports the chance to compete. London Lions Stonewall, the bronze medallists in the 1998 Gay Games football competition, or Rodney Brangwyn and Peter Ryan, gold medallists in the 1998 ballroom dancing event, should be included in any contemporary definition of sporting Englishness.[36] For as long as the mainstream sports establishment and media remain – if only implicitly – hostile to gay men, this development has created a setting for a new form of national sporting identity.

The growth of sporting opportunities for people with physical disabilities can also be seen in this context. People effectively excluded from traditional forms of sporting identity due to their bodies not working in orthodox ways have been able to represent England at elite levels, and have been accommodated (albeit with some reservations) by the media and the sporting establishment as part of the country's sporting identity. The application of traditional national epithets to them – bravery, determination, and stoicism, for example – has illustrated this accommodation. As with the able-bodied equivalent, Paralympics teams are organised around the United Kingdom, but the Commonwealth Games provides a relatively high profile event for English disabled sportsmen and women to compete for England. Gold medallists at Manchester in 2002 included Ruth Small in the blind singles bowls, and Sue Gilroy in the wheelchair singles table tennis.

Taken together, those pushing the boundaries of national identity in sport from the women's, gay, and disabled sports movements illustrate the fluidity of national identities, and the cultural and political importance of challenging orthodoxies which may have become obsolete. Taken with the integration of some ethnic minority groups within the sporting mainstream, this newly flexible English identity symbolised by 'veiled Muslim women wearing England tops' at a football match,[37] suggests that the links between sport and national identity remain strong in England. However, it is important to see this identity in the context of globalising trends in sport. Using Maguire's classic model of 'diminishing contrasts and increasing varieties', we should now consider how far English national identity in sport has been challenged.

The challenges of globalisation

The fluidity that surrounds current notions of English national identity within sport are not, of course, limited to England. The cultural and economic trends known as globalisation have made themselves felt in all areas of life, and can be seen to have had an impact on the ways in which people identify with the nation state.[38] Sport, which fulfils a leading role for many people in this process of identification, has been affected by these trends.

Globalisation has helped to create a setting in which English national identity has more sporting opportunities in which to express itself than at any previous point in history. The Olympics survived the Second World War, and have become consolidated as the premier multi-sport event in the world, with their winter version also increasing in popularity. The 2000 Summer Games in Sydney attracted teams from 199 nations, while at the 2002 Salt Lake City Winter Games 77 countries were represented. The Commonwealth Games have retained great popularity and media interest, particularly when they have been hosted in the UK. The football World Cup, set up in 1930 and now involving 32 finalists, has provided a template which has been successfully applied in regional events, such as the European Championships. The world cup format has been developed in rugby union, rugby league, and one-day cricket, as well as in the women's versions of all of these sports mentioned above. The more traditional international cricket format, the test match, has grown, with nine other countries now competing with England at this level. Individual sports, such as athletics and swimming, have all developed their own European and world championships alongside their Olympic presence. The professional circuits in lawn tennis and golf, and their national (or multi-national) contests in the Davis Cup and the Ryder Cup respectively, must also be seen in this context of increasing competition. This global setting has also given club sides in many sports opportunities to play across national borders. The introduction of competitive European club football in the 1950s, in which English clubs have an excellent record of achievement despite a five-year absence after the Heysel disaster of 1985, has been followed by European league and cup contacts for English clubs in other sports, including speedway, rugby union, rugby league, American football, and ice hockey. These are just a few of the more prominent examples of how the opportunities for English national representation have grown since the Second World War.

All of them have created settings in which players, supporters, and the media have been able to load sporting events with meanings informed by national identity. Flag-flying by travelling English spectators has become ubiquitous at international events in football, both rugby codes, cricket, athletics, and other sports. Many spectators continue to sport national colours, with replica shirts, red and white jesters' hats, and flag-based face painting all being common sights amongst spectators of all ages, genders, and various ethnic backgrounds at all of these sports. The contested revitalisation of English travelling cricket support associated with the Barmy Army must also be seen in this light, as indeed must hooligan and antisocial behaviour perpetrated by some sections of the England football team's travelling support. Political, media, and sporting agencies are always quick to condemn any forms of hooliganism linked to England fans, but their behaviour is so strongly linked to the idea of England that we cannot dismiss it so easily. Typically, many of the fans involved display both national colours and an orthodox loyalty to the idea of England. Most of their targets are those they perceive as un-English, with particular attention given to ethnic minority communities in the cities they visit, such as north Africans in France in 1998 and Belgium in 2000. They also draw on English history in many of their abusive chants, such as the aforementioned 'Two world wars and one world cup' at German fans, and 'If it wasn't for the English you'd be krauts' at Belgians. This has been particularly interesting at club level, where individual clubs have become – at least in the eyes of the Government and the media – proxy representatives of all of England. When 39 spectators died as a result of crowd trouble between Liverpool and Juventus supporters at Heysel in 1985, it was English – not British – clubs who were subsequently banned from European football; and when any English club does well in Europe, national media coverage assumes that all English fans will want them to succeed. In reality, of course, this does not always work: but the tone of the media assumes that national identity in sport is flourishing.

However, while globalisation may have created more spaces for national identity to be expressed in, it has also been the setting for a number of trends that challenge the notion of English national identity in sport. Two challenges in particular stand out: the flexible attitude towards nationality that some sportsmen and women take that is leading to a significant growth of sporting 'flags of convenience'; and the merging of commercial and national identities in sport. In relation to England, these are in their early stages at the time of writing, and this section must necessarily be speculative. It is hoped that by identifying trends from recent cases, we can fit the inherited model of English identity in sport into a wide contemporary context.

One of the most obvious ways in which globalisation is challenging national identity in sport is the migration of professional sportsmen and women along increasingly diverse routes.[39] This migration has the potential to cause an erosion of the historical relationship between sport and national identity in England. This erosion can come when individuals with complicated family histories choose to prioritise their English links above other, perhaps more obvious ones. The most controversial cases of elite sportsmen choosing Englishness have been boxer Lennox Lewis and lawn tennis player Greg Rusedski. Lewis, a London-born boxer of Jamaican origin, moved to Canada as a child, and boxed for Canada at the 1988 Olympic Games. His subsequent professional career, however, has been based in London, and he has fought for British and world titles as an Englishman. Rusedski was born in North America to an English-born mother who had moved to Canada as a child. After establishing himself as a professional, Rusedski chose to base himself in London and subsequently qualified to play for Great Britain in the Davis Cup. Media coverage and popular discourse surrounding both individuals, while happy with their successes, tend to treat their 'more' English contemporaries (such as Frank Bruno and Tim Henman respectively) more sympathetically. In some other cases, choosing Englishness through marriage or naturalisation has been more cynical, particularly where the individuals concerned have a greater chance of success if standards are lower in England than they are in their more obvious country. In February 2003, Chelsea FC's Italian manager Claudio Ranieri suggested that the club's Italian goalkeeper, Carlo Cudicini, should seek British nationality through residence, as he would have more chance of playing for England than he would for Italy.[40] While Cudicini subsequently rejected this idea, its public discussion highlighted the development of a 'flag of convenience' culture. This practice has been more prevalent in continental European football, particularly amongst club players from Latin America.

Of course, for every Greg Rusedski there is a Ryan Giggs. This Manchester United footballer was born in Cardiff, but moved to England as a child. Despite his residence qualification to play for England, he chose Wales, despite the knowledge that such a choice would severely limit his chances to play at the highest levels: like George Best, he is one of those great British players who has never been to the World Cup finals. While not everyone may wish to choose Englishness, the fact that some have for the sake of their careers suggests a potential erosion of English national identity in sport. English national teams using non-English coaches have intensified the debates around talent migration that these cases have sparked. The FA's appointment of Swede Sven Goran Eriksson has gained the most publicity here due to football's high profile. When he was appointed, Jeff Powell of the conservative tabloid newspaper the *Daily Mail* famously claimed that 'We've sold our birthright down the fjord to a nation of 7 million skiers and hammer-throwers who spend half their time in darkness'. John Barnwell of the League Managers Association was equally blunt: he saw the appointment of an overseas coach as 'a betrayal of our national heritage'.[41] Other sports that have experimented with putting overseas coaches in charge of English national teams – such as basketball with Hungarian coach Laszlo Nemeth – have sparked similar controversies.

Our second challenge comes from the merging of commercial and national interests in some sports. In the poor financial setting of the 1960s onwards, when gate receipts were falling and costs were rising, many sports accepted commercial sponsorship as a way of increasing income and diversifying audiences. This trend hit different sports at different times – for example, athletics and cricket in the late 1960s, rugby union in the 1970s, and football in the early 1980s. One of the effects of this has been the increasing presence of sponsors' names in various aspects of international events. In cricket, England's test matches accepted event sponsorship in 1981, with the insurance company Cornhill having its name as a prefix to all matches. Cricket, rugby union, and rugby league have gone on to allow commercial sponsors' names on playing kit, the size and design of whose logos often being more prominent than national badges. At the time of writing, the England cricket team has this link with telecommunications company Vodaphone, and the rugby union team with Vodaphone's rivals O2. Further opportunities come through perimeter and on-pitch advertisements, and through event sponsorship. The Football Association, in line with the sport's governing body's rulings, are unable to have shirt front sponsorship, but they have allied with the Nationwide Building Society for training kit advertisements and match sponsorship. So far, England's international teams have not experienced the degree of commercial influence that Nike wield over the Brazilian football team. However, the presence of sponsors' names next to national badges identifies this as a trend to watch for the future. As generations of sports enthusiasts grow up without a non-commercial model to look back on, commercialism represents a serious threat to the link between sport and national identity. The popularity of sports without formal links to nation states, such as Formula 1 motor racing, certain sailing events, and extreme sports, should also be seen in this context.

Despite these factors that can be seen to be eroding the idea of English sporting identity, we should return to our opening image: the proliferation of England flags during the 2002 football World Cup. Globalisation has created ever-increasing opportunities for national representation; and however much these events have been driven by commercial and media agendas and however much the idea of the nation may be under attack from migration, the media, and commercial interests, fans in many sports have maintained the links between the team and the nation. In any survey of the survival of English identity amongst English sports followers, we need to note the whole range of its manifestations, from the Sikh with the St George turban to the hooligan with the St George tattoo. It is a mark of England's diversity at the start of the twenty-first century that the nation and its sport can accommodate such extremes.

Notes

1 Billy Bragg, 'England, Half English', on Billy Bragg and The Blokes, *England, Half English*, Cooking Vinyl, 2002.
2 M. Billig, *Banal Nationalism*, London: Sage, 1995.
3 *Guardian*, 12 February 2003.
4 T. Edensor, *National Identity, Popular Culture and Everyday Life*, Oxford: Berg, 2002, p. 69.
5 K. Cameron, 'Introduction', in K. Cameron (ed.) *National Identity*, Exeter: Intellect Books, 1999, p. 1.
6 For various aspects of immigration and settlement, see P. Fryer, *Staying Power: The History of Black People in Britain*, London: Pluto, 1984; C. Holmes, *John Bull's Island: Immigration and British Society 1871–1971*, Basingstoke: Macmillan, 1988; C. Holmes, *A Tolerant Country? Immigrants, Refugees and Minorities in Britain*, London: Faber and Faber, 1991; P. Rich, *Race and Empire in British Politics*, second edition, Cambridge: Cambridge University Press, 1990; R. Skellington, *'Race' in Britain Today*, second edition, London: Sage, 1996; Y. Alibhai-Brown, *Who Do We Think We Are? Imagining the New Britain*, London: Penguin, 2001.
7 A detailed and highly accessible introduction to the history of the English in a British and European context can be found in N. Davies, *The British Isles: A History*, Basingstoke: Macmillan, 1999.
8 L. Allison, 'Sport and nationalism', in J. Coakley and E. Dunning (eds) *Handbook of Sports Studies*, London: Sage, 2000, p. 354.
9 B. Anderson, *Imagined Communities: Reflections on the Origin and Spread of Nationalism*, London: Verso, 1991. For sport, nationalism, and national identity, an excellent brief overview is Allison, 'Sport and nationalism'. See also A. Bairner, *Sport, Nationalism, and Globalization: European and North American Perspectives*, Albany NY: State University of New York Press, 2001.
10 J. Maguire, 'Globalization, sport and national identities: "The empires strike back"?', *Society and Leisure*, 1993, vol. 16 (2), p. 295.
11 For a survey of how sporting heroes have been represented in art, see J. Huntington-Whiteley (compiler), *The Book of British Sporting Heroes*, London: National Portrait Gallery, 1998. Richard Holt provides a scholarly introduction.
12 Quoted in Maguire, 'Globalization, sport and national identities', p. 296.
13 See M. Polley, *Moving the Goalposts: A History of Sport and Society since 1945*, London: Routledge, 1998, p. 3. For a narrative history of the Anglo-German footballing rivalry, see D. Downing, *The Best of Enemies: England v Germany*, London: Bloomsbury, 2000.
14 For an introduction to the debate on what constitutes a 'national' sport, see Bairner, *Sport, Nationalism, and Globalization*, pp. 17–20.
15 Office of National Statistics, *UK 2002: The Official Yearbook of Great Britain and Northern Ireland*, London: The Stationery Office, 2001, p. 116. *The Report*

of the Commission on the Future of Multi-Ethnic Britain (The Parekh Report) of 2000, using 1998 figures, provides a detailed analysis of ethnic groupings' distribution across the regions of England: see *The Future of Multi-Ethnic Britain*, London: Profile Books, 2000, pp. 372–7.

16 Quoted in *The Future of Multi-Ethnic Britain*, p. 229.

17 L. Colley, *Britons: Forging the Nation 1707–1837*, London: Pimlico, 1992, p. 17.

18 For an introduction to various aspects of northern English sport, see J. Hill and J. Williams (eds) *Sport and Identity in the North of England*, Keele: Keele University Press, 1996.

19 C. Marshall, A. Vowles, R. Del Naja, A. Thaws, 'Blue Lines', on Massive Attack, *Blue Lines*, Circa Records, 1991.

20 Z. Smith, *White Teeth*, London: Penguin, 2000, pp. 233–4.

21 E. Cashmore, *Black Sportsmen*, London: Routledge, 1982, pp. 11–36.

22 Englandneworder, 'World in Motion', Factory Records, 1990.

23 L. Christie, *To Be Honest With You*, London: Michael Joseph, 1995, p. 37.

24 Quoted in M. Marqusee, *Anyone but England: cricket, race and class*, second edition, London: Two Heads, 1998, p. 157. See also Maguire, 'Globalization, sport and national identities', p. 298–9.

25 Quoted in Marqusee, *Anyone but England*, p. 290.

26 Quoted in Marqusee, *Anyone but England*, p. 158.

27 'Highs and lows of London Welsh', London Welsh RFC, http://www.london-welsh.co.uk, accessed January 2003.

28 'The Club', London Irish RFC, http://www.london-irish.com/-new/html/the_club/n_introduction_01.html, accessed January 2003.

29 'History', London Nigerians RFC, http://www.londonnigerian.com, accessed January 2003.

30 London Kiwis RFC, http://www.londonkiwis.com.

31 London Springboks RFC, http://www.londonspringboks.com.

32 S. Bhachu, 'Talking balls', interview with Sunny Kanwal, 1 June 2001, BBCi Asian Life, http://www.bbc.co.uk/asianlife/sport/talkingballs/sunny_kanwal, accessed December 2002.

33 For an overview of the Jewish sport scene in England, see the sports section of *The Jewish Chronicle*, available on-line at http://www.jchron.co.uk.

34 G. Evans, *Prince of the Ring: The Naseem Hamid Story*, London: Robson, 1996, p. 39.

35 For a wide-ranging discussion of sport and homosexuality, and a historical analysis of the Gay Games, see B. Pronger, *The Arena of Masculinity: Sports, Homosexuality, and the Meaning of Sex*, London: GMP, 1990. This predominantly North American survey has yet to be developed by British scholars.

36 For results and statistics, see http://www.gaygames.com.

37 Ravi Deepres quoted, *Guardian*, 12 February 2003.

38 Globalisation has a vast literature. See, for example, K. Ohmae, *The Borderless World*, London: Fontana, 1990; K. Ohmae, *The End of the Nation State: The Rise of Regional Economies*, New York: Free Press, 1995; J. Bird, B. Curtis, T. Putnam, G. Robertson and L. Tickner (eds) *Mapping the Futures: Local Cultures, Global Change*, London: Routledge, 1993; R. Holton, *Globalization and the Nation-State*, Basingstoke: Macmillan, 1998; P. Preston, *Political/Cultural Identity: Citizens and Nations in a Global Era*, London: Sage, 1997; A. D. Smith, *Nations and Nationalism in a Global Era*, Cambridge: Polity Press, 1995; M. Waters, *Globalization*, London: Routledge, 1995. For an influential survey of sport and globalisation, see J. Maguire, *Global Sport: Identities, Societies, Civilizations*, Cambridge: Polity Press, 1999. For a brief introduction, see

J. Maguire, 'Sport and globalization', in Coakley and Dunning (eds) *Handbook of Sports Studies*, pp. 356–69.

39 For a collection of chapters on this theme, see J. Bale and J. Maguire (eds) *The Global Sports Arena: Athletic Talent Migration in an Interdependent World*, London: Frank Cass, 1994.

40 BBC Sport, 'Cudicini given England tip', http://news.bbc.co.uk/sport1/hi/football/teams/c/chelsea/2739845.stm, 8 February 2003; accessed 8 February 2003.

41 Both quoted in S. Hughes, 'Eriksson is a credit to the visionaries', *Daily Telegraph*, 2 September 2001. Online, http://www.telegraph.co.uk/sport, accessed December 2002.

2 'Your boys took one hell of a beating!'

English football and British decline, *c*.1950–80

Dilwyn Porter

Lord Nelson! Lord Beaverbrook! Sir Winston Churchill! Sir Anthony Eden! Clement Attlee! Henry Cooper! Lady Diana! Maggie Thatcher – can you hear me Maggie Thatcher! Your boys took one hell of a beating! Your boys took one hell of a beating![1]

The importance of football in its modern form as an identifiable element of English culture and signifier of Englishness has long been recognized. As a recent study of English society in the first half of the twentieth century has observed, sport was 'one of the most powerful of England's civil cultures' and football was 'the country's greatest sport'.[2] For many years the history of football dovetailed neatly with the complacent view that English people and the institutions they had created were innately superior to those found in other countries. Two Englishmen, it was said in the 1950s, left to their own devices on a desert island, would quickly organize a league and cup programme to be played according to the rules and regulations laid down by 'The Football Association', as the English governing body modestly styled itself. The success of football as a world game could be attributed, it seemed, to the fact that it had been 'made in England' and embodied a sense of orderliness that was supposed to characterise the English way of life. It was a product, according to the same source, of 'the English genius for organisation'.[3] A greater awareness that the game had developed a life of its own away from English shores developed later. Yet the stamp of origin remained important. In the making of the world game, it was argued, 'the English influence was central'.[4]

Football has also been seen as one of a number of artefacts which, taken together, help to define something that might be labelled 'English culture'. In the 1950s, Asa Briggs, one of the first social historians to take sport seriously, was delighted to discover that T.S. Eliot, no less, had discerned English culture in nineteenth-century Gothic churches, boiled cabbage, and also in the annual ritual of the Cup Final. Of these, the latter was by far the most important because, for many Englishmen, football was 'life itself'.[5] More specifically, sport in general and football in particular were increasingly recognised as components of English (and British) working-class culture. At work, Richard Hoggart explained in his classic account of working-class life in the north of England, 'sport vies with sex as the staple of conversation'.[6] High-minded politicians who forgot this did so at their peril. When, in the late 1940s, football matches on midweek afternoons were banned in an effort to curb rampant absenteeism, there were loud complaints from those who argued that the government 'had no right to interfere with the sport of the working man'. This was a timely reminder that football was England's most popular spectator sport and also, as A.J.P. Taylor put it later, its 'most democratic'.[7]

When they were not talking about sport or sex, and sometimes when they were, English people, and men in particular, have often been preoccupied with the idea of national decline. From the mid 1950s the daily diet of news and comment emanating from the mass media ensured that it was permanently on the agenda. Writing in the late 1960s, David Frost and Antony Jay, only slightly tongue-in-cheek, found signs of decay everywhere they looked.

> Ruin and misery the pundit sees as he gazes upon his England. Huge debts, inefficient industries, antiquated unions, uncompetitive managements, inadequate exports, depleted reserves, restrained wages, congested roads, decaying cities, irresponsible adolescents, irreligious clerics, escaped convicts, television addicts, and short-sighted bureaucrats. All trying to support the crumbling ruins of a derelict empire with an inadequate army, a doubtful currency and a Royal Mint with a hole in the middle.[8]

Though better fed, better clothed, better housed, better educated and better off than any previous generation, English people who lived through or were born into the post-war era became accustomed to the idea that they belonged to an old country that had seen better days.

Neither was this view the exclusive property of the fashionable pundit. As it has recently been observed of the post-war period: 'to live in England was to take part in a sort of wake'.[9] Sometimes a particular event – the retreat from Suez in 1956, the devaluation of sterling in 1967, the so-called 'Winter of Discontent' in 1978–79 – prompted anger and a sense of frustration to surface. More often, chronic discontent found expression in milder form as part of the common currency of everyday conversation. It was overlaid from the early 1960s by nagging anxieties arising from enhanced awareness of Britain's relative economic decline; relative, that is, in terms of the performance of its economy when compared to the economies of other developed nations. These experiences left their mark. There was, of course, 'practically no indicator of economic-related well-being on which individual British citizens have not vastly improved their situation over the post-war period'.[10] Opinion poll evidence suggests, nevertheless, that this benign state of affairs had little impact on public opinion. Asked, at the end of every year between 1960 and 1979, if they anticipated 'economic prosperity' or 'economic difficulty' in the twelve months to come, pessimists outnumbered optimists, often by a considerable margin, in every year but one (1964).[11]

It seems likely that coming to terms with the realities of the post-war era may have been more difficult for those who saw themselves primarily as 'English' rather than 'British'. Loss of empire and a dawning sense of Britain's diminished status in world affairs impacted especially hard on the English. 'We are at the end of a century', it was noted at the millennium, 'in which England lost the Empire it called British'.[12] It was also a century in which England's predominance as the most powerful of the separate national components comprising the United Kingdom was progressively undermined. Though nationalist sentiment in Scotland and Wales was insufficiently developed to secure majority support for political devolution in 1978, there was by then enough writing on the wall for some observers to anticipate 'the break-up of Britain' at some point in the not too distant future. 'There is no doubt', argued the Scottish socialist, Tom Nairn, 'that the old British state is going down'.[13] As the 'old British state' was largely an English creation, this required the English to make some painful adjustments, not only in the way in which they viewed themselves, but also in the way in which they viewed the Celtic nations with whom they shared the British Isles.

Moreover, as perceptions of economic decline became pervasive, it was difficult for England, as the dominant political and economic nation within the United Kingdom, to avoid taking the lion's share of the blame. As Nairn observed:

> That arcadian England which appeals so strongly to foreign intellectuals, is also the England which has, since the early 1950s, fallen into ever more evident and irredeemable decline – the United Kingdom of permanent economic crisis, falling standards, bankrupt governments, slavish dependence on the United States, and myopic expedients.[14]

When a cultural critique of Britain's declining economy emerged in the early 1980s, it was *English* culture that was at the heart of the problem, a culture that resisted systematic modernisation and discouraged industrial enterprise.[15] More often than not, Britain's ills were attributed to something called 'the English disease'.

In short, there may be something to be said for Jeremy Paxman's recent complaint that it is 'the obsession with decline that has poisoned the country's idea of itself since the war'.[16] Another way of putting it might be to say that what some have referred to as 'declinism' has helped to shape the evolution of English national identity throughout the post-war period. The business of this chapter is to indicate ways in which English football contributed to this process. Richard Holt and Tony Mason, in their study of sport in Britain since 1945, have implied that there was a discernible connection. Before the mid-1950s, the tendency was to take a fairly relaxed view of England's performances against foreign opposition. This changed after the short, sharp shock of Suez, the subsequent retreat from empire and the growing realisation that Britain counted for less than it once had in a world now dominated by the United States and the Soviet Union, the two post-war superpowers. Thereafter, it was much more diffi-cult for the English to view the efforts of their national side with detach-ment. A more chauvinistic tone became evident in the popular press. 'Winning became more important'.[17] Holt has noted elsewhere the tend-ency in recent years for nationalism in English sport to become more pro-nounced 'as the imperial role, through which it was formerly expressed, has disappeared'.[18]

The intention here is to show how the troubles besetting English foot-ball, along with its occasional triumphs, as mediated for the benefit of the British public, became part of the wider public discourse relating to national decline. Defeat for the national side, especially if it meant exclusion from the final stages of major competitions, served as a painful reminder that the world order had changed. In 1973, having con-ceded that England had no 'divine right' to success, *The Times* continued wistfully:

> Yet it is ironic to think that now sides like Morocco, Zaire or Zambia, on the one hand, and Australia or South Korea on the other – nations of little or no footballing tradition or distinction – should be in the final line up next summer while the pioneers of the game should be on the outside looking in.[19]

Increasingly, the game was written and talked about in a way that implied a sense of cultural bereavement, an awareness that something important had been lost or damaged beyond repair. From the late 1950s onwards there was much open criticism of the spirit in which the English game had come to be played. For the influential football journalist, Brian Glanville, a professional foul committed by Roy McFarland on a Polish forward at Wembley in October 1973 was symptomatic: 'once you have reached this stage of cynicism, games aren't worth playing at all'.[20] These themes were later developed powerfully in James Walvin's extended essay, *Football and the Decline of Britain*, itself a reflection of the despair that enveloped English football after the appalling stadium tragedies at Bradford and Heysel in 1985. A game that had once reflected the confidence and faith in progress of its Victorian founding fathers had come by the 1980s 'to repre-sent much of what ailed domestic life'. Walvin conceded that the problems he outlined were not confined to England; they were to be found to some extent in Scotland too. It could not be denied, however, that 'the disasters were English, and the subsequent punishments were properly directed at English football'.[21]

Much of the discussion relating to football seemed to give currency to the idea that to be English in the third quarter of the twentieth century was to belong to a once great nation that was incapable of living up to its past or competing effectively with its principal rivals. In this way, it will be suggested, English football and those who reported on it or interpreted it for public consumption, contributed to the prolonged angst about British decline and to the sense of crisis that it engendered. 'Of all the sports', noted Ted Croker, secretary of the Football Association, after England had failed to qualify for the final stages of the 1974 World Cup, 'football is the one we are expected to excel at internationally'. 'If we fail', he continued, 'we get criticised … and we deserve it'.[22] Though it might be argued that this can also be applied to cricket we are concerned here with the particular role of football, during a significant period of transition, in sustaining and replenishing those myths from which a sense of English national identity is derived and given shape. It acknowledges that the England team often serves as a metaphor for England itself and for Englishness.

Parallel narratives of decline

The idea that the course of its football history is somehow indicative of life in England more generally has been widely held by those who have written about it, in whatever genre, in the modern era. Since the late nineteenth century, as one of the game's gentlemanly scholars noted in the late 1960s, 'football has increasingly reflected the detailed pattern of social, political, and economic forces at work within the body politic'.[23] With growing awareness, after 1966, of the capacity of the English football team to generate a powerful and increasingly inclusive image of the imagined nation it was only to be expected that this theme should later be picked up and developed by other commentators. For John Clarke and Charles Critcher, looking back from the 1980s, the success or otherwise of the national team playing the national game in international competition had become 'a very sensitive popular indicator of the state of the nation'. The perceived decline of England as a power in world football 'provided a telling reminder of the failing fortunes of a Britain losing not only its Empire, but also its imperial role and status'. Here, then, writ large, was an example of the so-called 'athletic fallacy', a popular misconception characterised as 'the tendency to see English sporting performances as somehow symptomatic of the nation's health'.[24]

It is important to recognize at this point that there are competing or parallel narratives relating the story of Britain's decline, each of them constructed within a particular ideological framework, often with party political interests in mind. Over the years since the 1950s, the idea that the country was going to the dogs has proved especially useful to opposition parties, from both left and right, simply because it supplied an issue on which the government of the day was inevitably vulnerable. National decline could be 'used very loosely to appeal to a variety of worries' while generating simultaneously 'a vague sense of unease'.[25] It was, by nature, an all-embracing issue that could be pursued in many ways and linked to any number of themes, including football, as international rivalry intensified in the era of the Cold War. From the 1950s onwards, as Stephen Wagg has observed, Fleet Street journalists, as they explored the imagined subconscious of their readers, were increasingly inclined to exploit 'two highly promising anxieties: a wounded national pride associated with the dismantlement of the British Empire and a fear of communism'.[26] It proved relatively easy to assimilate the perceived decline of English football, where 'we' had once exercised an effortless superiority but were now sometimes beaten by teams from the Soviet bloc, like Hungary and Poland, into this disappointed, fearful way of looking at the world.

Recent work on the origins of the debate relating specifically to Britain's relative economic decline is also instructive here. Jim Tomlinson has suggested that 'declinism' took on the characteristics of an ideology. It embraced the political in the sense that the perception of decline as a problem implied 'that something could and should be done to improve economic performance'. He also notes that sustaining the idea of decline required an assessment of relative economic performance drawing on 'contemporary measurements and assessments of that performance'.[27] There are important parallels here with the ways in which the English team was written and talked about, much of which implied that 'something should be done', even if it was only to sack the manager. Donald Saunders of the *Daily Telegraph* encapsulated this neatly in 1973. 'Now England have been relegated to a place among soccer's second-class powers', he observed, 'while the elite prepare for next summer's World Cup summit meeting, the long difficult task of rehabilitation must begin immediately'.[28] At the same time, the growth of international competition, especially among European nations, generated a number of ways in which the performance of England's footballers relative to those of other nations might be realistically assessed. English participation in the World Cup, beginning in 1950, was an important development in this respect, its impact reinforced by appearances in the European Nations Championships after 1964. Since then, England's international competitiveness has been subject to more or less continuous assessment and intensive public scrutiny.

A variety of explanations have been advanced to explain Britain's fall from the position it once occupied as the world's first industrial nation. The complacency and short-termism of those who owned or managed industry was a feature of critiques emanating from the left; the inflexibility of Britain's unionised workforce and its stubborn resistance to change were the problems often identified by commentators on the right. Cultural explanations, like that associated with Martin Wiener, resorted to more complex historical arguments to explain why modernisation had been persistently frustrated in England's green and pleasant land. As the academic debate developed in the 1970s and 1980s, however, there was an increasing tendency to characterise the problem in terms of 'sclerotic tendencies inherent within the country's institutional arrangements'.[29] By then, it had become commonplace to explain the perceived underachievement of English football in comparable fashion, a tendency that remains evident in more recent literature.

The famous blank page in the autobiography of Sunderland's maverick, Len Shackleton, denoting 'the average director's knowledge of football' was an early sign of the times.[30] Press criticism of the assorted butchers, bakers and candlestick-makers to be found in the boardrooms of every club in England's Football League was commonplace, an integral part of the inquest that followed any serious setback for the national side. Elsewhere, the FA's resistance to change was well known. Walter Winterbottom, England's team manager from 1946 to 1963 became accustomed to the response: 'But, Walter, you've been doing it like that for years, so why change?'[31] After he had stepped aside to make way for Alf Ramsey, Winterbottom's claims on the vacant post of FA secretary were overlooked. Some argue that he 'could have revolutionized the way the game was run'; but, once again, Winterbottom was thwarted 'by the tin-pot gods of the FA'.[32] Ramsey, despite the success he enjoyed in 1966 and for a few years after, believed that he had been held back in the same way, complaining after his dismissal that 'the amateurs are back in charge'.[33] Brian Clough's story of his relationship with the FA makes sense in this context. Twice, in 1973 and 1977, he was passed over when the England manager's job fell vacant, despite an outstanding record in club football. Called to interview, he was confronted by a panel made up of elderly men who had 'bungled a few things in their time'.

> Those who refused to make me England manager in 1977 will never know what they would have missed. But they were scared to death of what would have hit them.[34]

Clough, it seems, saw himself as a moderniser frustrated by a football establishment displaying all the symptoms of institutional sclerosis.

1953 and all that

In this section and the one that follows, the intention is to track England's performances in key international matches from 1950 through to 1981 while cross-referring throughout to developments or historical moments that are more conventionally located within narratives of national decline.

This carries us from the totally unexpected defeat (0–1) by the United States at Belo Horizonte in 1950 to the failure in Oslo thirty-one years later that prompted the celebrated television commentary from which this chapter derives its title. At the start of the period, preoccupation with decline had yet to set in; at the end it appeared to have become a fixed item on Britain's political agenda. What is being suggested here is that international football, as experienced by newspaper readers, radio listeners and television viewers, provided a popular point of access to the complex of anxieties encapsulated by declinism as an ideology.

International football possessed a capacity to impact on the public mood in a powerful way throughout the period. Arguably, this effect became progressively stronger as television coverage expanded, given the tendency to address viewers 'in terms of national belongingness'.[35] As Niall Edworthy has recently observed: 'It does not take a political clairvoyant to work out that when half the public settles down to watch an England match, the nation's 'feel-good' factor will swing one way or the other according to the result'.[36] Factory output may or may not improve, tills may or may not ring more often in the High Street. It seems fairly safe to assume, however, that a satisfying performance leading to a good result by England in a major international match will leave a significant number of English people feeling more rather than less positive about their national identity and what it means. In defeat, this process goes into reverse. 'The whole country feels let down', claimed Birmingham City's manager, Jim Smith, after England had lost to Norway in 1981, 'and I mean everyone in England'.[37]

'The story of British football and the foreign challenge', Glanville concluded in 1955, 'is the story of a vast superiority, sacrificed through stupidity, short-sightedness and wanton insularity'.[38] These, along with a capacity for infinite self-deception', were the English failings exposed by the Hungarians at Wembley in 1953. There had, of course, been an earlier humiliation for England's footballers but the shock emanating from Belo Horizonte in 1950 had only a limited effect. Malcolm Allison, then playing for Charlton Athletic, later recalled that it made little impact on 'the dim, bland men whose voices were most powerful in English football'.[39] Or, indeed, on the British public whose engagement with an event happening on the other side of the world was minimal. Reporting facilities were primitive, thwarting Fleet Street journalists who might otherwise have given the story the sensationalist treatment it merited. There was, moreover, no television coverage. This helps to explain why the reaction to what is still regarded as the worst defeat in the England's football history was 'strangely muted'.[40]

Though it was possible to write off a freakish result at a distant South American venue, intensive press interest in England's home performances was inescapable. In the 1950s and early 1960s press coverage of sport expanded in mass circulation titles, like the *Daily Mirror* and the

Daily Express, as well as in middle and upmarket newspapers. Sports news, predominantly football, accounted for only about a quarter of the news in the *Mirror* at the start of the 1950s; by the end of the 1960s it accounted for more than half.[41] Those who wrote seriously about football for serious newspapers, like Geoffrey Green of *The Times* and Don Davies of the *Manchester Guardian*, encouraged the chattering classes to familiarize themselves with the people's game and helped raise its social status. Coverage in the quality press also tended to enhance awareness of continental football. Davies, 'delighted in the performance of star players on the continent' while Glanville, in the *Sunday Times*, reflected on 'the gradual decline of the British game as it was steadily overtaken by European and South American football'.[42] These developments coincided with the arrival of national decline as a significant political issue and anxieties arising from rising East-West hostility. On the sports pages, particularly at the *Mirror* and the *Express*, selling respectively 4.7 and 4.0 million copies daily in the mid-1950s, Peter Wilson and Desmond Hackett 'began to inject a patriotic invective into their reportage of the English team'.[43]

In this context, the defeats inflicted on England by Hungary at Wembley in 1953 (6–3) and Budapest in 1954 (7–1) were alarming in that they could be represented as a victory for communism. Before the match at Wembley, Wilson had expressed the earnest hope that the visitors would be beaten 'without any shadow of a doubt'. He had visited Hungary and knew 'how they, like other totalitarian states I have seen, regard a sporting triumph as a justification for their "superior" way of life'.[44] A win for Hungary would indicate powerfully that the people who had given the game to the world were no longer its masters. It was thus important to deny the regime in Budapest the opportunity to make propaganda at the expense of English football. Victory for England, on the other hand, would serve to reassure the unconscious believer in the athletic fallacy that all was well. The failure of the hoped-for conclusion to materialise in this instance may well have perplexed the 'ordinary man' who, according to a *Times* leader of the period, found 'the form of our professional footballers a more convenient indication of the state of the nation than all the economist's soundings'.[45] What all this suggests is that a disappointing performance in a high-profile match by those selected to represent England at football could now initiate a ripple effect, contributing to the 'vague sense of unease' regarding national decline.

On the day after Hungary's victory at Wembley, the first time that England had been defeated at home by a team from outside the British Isles, the *News Chronicle* published a photograph of Gyula Grosics, the Hungarian goalkeeper, walking on his hands. '6–3', ran the accompanying headline, 'NOW THE WORLD IS REALLY TURNED UPSIDE DOWN'.[46] It is important to retain a sense of the immediate historical context here. Public consciousness of national decline as a political issue was merely stirring in 1953, a year in which media coverage of the

Coronation of Elizabeth II guaranteed a succession of reassuring images of British power and Britain's place in the world. For those who looked to sport to provide an indication of the nation's condition there was great satisfaction to be derived from England's long-awaited Ashes triumph over Australia, the foundations of which had been laid by Watson and Bailey's heroic resistance in the second match of the series at Lords. All this, along with the conquest of Everest, helped to sustain an optimistic belief that the country was entering a glorious 'New Elizabethan' age. Thus the shock generated by Hungary's victory at Wembley was containable.

This is not to underestimate the significance of November 1953 as a critical turning point, readily recognizable both at the time and with the use of hindsight, by those within the game and close to it. The Hungarians, wrote former England captain, Charles Buchan, before the game, 'impressed me as great players', There was, nevertheless, 'nothing to rave about'. After the match he could only praise the team his headline writer had dubbed 'THE NEW WEMBLEY WIZARDS' and urge 'that something must be done with the England players before the World Cup'.[47] Perhaps it was Buchan that Glanville had in mind when he observed a little later:

> The result of this match gave eyes even to the blind who had ignored all those defeats which had taken place abroad. All at once ... everyone was wise, everyone casting round for scapegoats and explanations, everyone, in short, had discerned the crisis which had existed for over thirty years.[48]

Later still, Glanville remembered Buchan as 'a large, prosaic, amiably banal man' whose opinions 'were delivered ponderously in a South London accent'.[49] Yet Buchan was a respected football journalist and well known as a radio broadcaster. He was also more representative of English football than Glanville, a young tyro in the mid 1950s, whose interest in and knowledge of the game in Italy marked him out as unusual. If the Hungarians had caused the scales to fall from Buchan's eyes it was an important signifier.

'The Hungarian victory', Buchan recalled, ' – I almost said rhapsody – caused a flutter in official circles'.[50] The FA invited managers of England's professional clubs 'to confer on the means to improve the standard of English football in general and of International teams in particular'. A little later, after the 1954 World Cup finals had underlined the lessons taught by the Hungarians, reforms were introduced with the aim of enabling England's manager 'to concentrate much more on the preparation of International teams at all levels, during the next four or five years'.[51] It was a modest strategy but one which began to restore the prestige of English football in the eyes of its supporters. England performed creditably at the finals of the World Cup in Sweden in 1958; if they had not been denied the massive promise of Duncan Edwards and other Manchester United players killed in the Munich air disaster, they might have done better. John Moynihan, in an essay first published in 1966, located the emergence of Matt Busby's young team as a force in Europe in the context of other events of the mid-1950s that pointed to Britain's decline as a world power. At a time, he recalled, when British prestige was plummeting internationally after Suez, United had provided 'welcome consolation'.[52] It was an almost casual observation but it betrayed an awareness of national decline that would not have been apparent a few years earlier.

The road from 1966

Britain changed in many important ways between Sweden 1958 and England 1966. At some point its people joined the affluent society, an event signalled by a sudden surge in the sale of consumer goods hitherto regarded as luxuries. In 1957, the year in which Harold Macmillan, the Prime Minister, boasted that most people had 'never had it so good', the number of television viewing licenses issued totalled 6.9 million. 'Most of us', it should be remembered, 'spend a lot of time watching television ... so the way that television shows sport probably plays a part in shaping the way we see and understand the world'.[53] By 1966, the year that Bobby Moore lifted the Jules Rimet trophy in triumph on a sunny afternoon at Wembley, the number had risen to 13.5 million. Given the pervasive influence of declinism on accounts of recent British history it is important to remember 'what went right' as well as 'what went wrong'.[54]

Ironically, this transformation was accompanied by numerous reminders that Britain was no longer a Great Power on the world stage. In the immediate post-Suez era, independence was yielded to colony after colony. Britain had lost an empire; its role in a world dominated by the two post-war superpowers was a matter for nervous conjecture. These conditions generated a feverish debate about what was wrong and recognition of the need to revitalise Britain's flagging economy and strip out those institutions that were deemed to be holding the country back. Modernisation on these lines was the ticket that carried Labour to a narrow victory in the 1964 general election and it remained a keynote political issue throughout the 1960s. Some readings of England's 1966 victory locate it within this particular context with Alf Ramsey as the personification of 'scientific management' intent on innovation.[55]

One aspect of the continuing concern with the performance of the economy over this period was an enhanced interest in the comparative dimension. 'There is no excuse', argued *The Times*, 'for being unaware of the way in which other countries are forging ahead in the fields where Britain once led'.[56] As the government prepared its first, ultimately unsuccessful, bid to join the six states then comprising the European Economic Community, attention increasingly focused on Britain's relatively sluggish growth rate alongside that achieved in France, Italy and West Germany, at that time enjoying a well-publicised 'economic miracle'. Comparative indicators proliferated, helping to confirm the suspicion that the British had somehow missed out. For those for whom football supplied a rule-of-thumb measure of their country's standing in the league of nations, the expansion of European competition may well have had a similar effect.

Television was especially important here. It helped 'to break down the resilient barriers of insularity which for so long isolated British football'.[57] Televised European Cup football helped to spread an awareness of new standards of excellence. The 1958 final between Real Madrid and Milan, regarded as a classic by those who saw it, had been played in Brussels and attracted little attention in the British media. In 1960, however, Real's 7–3 victory over Eintracht Frankfurt was staged in Glasgow 'under the noses of the British press, radio and television'. Gerald Sinstadt, the football commentator, later recalled that it had generated huge interest.[58] Televised matches from England's unhappy 1962 World Cup campaign in Chile, a solitary win against Argentina aside, did not make comfortable viewing. 'We did not get a warm reception at home', recalled one member of the squad. Ray Wilson, England's left-back, was not alone in entertaining serious misgivings when Ramsey, not long after taking up his appointment as manager, predicted that England would win the 1966 World Cup. 'Obviously', he later recalled, 'he knew something that we didn't'.[59]

What had not yet changed by 1966 was a general acceptance of a British national identity in which Englishness remained the dominant characteristic. World Cup final day 1966 was essentially a moment in English rather than British cultural history. From the outset, Ramsey had declared his faith 'in England and Englishmen, as well as English football'.[60] He was sufficiently versed in the history of Anglo-Scottish rivalry, for example, to know that a victory for England, even over Germany, with whom the British had fought two savage wars in recent memory, was not a triumph that could, or should, be shared. 'This is the day we've all been waiting for', said Kenneth Wolstenholme as he opened his match day commentary for BBC television.[61] Some people, however, were resolute in their determination not to be included. Scotland's Denis Law took himself off to the golf course for the afternoon. 'I thought it was the end of the world', he said later, recalling his feelings as news of England's 4–2 win reached him. 'There was great rivalry between Scotland and England in those days', he explained, 'and I was not happy that they had done it, but of course it was the greatest thing that ever happened to English football'.[62]

And, of course, it was also one of the greatest things that ever happened to the English nation, supplying an occasion for a positive re-affirmation of national identity matched in modern times only by VE day in 1945 and the Coronation in 1953. England's progress was watched with growing interest by sections of the population previously indifferent to 'soccer' and it has been argued that this was indicative of 'a nationalism which incidentally happened upon football'.[63] The expressions of national identity that it generated were almost invariably benign, mercifully free of the beer-bellied aggression of later years. Moreover, it could be argued, Ramsey's team had succeeded, not by copying the continentals, but by exploiting what were widely considered to be the peculiar virtues of the English game. 'So', as Ramsey's biographer concludes, 'we had guts aplenty, power and stamina in every department, creating an environment in which our great players could operate most effectively, restoring belief in English qualities'.[64] Football had come home and it seemed immensely reassuring at the time.

How does England's triumph of 1966 articulate with the story of declinism and its grip on Britain in the 1970s and 1980s? Taken at face value, winning the World Cup, albeit with home advantage, seemed to suggest that the slide into relative backwardness so evident when Hungary had beaten England in 1953, had been arrested. The warm glow generated by England's victory lasted for as long as England retained the world championship and a little beyond, given a creditable performance in 1970. There was no shame in returning from Mexico having been narrowly defeated by Brazil, the eventual winners, and West Germany. It was disappointing, recalled Alan Ball, but 'we were part of a magnificent tournament and part of an England team that played some cracking football, and they were marvellous games'.[65] Thereafter, however, as success proved elusive, Wembley 1966 was increasingly characterized in the press and elsewhere as a peak from which England had now declined, another item in the collection of cultural clutter symbolic of national greatness once possessed but now lost.

Indeed, much recent writing on the history of English football at international level has suggested that the seeds of future disappointments were sown in 1966. 'There are certain thoughts an Englishman is best advised to keep to himself', the journalist Rob Steen observed in 1994, such as 'I wish that bomb had got Maggie' and 'God bless America'. 'Neither' he continued, 'above all, does it do to suggest that the 1966 World Cup was the worst thing ever to happen to our national game'. Since then, however, this view has surfaced more frequently in the football literature and is now almost a commonplace. 'Let me just say', wrote David Thomson mildly in his 1996 commemoration of the great day, 'that there are ways in which England's victory in 1966 made later defeats a little more likely'. For David Downing, writing four years later on the history of Anglo-German football relations, 1966 was 'the fatal victory', reinforcing notions of English superiority and making it difficult to adapt to or learn from the continuing development of the game elsewhere.[66] There are clear echoes here of the literature of decline dating from the 1980s, notably Correlli Barnett's *Audit of War* which argued that the root of Britain's post-war troubles could be traced to 'wartime British dreams, illusions and realities'.[67]

Precursors of this trend in football historiography were evident in press comment following England's European Nations Championship matches against West Germany in 1972 and the World Cup qualifiers against Poland in 1973. A 3–1 defeat by the stylish West Germans at Wembley in April followed by a dull, defensive and very physical performance to secure a 0–0 draw in Berlin a few weeks later seemed to suggest that England had stagnated since 1966 whereas West Germany had progressed. This paralleled much that was being written about the relative strengths of the British and West German economies at the time. Public opinion, on the question of joining the European Economic Community, for example, continued to be driven by the idea that Britain continued to eke out a miserable existence as 'Europe's economic invalid'.[68]

Since 1966, according to the *Daily Mirror*, old habits had re-appeared. 'As is so often the case', Peter Wilson declared, 'we have been content to dwell in the past and rest complacently on past triumphs until events – and other nations – overtake and surpass us'. In the *Sunday Times*, under the heading 'Brian James blames the 1966 World Cup Win', a similar analysis was offered. After 1966, England continued to believe in the 'triumphant manliness' that had secured victory for Ramsey's team. For West Germany, however, defeat had been followed by a critical re-appraisal. 'They have now moved nearer to the best of the Latins whom we beat in 1966 and then forgot'.[69] This message was reinforced when England, after failing to break down Poland's defence at Wembley in October 1973, were eliminated from the 1974 World Cup. It would be the first time since entering the competition in 1950 that England had failed to qualify for the final stages.

Though much criticism focused on Ramsey's tactics there was also a recognition that England had slipped backwards 'In eight years', as Dave Bowler observes, 'they'd gone from being World Champions to being nobodies'.[70] The most optimistic gloss that the press could put on these events was to suggest that England had been unlucky. The best hope for the future was radical reform. Under the heading 'WHEN FOOTBALL IS ALL KICKS', a leading article in the *Daily Mirror* suggested that if the result prompted 'a shake-up' then Poland 'will have done English football a good turn'.[71] It was the familiar knee-jerk reaction to defeat overlaid with a sense that 'we' had been there before. England, argued Geoffrey Green in *The Times*, had been given four years to re-examine its methods. 'If we can do that', he added cheerfully, 'and do it under intelligent direction there may yet be a rebirth before 1978 as came after the historic Hungarian defeat which shook English football to its foundations precisely twenty years ago'.[72]

This optimistic prospect largely disappeared from sight during the course of the 1970s. Not only did England fail to qualify for the 1974 World Cup finals, they were left behind in 1978 too. English football resolutely refused to be born again. A critical qualifying group defeat by Italy in Rome in November 1976 suggested that teams picked by Ramsey's successor, Don Revie, continued to exhibit the by now familiar deficiencies associated with the English game. 'We have men who can run and chase, battle and work', concluded Frank McGhee in the *Daily Mirror*, 'something they all did manfully, sweatily, in the match'. Unfortunately, the Italians had 'men who can play'. Strangely, this seemed to give them an advantage. The return match at Wembley a year later, largely empty of significance as it was already clear that England would not qualify, provided McGhee with an opportunity to indicate just how far expectations had diminished. 'The days when you could beat the drum for England', he wrote before the game, 'and make bold fighting forecasts with some certainty of success have long gone'.[73]

The press faithfully tracked the decline into what Norman Fox of *The Times* characterised as 'England's football poverty'.[74] It was little consolation for the English that Scotland succeeded in qualifying on both occasions. Gloomy introspection on the sports pages was perfectly in line with the plethora of decline literature that appeared towards the end of a decade in which governments of both the right and the left had struggled manfully, apparently without success, to deal with the intractable problems of the British economy. With unemployment rising to record postwar levels, it was easy to conclude that the British people had 'never had it so bad'. This was compounded by a growing realisation that the 'economic miracle' experienced by other industrialised nations after 1950 had left Britain behind.[75]

In these circumstances, the possibility of not qualifying for the World Cup finals for the third time running, after an unexpected defeat (2–1) by unfancied Norway in September 1981, simply supplied more kindling for the funeral pyre. By this time the *Sun's* circulation (3.7 million) had surpassed that of the *Daily Mirror* (3.6) and it had become the preferred quick read of the English working class. When following England, its journalists constructed a fantasy world based on atavistic notions of national greatness laced with contempt for those it accused of selling the country short. Its football writers demanded football of a quality befitting the nation that invented the game and then gave it to the world.[76] When this did not materialise the *Sun* put the boot in. Greeting defeat in Norway with the headline 'IT'S THE END OF THE WORLD FOR ENGLAND', criticism focused mainly on the players who were 'the laughing-stock of the world'. A comparative yardstick was offered with the claim that England were now 'down among the banana republics of world football'.[77] The Norwegian commentator's well-publicised coda, shouted into the microphone at the end of the match, not to mention his astute grasp of English history, was the final indignity. Beneath the sensationalism, however, the message was essentially the same as that with which readers of all sections of the British press had been regaled for years. 'Norway 2 England 1', declared Jimmy Greaves, outlining his plan to 'save' English football, 'could be just the result to start a revolution that is long overdue'.[78]

The importance of being English

England, it has been suggested, 'has ceased to be a mere country and become a place of the mind'.[79] In bringing this discussion to a close, the intention is to identify ways in which English football, as played at international level and interpreted for public consumption by the mass media, helped to shape a sense of England in the minds of the English in the late twentieth century. Consciousness of national identity, it might be argued, rather like consciousness of class, is shaped by shared experience, especially of the kind that creates a collective awareness that those people who constitute the nation are essentially different from others whom they encounter. International sport plays a part in this process, even if most people experience it only indirectly through the consumption of mass-produced words and images. Following the fortunes of the national football team helps to determine how English people see themselves and make sense of the world in which they live.[80]

In one of many contributions in the 1970s to the debate on Britain's decline and what should be done about it, Peter Jay described the British people in general as 'confused and unhappy'. What made them unhappy, he suggested, was evidence that the basis of their prosperity were being eroded while 'we can neither find nor agree upon any sure remedy for this decay'. What made them confused was the failure to come up with a satisfactory explanation of why this was happening to them, 'whether it is due to ... the incompetence of governments, defects of national character, the rhythms of history, the luck of the draw, or what'. These conditions had spawned a chronic malaise, 'Englanditis', characterised by a vicious circle in which the public expected more and more of leaders who were capable of supplying only less and less.[81] Though it is important not to push them too far, there are some suggestive parallels here with the unhappiness and confusion, albeit a more intermittent and significantly less important phenomenon, prompted by the progressive erosion, briefly interrupted in 1966, of England's standing in world football.

Football, a popular form of recreation and a mass spectator sport, supplied inadvertently a public point of access to the ongoing debate conducted at a higher level concerning the state of the nation. Though the loss of empire might be relatively easily grasped as the red areas on maps of the world diminished and former colonies tweaked the lion's tail, it was always more difficult to explain the problems of the British economy to a wide audience. 'I don't use the word 'City' if I can possibly help it', explained Robert Head, editor of the *Daily Mirror's* money page. For his readers, 'City were the team that beat United 3–0 on Saturday'.[82] Indeed, for *Mirror* readers, and for those who read the *Sun*, the idea of national decline was likely to be encountered first on the back rather than the front pages of their daily newspaper. It is significant in this context to recall that, of those who buy tabloid newspapers, a huge proportion are known to read them back-to-front; 'to them the back (sports) page *is* the front page'.[83] The post-disaster inquests, moreover, enabled some readers with an opportunity to engage directly, if in a rather narrow way, with the general issue of decline. England's defeat by West Germany in 1972, reported the *Daily Mirror*, 'produced easily the biggest postbag of the year'. And there was no doubting the nature of the message: 'Don't live in the past. Now is the time for change'.[84] If to be English in the 1970s was to be preoccupied with manifestations of national decline and what to do about it, concerns generated by the state of the national game were of at least symbolic significance.

This was important in reaching an understanding of what it meant to be English rather than Welsh, Scottish, Irish or British. Though some sports, like athletics and rugby union, provided opportunities to compete for Great Britain, international representation at football remained resolutely based on the four home nations. Thus, given the tendency of the media to describe sports action in terms of national stereotypes, those who followed English football were presented with a plethora of idealised images of themselves. As Liz Crolley and David Hand have argued, 'the discourse employed connects with a wider view of "Englishness" which is founded on a relatively simple set of beliefs about what it is to be English'. This incorporates a set of assumptions about the simple virtues of honest endeavour, physical courage and passionate commitment that together comprise what has long been referred to as 'the bulldog spirit'.[85] Victory for England, as in 1966, achieved in what was instantly recognisable as the English national style, was thus experienced via consumption of media output as a positive affirmation of Englishness. High profile defeats or a run of disappointing performances had a correspondingly negative impact. Thus, both triumph and disaster supplied periodic reminders of Englishness, the outcome of each match determining whether it was seen in a positive or negative light.

Moreover, British international football, organised as it was around the four home nations, routinely generated occasions that highlighted a particular awareness of Englishness.[86] One of the reasons why English-based clubs, some of which enjoyed great success in European competition in this period, could not function as a surrogate for a successful national team was that they often drew players from all four home nations, not to mention the Republic of Ireland. A Home International Championship was contested annually until 1984 and Anglo-Scottish rivalry remained a feature until the bitter end, denying the lazy option of blurring the distinction between English and British national identity. England's World Cup victory, the legitimacy of which was denied north of the border, and Scotland's swaggering 3–2 victory over the world champions at Wembley the following year marked a significant juncture in the relationship between the two nations. Geoff Hurst, credited with England's controversial third goal in the 1966 final, complained 35 years later that Scotsmen, total strangers, still sidled up to him in airport lounges to whisper, 'It never went in, wee man'.[87] Joy in Scotland, when England failed to qualify for the 1974 and 1978 World Cup finals in Germany and Argentina, was unconfined. The most popular line in 'Ally's Tartan Army', Andy Cameron's 1978 World Cup single, was the one that referred to the fact that England 'didnae qualify'. This was matched by English delight at the discomfort of the Scots when their campaign foundered in incompetence and scandal. 'Scotland are derided here', ran a front-page lead in the *Daily Mail*, 'as the dopers and no-hopers of the World Cup finals'.[88] Sir Alf had never had any illusions. Greeted at Prestwick Airport in 1967 with the words 'Welcome to Scotland', he is said to have responded in unusually robust language.[89]

All this ran counter to the bland assumption peddled by the media, that 'we', the English, were rooting for a 'British', i.e. Scottish success. It marked an untidy start to the painful but necessary process of disentangling a sense of Englishness from a British national identity that had been forged to meet the needs of an empire now long gone. It did not help that Englishness suffered from its association with the old British state as it experienced the discomforts of decline in the second half of the twentieth century. Loss of empire and a troubled economy, not to mention the 'thirty years of hurt' that began in 1966, have helped to ensure that positive affirmations of English national identity remain problematic.

Notes

1 Bjorne Minge, Norwegian television commentator, after Norway had defeated England, 9 September 1981. See 'The 10 greatest bits of commentary ever', *Observer Sports Magazine*, 6 October 2002; N. Edworthy, *The Second Most Important Job in the Country*, London: Virgin, 1999, p. 159, attributes the commentary to Borge Lillelien.

2 R. McKibbin, *Classes and Cultures: England 1918–1951*, Oxford: Oxford University Press, 1998, pp. 332, 339–50.

3 D. Batchelor, *Soccer: A History of Association Football*, London: Batsford, 1954, pp. 1–2.

4 J. Walvin, *The People's Game: A Social History of British Football*, London: Allen Lane, 1975, p. 112.

5 Briggs, 'Football and culture', *Encounter*, 1955, no. 16, p. 69.

6 R. Hoggart, *The Uses of Literacy*, London: Pelican, 1958, p. 84.

7 S. Fielding, P. Thompson and N. Tiratsoo, *'England Arise': The Labour Party and Popular Politics in 1940s Britain*, Manchester: Manchester University Press, 1995, p. 161; A.J.P. Taylor, *English History 1914–1945*, Oxford: Oxford University Press, 1965, p. 313.

8 D. Frost and A. Jay, *The English*, New York: Stein and Day, 1968, pp. 11–12.

9 J. Paxman, *The English: A Portrait of a People*, London: Penguin, 1999, pp. 233–4.

10 See I. Budge, 'Relative decline as a political issue: Ideological motivations of the politico-economic debate in post-war Britain', *Contemporary British History*, 1993, vol. 7 (1), pp. 10–12.

11 End-of-Year Poll: British trends, *Gallup Political Index*, Report no. 232, December 1979, p. 16.

12 N. Danziger, *Danziger's Britain: A Journey to the Edge*, London: Harper-Collins, 1996, p. 1.

13 T. Nairn, *The Break-Up of Britain: Crisis and Neo-Nationalism*, London: Verso, 1977, p. 13.

14 Nairn, *Break-Up*, p. 45. The seamless transition from 'England' to 'the United Kingdom' in this passage is highly significant.

15 See M.J. Wiener, *English Culture and the Decline of the Industrial Spirit*, Cambridge: Cambridge University Press, 1981, pp. 3–24.

16 Paxman, *The English*, p. 264.

17 R. Holt and T. Mason, *Sport in Britain 1945–2000*, Oxford: Blackwell, 2000, p. 129.

18 R. Holt, *Sport and the British: A Modern History*, Oxford: Oxford University Press, 1989, pp. 272–3.

19 *The Times*, 19 October 1973.

20 See D. Russell, *Football and the English: A Social History of Association Football in England 1863–1995*, Preston: Carnegie Publishing, 1997, p. 162; *Sunday Times*, 21 October 1973.

21 J. Walvin, *Football and the Decline of Britain*, Basingstoke: Macmillan, 1985, p. 128; preface. See also J. Moynihan, *The Soccer Syndrome*, London: Sportspages/Simon and Schuster, 1987, author's note.

22 Ted Croker interviewed, *Daily Mirror*, 19 October 1973.

23 P.M. Young, *A History of British Football*, London: Stanley Paul, 1968, p. 201.

24 J. Clarke and C. Critcher, '1966 and all that: England's World Cup victory', in A. Tomlinson and G. Whannel (eds) *Off the Ball: the Football World Cup*, London: Pluto, 1986, pp. 120–1; F. Wheen, 'The athletic fallacy', in A. McLellan (ed.) *Nothing Sacred: The New Cricket Culture*, London: Two Heads, 1996, pp. 107–8. See also M. Polley, *Moving the Goalposts: A History of Sport and Society since 1945*, London: Routledge, 1998, pp. 35–6.

25 Budge, 'Relative decline', pp. 14–15.

26 S. Wagg, 'Playing the past: the media and the England football team', in J. Williams and S. Wagg (eds) *British Football and Social Change: Getting into Europe*, Leicester: Leicester University Press, 1991, pp. 221–2.

27 J. Tomlinson, 'Inventing "decline": the falling behind of the British economy in the postwar years', *Economic History Review*, 1996, vol. XLIX, pp. 731–3.

28 *Daily Telegraph*, 19 October 1973.

29 See M.W. Kirby, 'Institutional rigidities and economic decline: reflections on the British experience', *Economic History Review*, 1992, vol. XLV, pp. 637–56.

30 D. Jack (ed.) *Len Shackleton, Clown Prince of Soccer: His Autobiography*, London: Nicholas Kaye, 1955, p. 78.

31 D. Bowler, *Three Lions on the Shirt: Playing for England*, London: Orion Books, 2000, pp. 110–11; see also Edworthy, *Second Most Important Job*, pp. 59–60.

32 See J. Greaves and N. Giller, *Don't Shoot the Manager: the Revealing Story of England's Soccer Bosses*, London: Boxtree, 1993, p. 18. See also Bowler, *Three Lions*, p. 111.

33 Greaves and Giller, *Don't Shoot the Manager*, pp. 45–6; D. Bowler, *'Winning Isn't Everything ...': A Biography of Sir Alf Ramsey*, London: Victor Gollancz, 1998, p. 293.

34 Clough, *Clough – the Autobiography*, London: Partridge Press, 1994, pp. 174–5. See also Roy McFarland's comments in Bowler, *Ramsey*, p. 287.

35 See G. Whannel, *Fields in Vision: Television Sport and Cultural Transformation*, London: Routledge, pp. 135–8.

36 Edworthy, *Second Most Important Job*, p. 5.
37 Smith quoted, *Sun*, 11 September 1981.
38 B. Glanville, *Soccer Nemesis*, London: Secker and Warburg, 1955, p. 1.
39 M. Allison, *Colours of My Life*, London: Everest Books, 1975, p. 27.
40 See Edworthy, *Second Most Important Job*, pp. 26–8; Holt and Mason, *Sport in Britain*, p. 115. Tom Finney, it should be recorded, recalled that the press had been 'very critical'. See Bowler, *Three Lions*, p. 48.
41 Russell, *Football and the English*, p. 197.
42 Ibid. pp. 140–1; J. Cox, *Don Davies: 'An Old International'*, London: Sportsmans Book Club, 1963, pp. 159–62; B. Glanville, *Football Memories*, London: Virgin, 1999, p. 96.
43 Wagg, 'Playing the past', p. 222. For national daily circulations see C. Seymour-Ure, *The British Press and Broadcasting since 1945*, Oxford: Blackwell, 1991, Table 3.2, pp. 28–9.
44 *Daily Mirror*, 24 November 1953, see also S. Wagg, 'Naming the guilty men: Managers and the media', in Tomlinson and Whannel, *Off the Ball*, p. 40.
45 *The Times*, 1 January 1955, cited in Clarke and Critcher, '1966 and all that', p. 120.
46 *News Chronicle*, 26 November 1953.
47 *News Chronicle*, 24, 26 November 1953.
48 Glanville, *Soccer Nemesis*, p. 182.
49 Glanville, *Football Memories*, pp. 2–3.
50 Buchan, *A Lifetime in Football*, London: Phoenix House, 1955, p. 209.
51 The Football Association, London: Senior, Intermediate and Technical Sub-Committees, minutes of meeting, 1 February 1954; International Senior Selection Committee and Technical Committee, minutes of meeting, 22 July 1954.
52 Moynihan, *Soccer Syndrome*, p. 31.
53 G. Whannel, *Blowing the Whistle: The Politics of Sport*, London: Pluto, 1983, pp. 62–3.
54 See the discussion in J. Obelkevich, 'Consumption', in P. Catterall and J. Obelkevich (eds) *Understanding Post-War British Society*, London: Routledge, 1994, pp. 141–54. For television licenses see Seymour-Ure, *British Press and Broadcasting*, Table 4.2, pp. 76–7.
55 See especially Clarke and Crichter, '1966 and all that', pp. 122–3.
56 *The Times*, 23 September 1964.
57 J. Walvin, *The People's Game: The History of Football Revisited*, Edinburgh: Mainstream, 1994, pp. 180–1.
58 *The Times*, 20 November 1977.
59 Maurice Norman quoted in Bowler, *Three Lions*, p. 108; Wilson quoted in Bowler, *Ramsey*, p. 162. For comment on this prediction and the reaction to it see D. Thomson, *4–2*, London: Bloomsbury, 1996, p. 70
60 Ramsey quoted in Bowler, *Ramsey*, p. 155.
61 Thomson, *4–2*, p. 9.
62 Law quoted in R. Taylor and A. Ward, *Kicking and Screaming: An Oral History of Football in England*, London: Robson Books, 1995, p. 173.
63 Clarke and Critcher, '1966 and all that', p. 121.
64 For an analysis of Ramsey's genius in harnessing the strengths of English football in 1966 see Bowler, *Ramsey*, pp. 301–2; also Clarke and Critcher, '1966 and all that', p. 123.
65 Ball quoted in Taylor and Ward, *Kicking and Screaming*, p. 242.
66 R. Steen, *The Mavericks: English Football When Flair Wore Flares*, Edinburgh: Mainstream, 1994, p. 27; Thomson, *4–2*, p. 221; D. Downing, *The Best of Enemies: England v. Germany, A Century of Football Rivalry*, London: Bloomsbury 2000, pp. 110–18.

67 C. Barnett, *The Audit of War: The Illusion and Reality of Britain as a Great Nation*, London: Macmillan, 1986, pp. 1–8, 304.

68 *Economist*, 30 December 1972, cited in K.O. Morgan, *The People's Peace: British History 1945–89*, Oxford: Oxford University Press, 1990, p. 340.

69 *Daily Mirror*, 1 May 1972; *Sunday Times*, 14 May 1972. For the press reaction to these matches see Downing, *Best of Enemies*, pp. 141–6.

70 Bowler, *Ramsey*, p. 287.

71 *Daily Mirror*, 19 October 1973.

72 *The Times*, 18 October 1973. See also Robert Oxby's article for some very similar thoughts on 1953 and the prospect of 'rebirth', *Daily Telegraph*, 18 October 1973.

73 *Daily Mirror*, 17 November 1976; 16 November 1977.

74 *The Times*, 18 November 1977.

75 See S. Pollard, *The Wasting of the British Economy: British Economic Policy 1945 to the Present*, London: Croom Helm, 1982, pp. 1–21. See also N. Tiratsoo, 'You've never had it so bad? Britain in the 1970s', in N. Tiratsoo (ed.), *From Blitz to Blair: A new history of Britain since 1939*, London: Weidenfeld and Nicolson, 1997, pp. 163–4. For a useful compendium of contemporary literature pertaining to decline see D. Coates and J. Hillard (eds) *The Economic Decline of Modern Britain: the Debate between Left and Right*, Brighton: Wheatsheaf, 1986.

76 Wagg, 'Playing the past', p. 225.

77 *Sun*, 10 September 1981. It was not quite 'the end of the world'; England went on to qualify.

78 *Sun*, 11 September 1981.

79 Dr David Starkey in *The Times*, 20 April 1996, quoted in Paxman, *The English*, p. 264.

80 See the discussion in J. Hill, *Sport, Leisure and Culture in Twentieth-Century Britain*, London: Macmillan, 2002, pp. 43–57.

81 P. Jay, 'Englanditis', reproduced in Coates and Hillard (eds) *Economic Decline*, pp. 115–22.

82 Cited in B. Calvert, *The Popular Press, Privatisation and Popular Capitalism in Britain during the 1980s*, unpublished PhD thesis, Coventry University, 2000, p. 65.

83 R. Grose, *The* Sun-*sation: Behind the Scenes at Britain's Bestselling Daily News-paper*, London: Angus and Robertson, 1989, p. 80.

84 *Daily Mirror*, 18 May 1972.

85 See the helpful discussion in L. Crolley and D. Hand, *Football, Europe and the Press*, London: Frank Cass, 2002, pp. 19–32.

86 For the home international championship and awareness of national diversity see H.F. Moorhouse, 'One state, several countries: Soccer and nationality in a "United" Kingdom', in J.A. Mangan (ed.) *Tribal Identities: Nationalism, Europe, Sport*, London: Frank Cass, 1996, pp. 70–2.

87 G. Hurst (with M. Hart), *1966 and All That: My Autobiography*, London: Headline, 2001, p. 3.

88 M.Wilson, *Don't Cry for Me Argentina: Scotland's 1978 World Cup Adventure*, Edinburgh: Mainstream, 1998, p. 139; *Daily Mail*, 8 June 1978.

89 See G. Tibballs, *'Do I Not Like That': One-Liners, Wise Words, Gaffes and Blunders from the World's Greatest Football Managers*, London: Virgin, 1999, p. 229. For another example of Ramsey's antipathy towards the Scots see Bowler, *Ramsey*, p. 159.

3 'Every day when I wake up I thank the Lord I'm Welsh'[1]

Sport and national identity in post-war Wales

Martin Johnes

'Wales is an artefact which the Welsh produce', wrote historian Gwyn A. Williams, 'the Welsh make and remake Wales day by day and year by year'.[2] Exactly what that artefact is and has been is a contentious question obscured by political debates about Wales's future, the absence of a nation state and internal geographic, linguistic and ethnic divisions. Wales as a unified entity is thus an 'imagined community' and Welshness has a plethora of different meanings for the people who possess and make it.[3]

However one defines Wales, it would be difficult to deny sport's place in the inventing, maintaining and projecting of the idea of a Welsh national identity in and outside of Wales's blurred borders, even if the Wales that sport has projected has varied according to time, place and context. Although the Welsh language, music and religious nonconformity have also played their part, few other cultural forms are as well equipped as sport to express national identity. Its emotions, national colours, emblems, songs and contests all make it a perfect vehicle through which collective ideas of nationhood can be expressed. Sport glosses over the different meanings that the people of Wales attach to their nationality, enabling them to assert, maybe even understand, their Welshness in the face of internal division and the political, social and cultural shadow of England. As Eric Hobsbawm put it, 'the imagined community of millions seems more real as a team of eleven [or fifteen] named people'.[4] This chapter explores the relationship between national identity and sport in Wales since 1945. It argues that sport has not simply been shaped by wider notions of national identity but that it has also been an active agent in actually creating and sustaining Welsh national identity.[5]

Rugby's golden age

The end of the Second World War brought first austerity and then prosperity to Britain. Welsh industry was revived practically through an economic boom and full employment and symbolically through nationalization. The depressed days of the 1930s seemed over and Welsh rugby shared in and perhaps symbolized the nation's rejuvenation. Rugby union's infrastructure and facilities were improved, clubs increasingly became social centres open to women and children, and a new generation of players emerged. In 1950, Wales won its first outright Championship and Triple Crown since 1911, with a team of fit ex-servicemen, manual workers and products of teacher training colleges. Between 1950 and 1956 Wales won the championship three times and shared it twice. Rugby was part of Labour Wales, a working-class, competitive but communal culture that celebrated and valued achievements in education, politics and sport. The ideals of rugby and Wales in this era were encapsulated by international fly half Cliff Morgan, who was brought up in a Rhondda Nonconformist home 'where Mam ruled and Sunday was for chapel'. Morgan later took up an influential radio career with the BBC, where he unashamedly celebrated the moral and traditional values of sport.[6] Nonetheless, for all the amateur principles of Morgan's world, Welsh rugby offered its players more tangible benefits. It could act as a form of freemasonry, opening doors to better jobs for even junior players, and there were often more direct payments for playing, such as cash in brown envelopes, generous travel expenses and free beer. The reality of Welsh rugby, like Wales itself, did not match its traditional and respectable ideals.

It was the teams that followed in the late 1960s and 1970s that ensured Wales and rugby would be umbilically linked in the popular imagination. Barry John, Gareth Edwards, J.P.R. Williams and a host of other stars established Wales as a world force in rugby union. Between 1968–69 and 1978–79 Wales won the Five Nations Championship six times, collecting three grand slams and six triple crowns in the process. The gulf between Wales and the other home nations became clear in 1971 when Wales supplied thirteen players for the British Lions's successful tour of New Zealand. It was not just the success that delighted rugby fans in and outside Wales, but the manner of it. Welsh rugby featured back play that was breathtaking by even the most staid of sportswriters' standards. For those lucky enough to get in, the National Stadium became a Welsh Mecca, adorned on matchdays with red rosettes and giant leeks and daffodils, and ringing to the sound of hymns and a newly invented tradition, former miner and poet/performer Max Boyce's 'Oggi-Oggi-Oggi, Oi-Oi-Oi!' Both players and spectators held the new stadium and its acoustics in special affection and to many it was 'the rugby shrine of the world'.[7] The Arms Park's role as a focal point for rugby, to which people descended from across Wales, contributed to a growth in the acceptance of Cardiff as the capital city that it had been declared in 1955.[8] The impact of the national XV's victories went far beyond those watching in the stadium. With interest bolstered by a patriotic media and regular victories, television now enabled international matches to become a national event that embraced areas outside the game's traditional hinterlands. Indeed, the BBC in Wales actively regarded rugby as an instrument for nation building.[9] For four Saturday afternoons a year, rugby seemed to bring much of

Wales to a standstill, as it won the interest of even those for whom sport was of marginal interest at all other times. The social base of the game was broadening and, in tune with the liberating ethos of the day, there were more women following and watching rugby from the late 1960s. Even in the traditional soccer hinterland of north Wales there was a fresh passion for the game emerging and new clubs, such as Bala and Bethesda, were formed.

For Barry John, known as 'the King', the adulation that the Welsh rugby stars received was too much. He retired prematurely to regain his freedom and privacy. Yet, for all their fame, the Welsh rugby stars of the 1970s were amateurs, still mostly working and living in Wales, and this kept them rooted in the society that worshipped them. A mixture of English and Welsh speakers and a combination of manual workers and the products of grammar schools, the players at the heart of this rugby fanaticism were a reflection of the nation they represented.[10] Thus the number of teachers, students, doctors and other public sector workers was on the increase, as industrial Wales slipped slowly into terminal decline. The developing importance of professional men for Welsh rugby, as well as the pull the British capital continued to exert on the young and ambitious of Wales, was symbolized by the emergence of London Welsh RFC as a regular source of players for the national side in the late 1960s and early 1970s.[11] Edwards, John, Gerald Davies and many of the other stars were the sons of manual workers who had, through education, gone into white-collar careers. In this they could be seen as symbolic of Wales's long established regard for education and social progress. Indeed, three of Wales's most successful coaches, Clive Rowlands, Carwyn James and John Dawes, were actually teachers. Hand in hand with respect for education had always been the importance of never forgetting one's roots, something which amateurism and the adoration of the Welsh people ensured its rugby heroes never did.

British press coverage of Welsh rugby drew heavily on certain national stereotypes but it also helped to dispel others. No longer were Taffy and his kin seen, in the words of historian John Davies, as 'puritan chapel-goers but rather as muscular boozers who were doubtful whether there was life beyond the dead-ball line'.[12] The Welsh XVs were described as 'magical', 'poetic', 'rhythmic', 'shrewd' and 'fighters'.[13] Many of the players themselves thought that rugby reflected the Celtic and emotional temperament of the Welsh. Barry John saw rugby as 'tough and fast, a man's game with its own controlled violence, its special skills and lore, its combination of brain and muscle, the emotional involvement of watchers and watched'. It had always, he noted, 'appealed strongly to the Welsh temperament'.[14] Such alleged national characteristics may have only been grounded in a distinctly limited reality but they formed part of a very real patriotism. Players spoke of their pride in donning the Welsh shirt and coaches appealed to such sentiments in trying to raise their game. Richard Holt has speculated that the sense of Welshness may have been particularly sharp for those players who made the break from the world of manual labour 'with its fierce solidarities and sense of place'.[15] In 1977, captain Phil Bennett rallied his team-mates before a match by declaring: 'These English you're just going out to meet have taken our coal, our water, our steel: they buy our houses and live in them a fortnight a year ... Down the centuries these English have exploited and pillaged us – and we're playing them this afternoon boys'.[16]

Drawing on such grievances, the 1960s saw a growth in political nationalism in Wales. A Welsh Office and Secretary of State for Wales had been created in 1964 but they did not stem the rise of the nationalist party, Plaid Cymru. From its first parliamentary victory in 1966, the pressure for a more revolutionary measure of devolution grew. Alongside this were the more radical but marginal campaigns of *Cymdeithas yr Iaith* (the Welsh Language Society) and the Free Wales Army. The former campaigned for greater recognition and use of the Welsh language, with tactics that included obliterating English-only roadsigns; the latter flirted with bombs and military uniforms in its inept campaign for a Welsh republic. Thus, as with many liberal causes worldwide, the 1960s represented a new, more pronounced and concerted era for Welsh national consciousness. Rugby both contributed to and reflected this. Rugby internationals became 'more overtly nationalistic', with Free Wales Army T-shirts visible in the crowd and the concerted booing of 'God Save the Queen'. This new world upset some of the conservative older generation, as did the decline in hymn singing at internationals.[17] Tom Jones's *Delilah* and the Max Boyce songs that often replaced the hymns may not have been as religious or as traditional but they were more representative of the modern, commercial popular culture of the 1960s and 1970s.

Change and transition

For all the popular pride in Wales, the enemy in mainstream Welsh politics was not the English but the Tories. Indeed, rugby in this period was seen by some as a safety valve for nationalistic sentiments. At the end of a decade where pride and success in Welsh rugby had probably been at its highest, only 11.8 per cent of the electorate (and 20.3 per cent of the turnout) voted in favour of the creation of a Welsh assembly at the 1979 devolution referendum. K.O. Morgan, writing in 1981, observed that:

> Welsh identity, so easily asserted in pounding the Saxon on the rugby field, was too easily diverted, in the view of more serious nationalists, from the quest for national independence. Rugby and investitures, the bread and circuses of the populace, became a peaceful therapy to suppress embarrassing political aspirations. Then [the Edwardian period]

and now most of the Welsh were content to have it that way. They rejoiced in their rugby skills, made no protest, and asked few questions.[18]

Sport may have been patriotism enough for some but there is little to suggest that it actually minimized political nationalism in Wales in any significant way. Identities are contextual and situational: taking pride in one's nation on the rugby field was one thing, taking a leap into the dark of devolution was quite another, especially when the Labour hegemony seemed incapable of running local government effectively, let alone a national assembly. Wales was not a nation of eighty-minute patriots, but simply one of economic and political pragmatists who understood the complex plurality of Welsh identity.

In the wake of the debacle of the 1979 devolution referendum, the 1980s were a period of dramatic change for Wales. Thatcherism's commitment to the free market spelled the end for the traditional heavy industries on which modern Wales had been built. Mines and steelworks disappeared to be replaced by rising unemployment and scattered modernist ventures, such as Japanese electronics factories that employed as many women as men. In 1981, there were 27,000 miners in Wales; by 1990, there was just one working pit in the whole country. By the mid-1980s in Mid Glamorgan, as many as one in three 16–19 year old men were on the dole in some former mining communities. As in the inter-war period, rugby seemed to reflect this economic downturn.[19] The sustained glories of the 1970s were not repeated and the 1980s were largely a dismal period for Welsh rugby. Rugby union's first ever World Cup, held in Australia and New Zealand in 1987, seemed to offer Welsh rugby some hope. Wales secured third place but it proved to be a false dawn, as anyone who looked at the 49–6 hammering by New Zealand in the semi-final could tell. There was a Triple Crown in 1988 but performances were resting too much on the shoulders of the talented Jonathan Davies. After he went north in 1989 to play rugby league, Wales failed to win a single Five Nations match for two seasons and England won at the Arms Park for the first time since 1963.

Many saw the seeds of the decline in rugby's grassroots. Gwendraeth Grammar School had produced Carwyn James, Barry John, Gareth Davies and Jonathan Davies, a world-class outside half in every decade since the 1940s. Trials for the school side would be attended by hundreds of boys and the school's achievements and fanaticism for rugby summed up how the sport was ingrained in the culture of Welsh education, much to the cost of Welsh soccer. But in the 1980s, Gwendraeth Grammar went comprehensive and the place and nature of school sport changed (as it did across Britain). Teachers' voluntary extra-curricular involvement in physical education lessened, at least partly in protest at the Thatcher government's management of education. Physical education itself diversified, as games and activities such as basketball and dance lessened the emphasis on competitive sports. Outside school, with video games, BMX bikes, skateboards and other new forms of globalised entertainment, there emerged a greater diversity of sporting and leisure interests amongst both boys and teachers. The net result was a more varied and cosmopolitan Welsh popular culture, where rugby occupied a more peripheral place and even Gwendraeth's first XV ceased to exist for a period. The school was not unique and, as other Welsh grammars disappeared, were amalgamated or changed, a cog in the conveyor belt of Welsh rugby was removed.[20] This may have hindered the expression of Welsh identity but it perhaps enabled a more democratic culture within schools that was less based on sporting ability.

The 1980s and 1990s saw Wales endeavour to adjust to the reality of a post-industrial society. The economy awkwardly adapted to make the most of foreign inward investment. The national curriculum, S4C (the Welsh television channel) and a second Welsh Language Act at least partly secured the future of the language, while the Labour Party and Plaid Cymru redefined their programmes to adapt to a modern world and the debacle of the 1979 referendum. Such changes were often accompanied by emotional and political arguments about whether they represented pragmatic adaptation or philosophical betrayals. Attempts to restructure Welsh rugby also brought similar dilemmas but with less success. After years of argument, it was not until 1990 that the much-needed national league was introduced. Such lack of vision in the game's hierarchy, the poor performances on the pitch and the weak Welsh economy encouraged a new glut of defections to rugby league. In 1985, Terry Holmes was the first leading Welsh player to head north for over a decade. A third of the 1988 Triple Crown team were lost to the professional game, including Jonathan Davies, who joined Widnes for a record fee of almost £200,000, disillusioned, like so many, at the management of the Welsh game.[21] Despite the obvious reasons to go, the players who did leave were often accused of profiteering or treachery. Scott Gibbs, on joining St Helen's from Swansea, said:

> It grates me that I am called a prostitute while players and officials keep on covering up what's going on in union. Every player in Wales knows that when you play on a Saturday, if you win you can get a few quid. Players get the cash after the game.[22]

In this wider climate of change and uncertainty, the definitions of amateurism were growing even more elastic and vulnerable. The fear of being exposed may have prevented some players from taking all they could but the desire to be open in their earnings continued to be an incentive for Welshmen to head north.

In 1992, the Campaign for a Welsh Assembly declared 'Welsh rugby, once a source of national pride, has now become part of that rapid erosion of identity which has thrown a big question-mark over what it means to be Welsh today'.[23] The decline in Welsh rugby fortunes after the 1970s may have lessened one traditional source of Welsh pride but more fundamental to any wider crisis of identity was the decline of the traditional Welsh industries and the rule of a Conservative government whose support across Wales was largely marginal. The social and political alienation brought about by the Conservative governments of 1979–97 was also critical in raising support for devolution and sharpened people's sense that Wales had political needs distinct from those of England.[24] Yet the 'Yes' vote at the 1997 devolution referendum was won by only 6,721 votes in a 50.3 per cent turnout. Evidently, the use of popular Welsh sports stars and other celebrities to mobilise support for devolution had not been entirely successful.[25]

Despite the narrowness of the referendum result, the election of the first Labour government for eighteen years and the subsequent devolution vote coincided with, or even brought about according to some commentators, a new patriotic confidence in Wales. While Tony Blair talked of 'Cool Britannia', the Welsh media invented 'Cool Cymru'. Its most obvious manifestation was the success of a number of Welsh rock bands. Catatonia, one of the most popular, declared to the world 'Every day when I wake up I thank the Lord I'm Welsh'. Wales's successful hosting of rugby union's 1999 World Cup in Cardiff's newly built, highly impressive and ultra-modern Millennium Stadium seemed to suggest that the nation had much to shout about again. By 1999 even BBC Wales felt bold enough to run a television trailer for its rugby coverage that centred on Kelly Jones of the Stereophonics singing 'as long as we beat the English we don't care'. When Wales did beat England in 1999, at Wembley no less with a last gasp try, a *Western Mail* editorial extolled: 'Confidence is a wonderful state of mind. The Welsh team now has it in abundance and, more importantly, it has rubbed off on the rest of the nation. It's a day to be proud'.[26] Much of this trumpeted pride in Wales had a lighthearted feel. In 1998, the *Western Mail* had made dramatic front-page associations between a rugby clash against England and the fifteenth-century rebellion of Owain Glyndŵr.[27] Yet, for all the paper's pride in Wales, its editorial line remained firmly committed to a devolved Wales within a wider British state. The hype and the moment of 'Cool Cymru' passed. By the millennium, the advent of a Welsh Assembly seemed to have changed little, Catatonia were taking time out because of exhaustion and the national rugby team had started losing again.

The brief rugby renaissances of the end of the 1990s seemed to owe much to the 1998 appointment of New Zealander Graham Henry as national coach. His appointment, although not unanimously welcomed, was a symbol that Welsh rugby was dragging itself into the professional age. Henry further demonstrated this by selecting players whose Welsh heritage was remote and sometimes somewhat dubious. Although this rankled with some fans and players (at least one of whom refused to play for Wales again), it was inevitable if Wales wanted to compete with the cream of the world's rugby nations. However, the policy backfired in the 'Grannygate scandal', when the Welsh ancestry of capped players Shane Howarth and Brett Sinkinson, both from New Zealand, was proved false.

The challenges of professionalism and the selection of overseas players raised questions about rugby's relationship with Welsh society. Did victory matter more than a team that represented the nation in a meaningful way? Such debates had added currency because rugby's relationship with Welsh identity had always been derived from the fact that it provided the nation with a popular culture that was distinct from that of England. Rugby's working-class base in south Wales made the sport different from its middle-class English counterpart and added a touch of social friction to national contests with the old enemy. Furthermore, much of the pride in Welsh rugby came from the fact that its players lived and worked in the communities they represented. No one begrudged players becoming financially removed from their roots but for capped players to have only tenuous connections with Wales raised new questions, particularly when the benefits on the pitch were not always apparent. Thanks to the new wage bills, rugby clubs were running into financial brick walls and struggling to recover from the concussion. They were in danger of going the same way as so many of the mines, factories and steelworks that they had existed alongside in the fabric of communities. Other symbols of Welsh identity were also in decline in an increasingly global popular culture. Many fans knew the words to soccer-like chants such as 'Wales-Wales-Wales' but not *Hen Wlad fy Nhadau*, the national anthem. When Wales played New Zealand at the Millennium Stadium at the tail end of 2002, tape recordings of hymn singing from the 1970s were played across the tannoys.[28] Despite the real patriotism, Welsh culture was subject to the realities and vagaries of market forces and fashion.

Wales, England and Britain

Reconciling the realities of professional sport with national ideals was a problem that Welsh soccer had long faced. Before the Second World War soccer in south Wales had sometimes been labelled a foreign sport because the professional players with Welsh clubs were often not Welsh, while the players in the national XI were usually employed by English clubs.[29] Yet, from at least the 1920s, association football was actually the most popular sport in Wales. This was especially clear in the north of Wales where Liverpool and Everton attracted devoted followings thanks to the cultural glamour and economic pull of English Merseyside. Even as far south as Aberystwyth, sales of Liverpool's *Daily Post* helped to determine the sporting loyalties of youngsters. Soccer's large following in Wales was not enough to create a perception of it as a Welsh sport. After all, the game enjoyed widespread support the world over. Had Wales ever enjoyed sustained success at the sport then this would not have mattered: a small nation living in the economic, political and cultural shadow of a larger neighbour latches on to any claim to glory with which she can associate herself. But Welsh soccer did not provide that success. Qualification for the 1958 World Cup and a quarter-final place in the 1976 European Championship stand out as Wales's only major feats in international soccer since 1945. While the national rugby team has offered as much glory as despair, the triumphs of the national soccer team have been fleeting moments in a general story of frustration. Wales has produced some world-class players, such as John Charles and Ryan Giggs, but they have generally played alongside a succession of journeymen, thus denying them the opportunity they deserved to perform successfully on the international stage. Such talented individuals may have become extremely popular in Wales but, with their personal achievements being largely with English teams, they alone were not enough to transform the image of international soccer in Wales. Instead, it was the unique, all-embracing rugby that was seen as the national sport, rather than a game played by most of the developed and developing world, in which context a small country like Wales could not hope to make a significant impact.

Soccer does however illustrate that Welsh identity is neither singular nor insular. The influence of the British popular press and the steady growth of football coverage on the radio ensured that the English First Division already attracted strong interest in south Wales by the 1950s. Television meant that English soccer became fully accessible to a Welsh audience that also possessed a sense of Britishness. The 1966 World Cup was enjoyed across Wales and a *Western Mail* editorial proclaimed England's 'superb victory' as an achievement which 'the whole of Britain can feel proud of' and which 'belongs to British football as a whole'.[30] In the 1990s saturation television coverage and the new fashionability of football furthered the passionate support for leading English clubs within Wales. By 2001 there were twelve official branches of the Manchester United Supporters' Club across Wales.[31] Manchester United and Liverpool shirts are even common sights on the home terraces at Swansea and Wrexham. There is substantial anecdotal evidence to suggest that when England has played important games in recent World Cups or European Championships, it has tended to find substantial numbers of supporters in the pubs and living rooms of Wales.

Yet despite the loyalty to the English game within much of Welsh football, nationality remains an issue for Welsh football fans, albeit in a complex and plural fashion. With the Welsh national XI not remotely on a par with England, fans could support the old enemy without feeling they were compromising their Welsh identity. There were, of course, substantial numbers of soccer fans who supported whoever England was playing, especially amongst the ranks of supporters of Wales's three Football

League clubs, but understandings of the requirements of being Welsh have always differed. Nonetheless, even amongst such fans (as well as supporters of the three semi-professional teams who play in English non-league), there has been strong opposition to their teams joining the League of Wales. Such a move would bring lower playing standards and smaller crowds; sporting standards and financial needs are clearly viewed as more important than any notion of standing independently on one's own feet. Indeed, to fans of Cardiff City, Swansea City and Wrexham, playing in an English rather than Welsh league, with all its opportunities to taunt and beat the English 'other', is actually a way of declaring one's Welshness. In the late 1960s a more aggressive and younger football fan culture developed in Britain. In Wales, in line with wider shifts in national identity, this took the form of a more assertive and provocative national consciousness. By the 1970s, chants at Cardiff City included 'Supertaffs' and 'Bloody English, all illegitimate ... Bastards every one'.[32] It is now commonplace for players and referees who commit fouls or give dubious decisions at Welsh grounds to be greeted with choruses of 'You cheating English bastard'. Away fans are taunted with the name of whichever team has last beaten England. Any attempt to respond is likely to be drowned out by 'England's full of shit', to the tune of the English football anthem, *Three Lions*. Although modern Welsh football demonstrates the complexity and perhaps contradictions of Welsh identity, it also needs to be judged within the context of a football culture that celebrates and even creates rivalries, hatreds and divides.[33] Even the aggressive assertions of fans (such as 'Being a Welsh football fan makes me hate the English with a passion'[34]) have to be taken with a pinch of salt, as fun and bravado. Other sports certainly do not feature such an aggressive anti-Englishness. In short, there is no single monolithic Welsh identity.

The relationship with England is crucial to an understanding of Welsh identity. Linda Colley has observed that:

> men and women decide who they are by reference to who and what they are not. Once confronted with an obviously alien 'Them', an otherwise diverse community can become a reassuring or merely desperate 'Us'.[35]

Thus one of the agencies that has driven the Welsh to make and remake Wales is a sense of being different to England. This may derive from some sense of a common inheritance or even, at times, alleged racial Celtic qualities, but these are vague and, arguably, mythical attributes that are certainly not inclusive in a nation with a rich history of immigration. What sport has done, more tangibly and inclusively, is to bring alive a sense of 'otherness' and difference in the relationship between Wales and England that would otherwise be almost invisible and often alienating.

How Wales responds to that 'other' has varied across sports, place and time. There is little evidence of any active tension between the Welsh and English immigrants in the south Wales coalfield before the Second World War. Probably thanks in part to such movements of people, sporting contests against England in this period seem to have been imbued with friendly rivalry rather than the passionate anti-English antagonism found in contemporary England-Scotland football matches.[36] The growth of anti-Englishness in Welsh sport seems to date from the 1960s, when wider Welsh nationalism took on the more overt, confident and even confrontational character. Today, the healthy state and prominent television coverage of Welsh club rugby (at least in comparison to Welsh soccer) mean that very few people in Wales support an English rugby club and thus there is little individual identification between Welsh fans and English players. Welsh rugby sees itself on a par with England. Even where there are not current successes to match such rhetoric, there are shared memories of victories from the past. Thus the English national XV takes on the persona of the arrogant neighbour who must, and can, be cut down to size. This persona is further developed by English rugby's middle-class and establishment associations which contrast unfavourably with the more populist image of rugby in Wales. By the 1990s, while the traditional hymn singing was in decline, 'Shove your chariots up your arse' had joined the witty repertoires of Welsh international crowds watching contests against England.[37] Arguably, few Welsh rugby fans would support England against non-British sides, let alone other 'Celtic' nations. And yet there is widespread support for a British league because of its potential to develop Welsh players more fully than a Welsh league. Anti-Englishness is not, then, incompatible with an appreciation of Britain. Indeed, Britain can be a forum in which people can vent a sense of anti-Englishness.

In 1997, Robert Croft, the England and Glamorgan cricketer, said that when he and his fellow players turned out for Glamorgan they were representing Wales, while being chosen to play for England in a test match was like being picked for the British Lions.[38] Welsh sport has consistently required fans and players to make such rationalisations about their national identity, even if only subconsciously. The pride players have declared on being picked for the British Lions also perhaps suggests a pride in Britishness that extends beyond the achievement of being honoured at one's profession. Sport has certainly signalled the popular Britishness that was so evident in Wales during times of war. Welsh athletes compete for Great Britain at the Olympics, while Welsh fans cheer on English, Scottish and Northern Irish athletes running and jumping for the Union Jack. The 1996 British Social Attitudes survey showed that 69 per cent of Welsh respondents were 'very' or 'somewhat' proud of Britain's achievements in sport. Yet this compared to a figure of 85 per cent when asked about Britain's history and 86 per cent when asked about Britain's armed forces.[39] Sport, an arena where Wales does have its own identity, was not the keenest outlet for the nation's sense of Britishness.

Table 3.1 Self-description of national identity by respondents in 1997 Referendum Survey

	%
Welsh, not British	17
More Welsh than British	26
Equally Welsh and British	34
More British than Welsh	10
British, not Welsh	12

Source: J. Curtice, 'Is Scotland a nation and Wales not?', in B. Taylor and K. Thompson (eds) *Scotland and Wales: Nations Again?*, Cardiff: University of Wales Press, 1998, p. 125.

The 1997 Referendum Survey suggested that Welsh people are very divided in how they see their national identity, with only 17 per cent denying that they had any British identity at all. Furthermore, 23 per cent of the sample who saw themselves as Welsh not British still voted 'No' in the devolution referendum.[40] In contrast to Scotland, popular doubts remain about whether devolution has had any positive benefits for Wales. The nation might have its own Assembly, not to mention a world-class stadium, but it remained committed to the British state and a British culture within which it could take pride in its multiple identities.

An inclusive nation?

These multiple identities extended beyond simple ideas of Welshness and Britishness. The large-scale Commonwealth immigration of the 1950s and 1960s saw Wales become a multi-cultural nation and gave birth to many current Welsh sport stars. In the wake of this immigration, sport has played a part in promoting racial integration. The popular sporting success of the likes of Colin Jackson, Nigel Walker, Steve Robinson and Ryan Giggs have ensured that not all the symbols of Welsh national identity are white. An apt illustration of the integration that sport can promote was the treatment of Pakistani bowler Waquer Younis. His contribution to Glamorgan's 1997 county championship was celebrated by crowds with chants of 'Waquer is a Welshman'. Yet sport has not always been so progressive in its attitudes towards race and it has also demonstrated some of the uglier responses to immigration. Billy Boston was born in Wales to West Indian and Irish parents in 1934. Although he had played rugby for Neath and captained the Welsh Boys Clubs, racial attitudes meant that he saw little chance of realizing his ambition of playing cricket for Glamorgan and rugby for Wales. He thus joined Wigan rugby league club, where he became one of the game's finest wingers.[41] Boston was just one of a number of talented black Welsh rugby players who were 'overlooked' in the union game before making their names in rugby league. It was not until 1983 that Mark Brown of Pontypool RFC became the first black player to be capped by Wales at rugby union. On the pitch, black players in both Welsh football and rugby have, on occasions, suffered considerable racist abuse, particularly in amateur and park games. As late as the 1990s, Bobby Gould, the Welsh national soccer manager, was accused of racism by his striker Nathan Blake.[42]

Like sport in England, Welsh sport has often been shaped by the social cleavages of, not only ethnicity, but also class, gender and region. Furthermore, sport's role in building and sustaining national identities is also limited by the simple fact that not everyone likes sport. The 1999 Wales versus England rugby international at Wembley attracted 600,000 television viewers in Wales. Although this did not include people watching in pubs and clubs and was a significantly higher proportion of the viewing audience than in England, it still only represents around one in five people in Wales.[43] Even in rugby's 1970s heyday less than half of Welsh households were watching international matches on television.[44] In the 1997 Welsh Referendum Study, only 49 per cent of the representative sample claimed to be very proud of the Welsh rugby team.[45] Neither rugby nor sport are quite the dominant Welsh obsessions that many would like to believe.

Rugby and football have continually attracted female support but the sports have always been male-dominated and have even at times deliberately excluded women. David Andrews has argued that the new Welsh national identity of the late Victorian and Edwardian periods was very much a male construct, which ignored women and reinforced the patriarchal nature of society. The role of rugby in promoting this identity was particularly illustrative of this male domination.[46] Female support and involvement in traditionally male sports may have increased in the late twentieth century but women remain marginal within the culture of those sports and thus the national identity that they project. Furthermore, as sexual discrimination increasingly became socially unacceptable, sport could even act as something of a last bastion of traditional ideas of male domination and gender roles. After Wales had beaten England in 1993, a Welsh rugby correspondent at *The Observer* wrote: 'Once it has sunk in today, the singing in the chapels will be heavenly and afterwards the pubs will be joyfully overflowing and the Welsh womenfolk will be baking their Welsh cakes and taking their men to their bosoms'.[47] This may have been tongue-in-cheek journalism but at another level such rhetoric illustrates and perhaps perpetuates the male chauvinism that still dominates popular perceptions of what Welshness is and of where sport fits into that Welshness. Sport alone has not been responsible for the marginalisation of women in the national identity – economic inequalities and physiology are more important in that respect – but it is a symbolic reflection of a secondary status in Wales from which women are yet to fully emerge. Nonetheless, one does not have to be liberated by or actively interested or involved in sport to be aware of its existence and proclamations of nation-hood. As media coverage of sport, and indeed the actual audience of the popular media, grew in the post-1945 period, it became far harder for people to be unaware or untouched by sport. Many women may not have not felt directly included in the process but extensive media coverage ensured that sport maintained and developed its role as an agent in pro-jecting national identity.[48]

Thus sport illustrates and contributes to the complexity of Welsh iden-tity. Despite the enthusiasm with which many people throughout the twen-tieth century have voiced their patriotism, Wales also exists within a British and increasingly global culture. Tim Williams, a leading anti-devolution campaigner, argued:

> For most of us, Wales is a team and a nice place from which to get a letter. It exists for the purposes of sport and sentiment. Our 'country' for every serious purpose from voting through to fighting a war is our state, the United Kingdom.[49]

Williams' opinion is controversial on many levels but he is right when he goes on to contend, with reference to popular television soap operas, that 'we see in the trials, tribulations and triumphs of our fellow citizens in a Salford street, a Liverpool close and a Cockney borough, a more satisfac-tory mirror of our concerns and characters' than anything on Welsh-language television. The historical experience of the people of south Wales has certainly been much closer to the other industrial regions of Britain than it has to rural west and north Wales. As Neil Evans put it, Wales is more of an idea than a unified society.[50] For many, sport made this idea seem real. Merfyn Jones has argued that the Welsh are increas-ingly becoming defined 'not in terms of shared occupational experience or common religious inheritance or the survival of an ancient European lan-guage or for contributing to the Welsh radical tradition, but rather by ref-erence to the institutions that they inhabit, influence and react to'.[51] Wales may not have a presence on the international political stage but it does have a long history of its own national teams and associations, many of which have attracted considerable media attention. These institutions formed an integral part of the limited civil Welsh society that existed over the course of the twentieth century. They were something that the Welsh could use to define Wales and their own Welsh nationhood. Cultural iden-tity is a two way process and sport has also helped others accept Welsh nationhood too.[52] Moreover, sporting institutions have enjoyed a more popular relevance than the host of national bodies that grew up after the administrative devolution of the 1960s and beyond. It is because the 'bureaucrats, quangoroos and language entrepreneurs' that define the nation struggle 'to capture our attention let alone our imagination' that sport is so important in making Wales relevant and something more than a simple sentimental place from where we come.[53] The most popular sports in Wales were a collective experience that helped sustain a popular Welsh national identity that, at least partially, crossed the social and political divisions of everyday life.

Notes

1 Chorus to title track on Catatonia's *International Velvet* album, Blanco Y Negro, 1998.
2 G.A. Williams, *The Welsh in their History*, London: Croom Helm, 1982, p. 200.
3 B. Anderson, *Imagined Communities: Reflections on the Origins and Spread of Nationalism*, London: Verso, 1983.
4 E.J. Hobsbawm, *Nations and Nationalism since 1780*, Cambridge: Cambridge University Press, 1990, p. 143.
5 For the social history of sport in Wales see M. Johnes, *Sport in Wales, 1800–2000*, Cardiff: St. David's Press, 2004.
6 D. Smith and G. Williams, *Fields of Praise: The Official History of the Welsh Rugby Union, 1881–1981*, Cardiff: University of Wales Press, 1980, p. 340. This book is the classic social history of Welsh rugby.
7 J.P.R. Williams, *JPR: The Autobiography of J.P.R. Williams*, London: Book Club Associates, 1979, p. 15.
8 J. Davies, *A History of Wales*, Harmondsworth: Penguin, 1993, p. 644.
9 J. Davies, *Broadcasting and the BBC in Wales*, Cardiff: University of Wales Press, 1994, p. 320.
10 The careers, lives and context of some of the stars of this era are explored in H. Richards, P. Stead and G. Williams (eds) *Heart and Soul: The Character of Welsh Rugby*, Cardiff: University of Wales Press, 1998; and *More Heart and Soul: The Character of Welsh Rugby*, Cardiff: University of Wales Press, 1999.
11 E. Jones (ed.) *The Welsh in London*, Cardiff: University of Wales Press, 2001.
12 Davies, *History of Wales*, p. 644.
13 J. Maguire and J. Tuck, 'Global sports and patriot games: rugby union and national identity in a United sporting Kingdom since 1945', in M. Cronin and D. Mayall (eds) *Sporting Nationalisms: Identity, Ethnicity, Immigration and Assimilation*, London: Frank Cass, 1998, pp. 103–26.
14 B. John, *The Barry John Story*, London: Fontana, 1975, pp. 13–14.
15 R. Holt, *Sport and the British: A Modern History*, Oxford: Oxford University Press, 1989, p. 253.
16 Quoted in M. Polley, *Moving the Goalposts: A History of Sport and Society Since 1945*, London: Routledge, 1998, p. 60.
17 Smith and Williams, *Fields of Praise*, p. 375.
18 K.O. Morgan, *Rebirth of a Nation: Wales, 1880–1980*, Oxford: Oxford University Press, 1981, p. 134; also see p. 348.
19 For Welsh rugby in the 1980s and 1990s see D. Smith and G. Williams, 'Beyond the fields of praise: Welsh rugby, 1980–1900', in Richards *et al.* (eds) *More Heart and Soul, pp.* 205–32.
20 R. Holt and T. Mason, *Sport in Britain, 1945–2000*, Oxford: Blackwell, 2000, p. 50; Smith and Williams, 'Beyond the fields of praise', pp. 219–20.
21 J. Davies with P. Corrigan, *Jonathan: An Autobiography,* London: Stanley Paul, 1990.
22 Quoted in A. Smith, 'Civil war in England: the clubs, the RFU, and the impact of professionalism on rugby union, 1995–99', in A. Smith and D. Porter (eds) *Amateurs and Professionals in Post-War British Sport*, London: Frank Cass, 2000, p. 150.

23 Quoted in M. Stephens, *Wales in Quotation*, Cardiff: University of Wales Press, 1999, p. 128.

24 For accounts of the changing political climate in Wales, 1979–99 see J.B. Jones and D. Balsom (eds) *The Road to the National Assembly for Wales*, Cardiff: University of Wales Press, 2000, Chapters 1 and 2; and K. Morgan and G. Mungham, *Redesigning Democracy: The Making of the Welsh Assembly*, Bridgend: Seren, 2000, part one. For changing attitudes in Wales see also G. Evans and D. Trystan, 'Why was 1997 different?', in B. Taylor and K.Thomson (eds) *Scotland and Wales: Nations Again?*, Cardiff: University of Wales Press, 1999, pp. 95–117.

25 L. Andrews, 'Too important to be left to the politicians: the 'Yes' for Wales story', in Jones and Balsom, *Road to the National Assembly*, pp. 50–69. The No campaign also tried to use celebrities, with footballer Gary Speed countering Ryan Giggs' support for a Yes vote. D. McCrone and B. Lewis, 'The Scottish and Welsh referendum campaigns', in Taylor and Thompson, *Scotland and Wales*, p. 32.

26 Quoted in Stephens, *Wales in Quotation*, p. 135.

27 *Western Mail*, 21 February 1998.

28 *The Independent*, 3 December 2002.

29 See M. Johnes, *Soccer and Society: South Wales, 1900–39*, Cardiff: University of Wales Press, 2002.

30 *Western Mail*, 1 August 1966.

31 Manchester United official website. Online. Available HTTP: http://www.manutd.com/supporters/brancheswales.sps (accessed 9 October 2001).

32 P. Harrison, 'Soccer's tribal wars [1974]', in P. Barker (ed.) *The Other Britain: A New Society Collection*, London: Routledge: 1982, p. 246.

33 G. Armstrong and R. Giulianotti (eds) *Fear and Loathing in World Football*, Oxford: Berg, 2001.

34 Cardiff City fan in D. and E. Brimson, *England, My England: the Trouble with the National Football Team*, London: Headline, 1996, p. 192. Occasionally, anti-English chanting throws up debates on fan websites about whether it constitutes some form of racism. The dominant opinion seems to be that such behaviour should be regarded light-heartedly.

35 L. Colley, *Britons: Forging the Nation, 1707–1837*, London: Pimlico, 1992, p. 6.

36 C. Williams, *Capitalism, Community and Conflict: The South Wales Coalfield, 1898–1947*, Cardiff: University of Wales Press, 1998, p. 70. For national identity and sport in Wales pre-1939 see Johnes, *Soccer and Society*, Chapter 6.

37 This is a reference to the song 'Swing low, sweet chariot', which English rugby union fans have adopted as an unofficial anthem.

38 Quoted in *The Times*, 29 December 1997.

39 L. Dowds and K. Young, 'National identity', in R. Jowell *et al.* (eds) *British Social Attitudes: The 13th Report*, Aldershot: Dartmouth Publishing Co., 1996, p. 145.

40 Curtice, 'Is Scotland a nation?', in Taylor and Thomson, *Scotland and Wales*, p. 129.

41 P. Melling, 'Billy Boston', in Richards *et al.*, *Heart and Soul*, pp. 47–58; R. Gate, *Gone North: Welshmen in Rugby League,* vol. 1, Ripponden: published by author, 1986, pp. 108–20.

42 N. Evans and P. O'Leary, 'Playing the game: sport and ethnic minorities in modern Wales', in N. Evans, P. O'Leary and C. Williams (eds) *A Tolerant Nation? Ethnic Diversity in Wales*, Cardiff: University of Wales Press, 2003; M. Burley and S. Flemming, 'Racism and regionalism in Welsh soccer', *European Physical Education Review*, 1997, vol. 3, (2), pp. 183–94.

43 Communication with BBC Information Wales, 8 July 2002.

44 Davies, *Broadcasting and the BBC*, p. 358.
45 Although the survey identified rugby as second to the landscape in prompted cultural sources of national pride, the response was only three per cent higher than for male voice choirs. Curtice, 'Is Scotland a nation ?', in Taylor and Thomson, *Scotland and Wales*, p. 127.
46 D. Andrews, 'Sport and the masculine hegemony of the modern nation: Welsh rugby, culture and society, 1890–1914', in J. Nauright and T.J. Chandler (eds) *Making Men: Rugby and Masculine Identity*, London: Frank Cass, 1996, pp. 50–69.
47 Quoted in J. Maguire, 'Sport, identity politics, and globalization: diminishing contrasts and increasing varieties', *Sociology of Sport Journal*, 1994, 11 (4), p. 412.
48 Such ideas are briefly developed in G. Whannel, 'Individual stars and collective identities in media sport', in M. Roche (ed.) *Sport, Popular Culture and Identity*, Brighton: Meyer and Meyer, 1998, pp. 34–5.
49 T. Williams, *The Patriot Game: Reflections on Language, Devolution and the Break-up of Britain*, vol. 1, Beddau: Tynant Books, 1997, p. 16.
50 N. Evans, 'Writing the social history of modern Wales: approaches, achievements and problems', *Social History*, 1992, vol. 17 (3), p. 485.
51 R.M. Jones, 'Beyond identity? The reconstruction of the Welsh', *Journal of British Studies*, 1992, vol. 31 (4), p. 356.
52 Holt, *Sport and the British*, p. 237.
53 Williams, *Patriot Game*, p. 17.

4 'Cry for us, Argentina'

Sport and national identity in late twentieth-century Scotland

Ronald Kowalski

Even after the Union of the English and Scottish Parliaments in 1707 Scotland retained a strong sense of national identity. This was especially evident in lowland Scotland, the site of the Scottish Enlightenment and the Industrial Revolution. In part, this identity may have been 'cramped, stagnant, backward-looking, parochial', as Tom Nairn claimed, but the Scots also created a sparkling intellectual ethos that Arthur Herman recently has identified as central to the 'invention of the modern world'.[1] Scottish identity was also underpinned by the continued existence of a set of Scottish institutions distinct from those in England, notably, the Church, and the legal and educational systems. Yet, despite this, it was more than two centuries before Scotland generated a dynamic nationalist movement to match those that had vigorously pursued self-determination in many other small European nations during the nineteenth and early twentieth centuries.

Many historians have attributed this 'peculiarity' of the Scots to the fruits of the Union with England. In the nineteenth century, as Nairn again pointed out, the rapidly growing Scottish bourgeoisie profited both within the Union, and in its Empire. By the early twentieth, John Foster concluded, Scotland's capitalist class were firmly at the centre of the decision-making process at Westminster. Moreover, the Union, English-dominated as it was, did not frustrate the ambitions of Scotland's forward-looking intellectual elite, the inspiration behind nationalist movements elsewhere. On the contrary, it was co-opted into Britain's burgeoning imperial bureaucracy, whilst Scots soldiers came to play a prominent and at times savage role in the army of Empire. Scotland, as Michael Fry remarked, was no mere colony of England, in the service of some greater English design. The benefits of industry and empire had emasculated Scottish *political* nationalism and contributed to many Scots subscribing to what Linda Colley has described as a British nationalism. What survived was a sub-cultural nationalism, one in which football was by far more important than politics, as Nairn, no *afficionado* of the game, lamented.[2]

In 1992, Jim Sillars, then leader of the Scottish National Party (SNP), elaborated on Nairn's analysis, with an added vitriol. In his much-cited 'ninety minute patriots' speech delivered after the general election of that year, he denigrated the influence of sport, especially football. The fleeting 'nationalist outpourings' that 'major sporting events' engendered (at Hampden Park in Glasgow, the national football stadium, and latterly at Murrayfield in Edinburgh, the home of Scottish rugby) had deflected far too many Scots from rallying decisively behind the movement for independence. His outburst was prompted by disappointment at the outcome of the election. Three-quarters of the Scottish electorate had rejected the staunchly pro-Union Conservative Party of John Major yet it was returned to power by the voters of England. Unwittingly, his intervention echoed an emerging consensus among historians that sport has served as an important constituent of national identity. Precisely how it has done so remains highly contested. However, as Martin Polley, among others, has reminded us, sport does not function in a socio-economic or politico-cultural vacuum.[3] Hence, before addressing its role in shaping Scottish identity in the late-twentieth century, it is necessary to consider briefly the rapidly changing circumstances in which Scotland and the Scots found themselves – these circumstances, despite Sillars' despair, had led to a marked growth in support for devolution, if not outright independence.

Economic decline has proved to be a major formative influence on the emergence of political nationalism since the 1960s. The collapse of Scotland's heavy industries, especially mining, shipbuilding and railway engineering, caused the loss of tens of thousands of jobs which government-backed investment in car, truck and strip steel plants did not adequately replace. As fears of economic insecurity mounted, the main political beneficiary was the SNP, which polled a remarkable 34 per cent of the vote in the May 1968 local elections. The economic failures of Edward Heath's Conservative administration, elected in June 1970, especially its refusal to support old 'lame duck' industries, provided a renewed fillip to the SNP which garnered almost one-third of the vote in the general election of October 1974. The Westminster government, it seemed, had little concern for Scotland's particular needs, a perception reinforced by its decision to sell the newly discovered oil fields in the North Sea, off the north-east coast of Scotland, to the large multi-national oil companies. In response, as opinion poll evidence suggested, more and more Scots swung behind devolution, if not independence. The SNP wanted an elected Scottish parliament with the power to safeguard the country's future. Afraid that the alternative to devolution would be the disintegration of the Union, the Labour government elected in 1974 eventually and grudgingly agreed to a referendum on the issue which took place on 1 March, 1979.[4] The devolutionist cause failed. In large part it was prejudiced from the outset by an amendment proposed by the Labour backbencher George Cunningham, a Scot but representing a London constituency. This required that a minimum of 40 per cent of the Scottish electorate had to vote for the creation of a new Scottish Assembly. Only 63.8 per cent turned out, with barely over half in favour. Whether Scotland's disappointing performance in the 1978 football World Cup finals in Argentina had any significant impact on the outcome remains conjecture.[5]

The ensuing general election in May 1979 saw the return of a Conservative government, and a precipitous decline in SNP fortunes. It polled less than one-fifth of the vote, returning only two of its previous eleven MPs to Westminster. Political nationalism, it appeared, was dead in the water. Margaret Thatcher, now Prime Minister, and an intransigent champion of the Union, came to be regarded as a new 'hammer of the Scots' (the epithet was first applied to the English king, Edward I, in the early thirteenth century). Paradoxically, Thatcher was the saviour of the nationalist cause. Conservative victories in United Kingdom general elections between 1979 and 1992 were not mirrored in Scotland, where the party's support plummeted. An increasing majority of Scots rejected Thatcherite policies which had led to the virtual destruction of the remnants of traditional industry, savage cuts in public services, and the imposition of the community charge, the infamous 'poll tax', levied in Scotland in 1988, a year before it was introduced in England. Moreover, as William Keegan pointed out, the windfall of North Sea oil was dissipated too. Much of the oil revenue went to finance the rising unemployment wrought by Thatcher's emphasis on free market economic policies, while the 'petro-pound' rose to such levels as to make British industry uncompetitive abroad.[6] All Scottish protests were ignored. The Scottish Conservative Party consistently endorsed a policy of 'no surrender' on the question of devolution and, in turn, the majority of Scots saw Thatcherism as a manifestation of an English nationalism insensitive to Scottish interests.

It was little surprise that support for the devolutionist and nationalist causes gained a new momentum from the late 1980s, with all Scottish political parties, except the Conservatives, and the trade unions and the Churches, firmly behind home rule in some shape or form. The conclusion of Charles Kennedy, himself a Scot and currently leader of the Liberal Democratic Party, that Mrs Thatcher had turned out to be 'the greatest of all Scottish nationalists' was somewhat tongue in cheek, but not without foundation.[7] However, it took the landslide victory of the Labour Party in the general election of May 1997 (not one Conservative MP was returned from Scotland) to unfreeze the Union. A referendum on Scottish devolution was held in September 1997. In contrast to 18 years earlier nearly three-quarters of Scots voted for a new Scottish parliament, with almost two-thirds in favour of it having the right to raise taxes. Scotland's recent qualification for the 1998 World Cup Finals in France arguably had little influence on the outcome, though unlike Sillars before him Alex Salmond, the SNP leader, argued that success in football had fuelled pro-devolution sentiment.[8]

Sport and Scottish identity

Scotland's political evolution since the 1970s has been refracted through the prism of sport, in particular football and rugby union. Snooker, where Scots were dominant in the 1990s, never struck a significant national chord, largely because it was a game of individuals, not teams. As Jarvie and Reid insist, ' … sporting culture … is invariably political', and that of 'stateless nations, arguably, is more acutely political'.[9] The question is, political in what way? Polley identified three broad ways of understanding the interaction between sport and politics: sporting rivalries can act 'as a surrogate for nationalism; as the only real forum for national identity; and as a symbol of national difference'.[10] Jim Sillars, in his 1992 speech, had clearly plumped for the first of these theories. Christopher Harvie tended towards the second point of view. Gently rebuking Tom Nairn, he argued that football, especially after the creation of an independent Scottish league in the late nineteenth century, had contributed to a continuing sense of 'Scottishness'. Bert Moorhouse further developed this point emphasising that, as far as Scotland was concerned, sport had nurtured a continuing sense of national resentment against England.[11] Scots, unquestionably, have taken great delight in any victory over the 'auld enemy', such occasions often evoking folk memories of Bannockburn in 1314 when Scottish forces under Robert the Bruce defeated those of Edward I. The most recent example came against all the odds when Scotland denied England rugby union's 'Grand Slam' at Murrayfield in 2000. Echoing the thoughts of the outstanding Scottish sports journalist, Hugh McIlvanney, an unnamed Scot remarked: 'There's only one thing better than beating England … , and that's having to sit with nine Englishmen at the post-match dinner.'[12] This sentiment reappeared during football's 2002 World Cup Finals when the appeals of numerous politicians, including leading members of the SNP, for the Scots to grow up, jettison their antipathy and support England (Scotland had failed to qualify) were met with near universal derision. A minority was inspired by a deep-rooted Anglophobia. The majority, however, was simply weary of the 'hype' propagated by the English media. The all too predictable recollections of victory in the 1966 World Cup, repeated *ad nauseam* every time England qualified for the finals of a major championship, stuck in the craw of many Scots.[13]

Sport, therefore, is not always the 'benign' symbol of the nation posited by Mike Cronin and David Mayall. Neither has the attitude of the Scots towards England been unique. A similar resentment has been observed amongst other 'submerged nations' living in states dominated by an 'alien' nation. In Spain, as Simon Kuper pointed out, Barcelona has been a symbol of Catalan identity since the days of the Franco regime.[14] The Dinamo Kiev football team acquired a similar iconic status in the Ukraine when it was under Soviet tutelage. The English themselves did not invest Anglo-Scottish sporting encounters with as much passion. Where football is concerned Germany has been their *bete-noire* for the last thirty years – and for rugby, Wales in the 1970s and latterly France.

Whilst a degree of xenophobia towards England continues to lurk in the psyche of some Scots, sport has contributed more positively to Scottish identity in the last three decades. For a small nation of some five million people, qualification for six of the last eight football World Cup Finals engendered a real sense of national pride.[15] So too did the fact that Scotland reached the semi-finals of the rugby union World Cup in 1991. The members of the self-styled 'Tartan Army', who followed Scotland's football team abroad, took great pains to present themselves as ambassadors for Scotland, self-consciously and self-professedly different from the hooligan fringe that has blighted England's travels. However, as John Burnett and Grant Jarvie recently reiterated, it would be unwise to assume that sport has created 'a homogenous community that is Scotland'. Divisions based on gender, region, religion, even race, persist. Football, the so-called 'national game', still provides an important focus for the perpetuation of the sectarian divisions that have marred Scotland since the second half of the nineteenth century. These are most apparent in the continuing 'Old Firm' rivalry between the Scots-Irish Catholics of Glasgow Celtic and the Protestant (and Unionist) ascendancy associated with Glasgow Rangers. A similar divide exists in Edinburgh, where Hibernian represent the Scots-Irish and Heart of Midlothian the Protestants. Women have remained largely impervious to the appeal of football, while rugby union, with the exception of the textile and farming communities of the borders, for long was the domain of the more Anglicised middle-classes of Edinburgh and Glasgow. In the Highlands, distinctive and very much minority sports predominated.[16] The remainder of this chapter will explore the ways in which the positive and negative sides of Scottish identity have manifested themselves through football and rugby. Questions of sectarianism and racism provide a sub-theme, as Scottish political culture has not yet fully come to terms with those of another 'persuasion' (Catholics), or ethnicity.

Football

Since the late nineteenth century 'fitba' (football) has been the 'national' game, though one mainly associated with the central belt of the country, especially Glasgow and the west, and its male working class. As one journalist pointed out on the occasion of the annual fixture against England in 1974, it had become a Scottish 'virility symbol', albeit 'elevated out of all proportion'. Victory, especially against England, 'brought hope and stature to a nation so often insecure and concealing of its insecurity' and provided solace 'for a lost and neglected land'.[17] Such a view presaged what Neal Ascherson, in his *Stone Voices – the Search for Scotland*, identified as 'the St Andrew's Fault'. Scots, he argued, are full of 'self-doubt', and lack 'self-confidence' about their own identity. Compensation was sought by an emphasis on what became known as the 'wha's [who is] like us' syndrome.[18]

For many Scots, football epitomised this syndrome. The national side has suffered some humiliating defeats: 7–0 to Uruguay in the 1954 World Cup finals, and, even worse, 7–2, 9–3 and 5–1 to England in 1955, 1961 and 1975 respectively. Moreover, it has failed repeatedly to advance beyond the initial stages of World and European Nations finals. Yet, despite these setbacks, the view has long persisted that Scottish football remained exceptional. Since the late nineteenth century, so the story goes, skilful and imaginative Scots were at the heart of virtually every successful English club side, some solace for the fact that Scottish clubs themselves, even the mighty Celtic and Rangers, lacked the financial clout to keep their most gifted players. The myth was reinforced by the legend of the 'Wembley Wizards', whose flair and extraordinary abilities had humbled England 5–1 at Wembley in 1928. (Ironically both teams were playing to avoid the wooden spoon in the Home Nations Championship). Their example allegedly had inspired later outstanding teams, such as the Hungarian 'golden team' of the early 1950s, even though the often-chauvinistic Scottish tabloid press took a surprisingly sober view of this comparison.

While belief in the superior qualities of Scottish football was much exaggerated, it persisted long after 1945. It was reinforced by Scotland's victory over England, the then World Champions, at Wembley in 1967. Writing in the Scottish tabloid, the *Daily Record*, Hugh Taylor lauded Scotland's performance, and singled out Bobby Brown, the new Scotland manager, for special praise. His tactics, he hyperbolically concluded, had 'revealed a style that [would] go a long way in helping us to win the World Cup in 1970'. Taylor would have preferred a 6–2, rather than the actual 3–2 victory, but was consoled by the fact that the Scots had outplayed the English. Jim Baxter was identified as the fulcrum of England's humiliation, though in the *Daily Mirror* Ken Jones was scathing of his performance: 'Baxter's less-than-adult approach led to "taking the mick", rather than a massacre'. Denis Law shared this view as he wanted a 'massacre' to atone for the 9–3 debacle four years earlier but forgave Baxter afterwards for his attitude. Developing an inimitable style, 'wha's like us', still was of paramount importance for many Scots.

It was 'that peculiar Scottish thing', as John Rafferty, football correspondent for the *Scotsman*, later remarked, 'in which the score line is not as important as toying with beaten opponents, tormenting them, humiliating them'.[19] Just over five weeks later this keen sense of Scottish superiority was confirmed. Celtic, a team composed of 11 native Scots all born within 30 miles of Glasgow, not only won the European Cup, but did so against a rigidly defensive Inter Milan in a sustained attacking performance that caught the imagination of virtually all observers, English and continental as well as Scottish.[20] The Scots had little to crow about for some years after, with the notable exception of Rangers' victory in the final of the European Cup Winners' Cup in 1972, though this was soured by violent clashes between Rangers' supporters and the Spanish police. Yet pride in the supposed virtues of Scottish football before the 1970s should not be confused with the desire to 'break up' Britain. Baxter and Law, the architects of 1967, were passionately Scottish, but neither questioned the virtues or permanence, of the Union. There is no evidence that the bulk of the supporters did either, and it was only from the early 1970s that they began to jeer the British national anthem.[21]

1974 witnessed a resurgence of belief in football as a symbol of Scottish nationhood. In May, Scotland convincingly defeated England 2–0 at a passionately nationalist Hampden bedecked with Lion Rampant flags. The victory, however, was marred by chants of 'We hate the English', a recurring phenomenon which a junior minister at the Scottish Office later condemned as an 'ugly manifestation of Scottish nationalism'.[22] The identification of football more healthily with the 'nation' was reinforced by Scotland's performances in the 1974 World Cup in West Germany. Crude tactics by Brazil and Yugoslavia, combined with weak refereeing, resulted in a disciplined, gifted and thoughtfully organised Scottish team failing to progress to the quarter-finals on goal difference. One could add that Scotland's failure to beat Zaire by more than 2–0 played its part in the disappointment. However, the team had represented Scotland proudly on the world stage.[23] Its thousands of supporters had done their country proud too. They drank, they sang, they danced, and they fraternised, in particular with the Brazilian supporters. The authorities in Dortmund and Frankfurt were pleasantly surprised – probably also immensely relieved – by the behaviour of this embryonic 'Tartan Army'.[24]

The rise of nationalist sentiment, combined with a noticeably growing anti-English feeling, continued during the 1976 Home Nations Championship. When England came to Hampden, the national anthem was greeted with a barrage of booing. In part, this was caused by the refusal of the Scottish Football Association to adopt 'Flower of Scotland' as its own anthem, a move favoured by much of the local press and Willie Ormond, the team manager. During the game, which ended in a 2–1 victory for Scotland, the crowd repeatedly sang the 'Flower' and so mastered it.[25] Scotland's performance again led to grossly inflated expectations, and the speculation that Scotland had a pool of players good enough, with a bit of luck, to win the 1978 World Cup.[26]

1978 proved to be a landmark in football's function as the symbol of Scottish identity. In retrospect, a scarcely believable euphoria had gripped much of the country after a good Scottish side qualified for the World Cup Finals in Argentina. The belief that Scotland could progress to the last four, if not win the Cup, was widespread; a view more cautiously expressed by the then manager, Ally McLeod, than myth would have it. Many neutral experts concurred that the Scots had the talent to do well, despite recent poor performances.[27] A few words of caution were heard, with some columnists concerned that 'commercial ventures' or 'cash grabbing schemes' had taken precedence over preparation for the World Cup itself.[28] Their concerns proved to be well founded. Scotland lost to a decent but not outstanding Peru side; drew with the minnows in their group, Iran; defeated the eventual runners-up, the Netherlands, which restored some of the nation's shattered self-esteem; and again went out on goal difference. The sense of national tragedy was compounded by the fact that Willie Johnston, Scotland's left-winger, was sent home in disgrace after testing positive for drugs in the wake of the Peru game.

The post-mortems swiftly followed. Blame for Scotland's failure was attributed, variously, to McLeod's failure to study the opposition in person and poor team selection, and to arguably inflated allegations of indiscipline, even drunkenness in the Scottish camp. As James Naughtie reported, an overwhelming depression gripped much of Scotland, especially after the failure to beat Iran.[29] A series of conflicting observations on the role of football in shaping Scotland's sense of identity quickly surfaced. An editorial in the *Glasgow Herald* was highly condemnatory of a nation that allowed football to become such an influential determinant of its pride. Less critical voices were also heard. A letter to the *Scotsman* soberly noted that, while Scotland lacked its own parliament, international football would always be more than a game. It would remain one of the few fields in which Scotland possessed an individual identity, with its footballers as its only ambassadors. This prompted another reader to argue that football was simply a game and thus an inadequate substitute for the sense of nationhood that only self-government would bring. To contend otherwise only imposed an overwhelming burden on the shoulders of the country's footballers.[30]

What Argentina conclusively demonstrated, as Hugh McIlvanney pointed out, was that football was 'hopelessly ill-equipped to carry the burden of emotional expression the Scots seek to load upon it'. It marked, as the *Scotsman* reaffirmed some 12 years later, the turning point in the old 'wha's like us' mentality. Footballers continued to be seen as representatives of nation, which demanded good behaviour on and off the field, but expectations of what they might achieve were gradually reduced. Jock Stein, when he took over as manager of the national team in 1978, made an important contribution, insisting that a small nation could not expect to be world-beaters. Stein's realism has proved to be well considered. Despite qualification for four further World Cup finals, and two European Nations Championships, itself a respectable record, Scotland's displays became increasingly erratic. The question in most Scots' minds no longer was about ultimate triumph, but more and more about whether Scotland might progress, and if not whether there would be dignity in defeat.[31] Paradoxically, as the performances of the national team declined, the conduct of their supporters markedly improved, with remarkably few exceptions. Violence was dramatically reduced at home after a ban on the consumption of alcohol in football grounds was introduced in the mid-1970s. The end to the Home Nations Championship in 1988 led to the demise of the biennial, invariably drunken, and sometimes violent, descents on London. Writing in the *Daily Mirror* on the morning of the England-Scotland game at Wembley in 1977, Frank McGhee concluded that the occasion had become 'unpleasant, ugly and idiotic', with London under siege from hordes of lurching and drunken Scottish hooligans. It would be naïve to deny a degree of truth in McGhee's assessment, but his reports on the Monday after the game were disproportionate. Admittedly, many inebriated Scottish fans had invaded the Wembley pitch after a comfortable 2–1 victory, dug up parts of the pitch as souvenirs and broken the goalposts. The headline run by the *Mirror* was 'Jock the Ripper', and McGhee castigated the Scottish supporters for their stupidity and violence, although the Metropolitan Police conceded that the Scots had been euphoric rather than vindictive.

As the *Glasgow Herald* reflected many years later, the English media reaction to 1977 had been 'vicious and unjust'.[32] When violence again marked the last Home Nations fixture in 1988, the reaction was equally disproportionate, with the Conservative MP, Terry Dicks, condemning the Scots as 'pigs and animals'. A minority of Scots 'fans' had gone to London intent on wreaking mayhem, as the Scottish press conceded, though not necessarily for 'xenophobic' reasons. More likely, organised hooligans, the so-called 'casuals', who had grouped around leading clubs north and south of the border, sought to use the occasion to knock lumps out of their rivals. The truth is difficult to untangle, though there are grounds to suggest, as the *Scotsman* did, that racist National Front 'hangers-on' who had infiltrated the English support were more culpable for sparking off the violence than the 'lunatic fringe' which had followed Scotland to London.[33] To the relief of many Scots, 1988 marked the end of the annual encounter with England.

As relieved as any were the members of the 'Tartan Army', a large and heterogeneous group of Scottish fans, encompassing professionals, workers, some women, the unemployed, and even the unemployable, but with few Celtic or Rangers supporters in its ranks. When the Army emerged is still uncertain. One of its members, Ian Black, who has chronicled its history, argued for its existence in the 1982 World Cup finals in Spain, though it was evident in embryo in West Germany eight years earlier. According to Hamish Husband, chairman of the 'West of Scotland Tartan Army', 20,000 fans, including many families on holiday, had travelled to Spain. What is more certain is that Scottish football supporters increasingly developed an image of themselves as representatives of the nation. They drank copiously, as always, and continued to sing and dance, as they sought to 'entertain' the locals. Yet they rarely, if ever, engaged in acts of vandalism. Its more mature members took responsibility for controlling any potential excesses. They followed the national team in most of its travels, though rarely to London. The reason, as Black pointed out, was a measured decision, as the members of the 'Army' sought to distance themselves from the racism and xenophobia that gripped the 'amateur brigade' which descended on Wembley every two years. One may surmise that as the team's performance deteriorated, while that of England arguably improved, many of its followers sublimated this by self-consciously distinguishing themselves from the hooligan fringe that blighted the 'Auld Enemy's' sallies overseas and embraced what Husband described as a 'positive, ambassadorial nationalism'.[34]

The paths of England and Scotland, however, have crossed on three occasions since 1988. In the European Nations finals held in England in 1996, a 2–0 defeat at Wembley was disappointing, but led to little violence. Nor did the Scottish tabloid press display its former levels of chauvinism, either before and after the match, apart from feeble efforts to stoke up anti-English resentment. Sporadic outbursts of fighting did occur, in all probability between 'casuals' from north and south of the border, with those associated with Chelsea and Aberdeen apparently in the forefront. The 'Tartan Army', which had little choice but go south of the border to support Scotland, stood aside.[35] These few clashes, nevertheless, reinforced the belief of the football authorities in both countries that it would be unwise to revive an annual fixture. The teams did not meet again until November 1999, when they were paired in a two-game eliminator for the Euro 2000 finals. Scots everywhere may have passionately desired victory over England but post-devolution there was remarkably little xenophobia. Some anti-English resentment was evident. Most of it was a response to the all too typical arrogance of the English media, especially the reported comments of Tony Adams, the English captain, who proclaimed England's undoubted superiority – and to England 'usurping' the national anthem for its own use. Even the Scottish unionists were moved to protest about the latter.[36] Scotland lost in typical fashion. Having performed dismally in a 2–0 defeat at Hampden – (one female columnist claimed that watching it was worse than childbirth) – the nation 'regained its pride on the park', to quote Alex Salmond, in a 1–0 victory at Wembley.[37]

Two conclusions can be drawn from these last encounters with the 'Auld Enemy'. First, the violence in Glasgow and London surrounding the games, albeit caused by a minority, determined that there would be no resurrection of the annual fixture. It could do little to promote a more mature relationship between the two nations. Second, despite the Scots drowning out the national anthem at Hampden, the game simply did not matter as much to the Scots as it had 30 years earlier. Defeat did hurt and victory would have been sweet, but the pain swiftly dissipated. The nation may not have reached maturity quite yet but, as Ian Bell cautiously pointed out in the *Scotsman*, 46 per cent of Scots looked to the new parliament in Edinburgh to provide a better future, 31 per cent to Europe, and only 8 per cent to London. The Scots may not have abandoned their adolescence totally, but there are some grounds for hoping that, as Ascherson argued, for most Scots 'there is more to being Scottish than a desire to thump Englishmen', even on the football field.[38]

Rugby Union

Rugby too has acquired an overtly national patina, to which even the infamously conservative Scottish Rugby Union (SRU) responded by adopting 'Flower of Scotland' as its official anthem in 1990 instead of 'God Save the Queen'. Before the 1970s, the annual Calcutta Cup match against England was not gripped by the popular frenzy that football against the 'Auld Enemy' generated. Richard Holt explained the more 'gentlemanly', atmosphere surrounding rugby union by the fact that outside the Borders it had for long remained the domain of the elite public schools of Edinburgh, and later of Glasgow. The historical function of these schools, as J.A. Mangan argued, was to breed an elite to staff the Empire. Sport, especially 'rugger' and cricket, played its part in nurturing the qualities, the 'clubability', required of the ruling class. The products of these schools, however, were not simply English clones, but neither were they dyed in the wool Scots. Rather, what they acquired was a sense of British identity, and duty and service to Empire.[39]

This legacy was to mute the intensity of Anglo-Scottish rivalry on, and off, the rugby field. More recently, however, rugby itself has become caught up in the swell of the new nationalism, especially evident when England visits Murrayfield. Its politicisation certainly pre-dated the 1990s. The first portents emerged in the 1970s. Commenting on Scotland's 26–6 hammering of England in the game organised in March 1971 to mark the centenary of fixtures between the two countries, the *Scotsman*, in a front-page article, complained that the evening news on the BBC had failed to make any reference to the result. Two days later, correspondents criticised the BBC for its perennial pro-English bias.[40] Five years later, in February 1976, when the Queen visited Murrayfield for the Calcutta Cup match, the Scottish press feared that her visit would turn into a national embarrassment, anticipating that much of the crowd would boo the national anthem. To defuse this possibility, the SRU agreed that 'Scotland the Brave' was to be played immediately before the anthem. The extent to which this ploy succeeded is a matter of debate. The *Sunday Post* and *Glasgow Herald* considered that it had been successful. The latter claimed that 'civility had triumphed over ill-mannered chauvinism', yet added that it was quite proper for the Scots to have their own anthem. The *Scotsman*, more accurately, if my memory serves me correctly, reported that while those sitting in the stand 'lustily' sang the anthem many on the terraces whistled and jeered.[41] Middle-class Scotland, it seemed, or part of it, was turning.

The 'turn' accelerated during the Thatcher years, arguably reinforced by the pride taken in Scotland's 1984 success in winning the 'Grand Slam', the first since 1925. Nationalist fervour reached extraordinary heights of intensity in March 1990, when the English came north again, for a match of unprecedented importance. At stake then was not just the Calcutta Cup, but the Triple Crown, the 'Grand Slam', and the (unofficial) title of 'Champions of Europe' as both England and Scotland went into the game undefeated. The fervour was fuelled by two quite disparate sources. The first was the 'poll tax', which according to the *Scotsman* had become a real threat to the Union. The second was the hubris of the English press which, as even *The Times* conceded, had no doubts that the all-conquering English XV would destroy the Scots. The Bannockburn spirit was roused – another Flodden, when the Scots had been crushed by the English, was unthinkable – with the *Daily Record* invoking 'Flower of Scotland' and imploring the Scottish team to send the English home 'tae think again'.[42]

The Scottish team itself was conscious enough of its potential place in history. It had prevailed upon the SRU to agree that two verses of the 'Flower', just adopted as the official anthem of Scottish rugby, be sung on the day – and the *Glasgow Herald* obligingly printed them on its front page. When the teams took the field, with the Scots marching out like gladiators, the crowd erupted into voice. The singing of the 'Flower' 'certainly stirred the blood of every Scot', as Bill McLaren, the doyen of rugby commentators, recalled. The Scottish XV was inspired and, contrary to English predictions, defeated an England team that hitherto had seemed unstoppable. As John Jeffrey, a Scottish wing-forward on the day, recollected: 'The English were more talented than us but they believed the [media] hype ... They thought they only had to turn up to win ... They were cocky, way beyond arrogant',[43] First hubris, then the fall. Many Scots on Saturday night were seen sporting badges with the inscription: 'Bannockburn 1314 Murrayfield 13–7'. While the result was important to the Scots, the occasion itself had greater significance. The stance of the *Glasgow Herald*, which a mere 14 years earlier had defended the singing of the national anthem, was illuminating. In an editorial on the morning of the game it had come out vehemently against 'God Save the Queen'. It described it as an 'awful dirge', an 'obsequious hymn' lauding the vanquishing of Scotland by its oldest enemy, which Scots had sung for far too long. It applauded the highly conservative SRU for coming to its senses and embracing the 'Flower', which would help all Scots reacquire an identity long 'suppressed'. Middle class Scotland, or a significant part of it, had found one voice.[44] The *Herald* was not alone. As some 20 years earlier, the *Scotsman* published correspondence critical of the 'English Broadcasting Corporation' (the BBC) for the notable absence in its 5.00 p.m. Saturday national news broadcast of any mention of Scotland's triumph. An England victory, it was said, would in all probability have been a leading item.[45] Media bias, it appears, was as galling to Scotland's rugby supporters as it was to its football supporters.

Rugby union precipitated a similar outpouring of national passion in October 1991. Before the semi-final of the World Cup between England and Scotland, played at Murrayfield, Gordon Brown, an ex-international forward, declared:

> The people see this game as more than a rugby match. This is about life and politics in Scotland, the poll tax and Whitehall rule. Even the players say, while they like to beat anyone, even Japan, and love to beat the Welsh or Irish, they live to beat the English.

A current Scottish player agreed. Given the sad decline of the Scottish football team, he stated anonymously, rugby had become the symbol of nationhood. 'So I dare say,' he continued, 'we have been chosen in this match to right the ills of Thatcherism, the poll tax and the Westminster government. You might say the people see us playing for the rugby-loving Celt Kinnock (then leader of the Labour Party) against the cricket-loving, po-faced English government'.[46] Yet there was a darker side to this upsurge of national identity. In the *Scotsman*, Nick Cain feared that Scottish patriotism was turning into a blind hatred of all things English, while Brian Meek in the *Glasgow Herald* cautioned against 'tribal outpourings of bile about the English'. If so, it was not confined to Scotland. Messages of support for the Scots, so the *Glasgow Herald* claimed, were received from Ireland, Wales, Australia, New Zealand, and even the United Arab Emirates, a testimony to the near-universal satisfaction to be derived from beating the English.[47] Scotland lost by the narrowest of margins, 9–6, and was not to defeat England again until 2000.

The game in 2000 again evoked much national fervour, but on this occasion most Scots were fearful of the outcome as their team had lost its previous four internationals. The hitherto rampant English were 14–1 odds-on favourites and, it seemed again, only had to turn up to walk off with the 'Grand Slam'. Astonishingly, Scotland won, inspired, as Andy Nicol, the Scottish captain declared, by the zeal of the crowd, which sang the 'Flower' with a gusto and passion not heard since the early 1990s. Victory caused great rejoicing, yet it was also occasion for more mature reflection about Scottish identity. John Beattie, a former international forward and then rugby correspondent for the *Herald*, admitted that denying England the 'Grand Slam' had been 'so sweet'. But he also raised serious questions about the nature of Scottish national feeling in the twenty-first century. Echoing Nick Cain's observations some nine years earlier, he was highly critical of the apparent xenophobia of many Scots:

> The trouble with hating the English is that if that's your sole reason to cheer on a Scottish team, then we are sunk as a country. When things get so bad that the English race is the target of our hatred, then it just goes to prove that we have reached an all time low.[48]

It was time, he implied, for the 'new Scotland', with its devolved assembly, to transcend defining itself simply by antagonism to England. Scots should grow up and take a more positive view of themselves, as the SNP earlier had urged with its vision of Scotland in Europe. What he might have added was that there were issues at home, of sectarianism and racism that Scotland would also have to address if a healthier sense of national identity was to be created.

Sectarian and racist divisions in sport

Football in particular has been a locus of longstanding sectarian and more recent racist fissures in Scottish society, which casts doubts on its status as the 'national' game, the lynchpin of a unified national identity. The bulk of research into this issue has focused on the Old Firm of Celtic and Rangers. Nearly half of Celtic supporters, surveys suggest, are more concerned with the fortunes of the Republic of Ireland than of the Scottish national team. On the other hand, many of Rangers' supporters, and its directors, remain committed to the Union and are wary of the SNP. Few Celtic and Rangers fans, as we have seen, are to be found in the ranks of the Tartan Army, the latter having comprised the bulk of Scotland's support until the early 1970s.[49]

Sectarianism, in particular anti-Catholicism, has been a persistent feature of Scottish society since the Reformation. It was brought to the fore in the nineteenth century by the influx of hundreds of thousands of Irish Catholics, fleeing poverty, and famine, for employment in Scotland's new industries. In a staunchly Presbyterian country they were subject to discrimination by the dominant majority which looked down upon the Irish as an inferior species. This fault line was later reflected in the bitter rivalry between Rangers and Celtic, which came to symbolise the clash of two different cultures.[50] Established in 1888 to raise money for the Catholic poor and to maintain the faith, Celtic ever since has acted as a focus for Irish Catholic identity. Yet, as Joseph Bradley has argued, it also betokened the readiness of many Irish Catholics to integrate into their new home, most marked in Celtic's willingness to sign players who were neither Irish nor Catholic. Jock Stein, its most famous and successful manager, was a Protestant.[51] Rangers, the quintessential representative of Protestant supremacy in sport, displayed an intolerance that had roots which went deeper than merely being a response to the success of Celtic in mobilising the loyalties of Irish Catholics. This was displayed most starkly in its refusal for most of the twentieth century to sign a player of 'the other persuasion'.

Undoubtedly, sectarianism did recede during the twentieth century. Paul Dimeo and Gerry Finn, who remain highly critical of the divisions that continue to bedevil Scotland, concede that remarkable advances have been made in inter-communal and inter-faith relations, 'especially over the last thirty or so years'. Recent statistics, as Bert Moorhouse has pointed out, suggested that 40 per cent of all marriages in Scotland were now 'mixed', that is, between Protestants and Catholics. John Foster concurred with these optimistic views, contending that sectarianism was generally held in check, even in the grim 1970s when unemployment rose to over 100,000 and 'the troubles' in Northern Ireland escalated into terrible violence.[52] Sadly, recent episodes in sport have run counter to these heartening trends. Despite initiatives sponsored by the directors of both Celtic and Rangers to clamp down on sectarianism and racism, and Rangers' abandonment of its Protestants only policy, there has been a resurgence of sectarian violence since the mid-1990s. Stabbings and arrests have frequently followed matches between the two clubs. A Glasgow schoolboy, Mark Scott, died in one such incident in October 1995. In May 1999 a Rangers fan, and another 16-year old Celtic fan, Thomas McFadden, were also stabbed to death.[53]

Racism has been an unacknowledged blight within Scotland too, one to which football has not been immune. Black players have often been subjected to racial taunts. In September 1983, in a UEFA cup-tie at Paisley, St Mirren supporters hurled abuse at the Dutch international, Ruud Gullit, then playing for PSV Eindhoven. Later, other black players in Scotland were greeted with bananas thrown from the crowd and a barrage of 'monkey grunts', notably Mark Walters of Rangers and Paul Elliott of Celtic. In defence of Walters, Rangers' fans, with an unconscious racism, sang 'I'd rather be a darkie than a Tim (a Catholic)'.[54] Racism was also evident at boardroom level, most notoriously in 1995 when Jim Oliver, chairman of nearly bankrupt Partick Thistle, opposed the efforts of Asian-Scottish businessmen to invest in the club. He reportedly said that he would not hand over the club to 'some Indian with a curry shop'.[55] However, it would be unwise to assume that racism was directed only against those of African and Asian descent. It was also in evidence when Scotland played Italy in a World Cup qualifying match at Ibrox Park, Rangers' ground, in November 1992. As Giancarlo Rinaldi recalled, the Italian players, along with their supporters from Scotland's large and 'well integrated' Italian community, suffered 'a non-stop barrage of racial abuse', including choice epithets such as 'Wops', 'Dagos' and, of course, 'Fucking Fenian bastards'. Equally disturbing was the fact that both the SFA and the Strathclyde police kept their heads firmly in the sand, denying that any abusive language had been used.[56]

The incontrovertible existence of sectarian and racial divisions has not been confined to sport, and it has become a matter of more general, often passionate, but possibly healthy, debate in recent years. It hit the headlines during the Edinburgh Festival in August 1997 when James Macmillan, the Catholic composer, launched an extreme, if exaggerated, assault on the bigotry of Scotland's Protestant majority that he saw as all-pervasive. In response to heightened criticism of separate, state-funded Catholic schools, he defended the excellent education that they offered.[57] This issue, however, remains highly contentious, despite surveys suggesting that four-fifths of all Scots, and almost three-fifths of Catholics, are in favour of phasing out such schools. The Catholic Church hierarchy has rejected even the most cautious of moves towards integration, notably the idea of locating separate Catholic and Protestant schools on the same campus.[58] Whatever rationale there was for separate Catholic schools in the past, whether they have a positive role to play in the Scotland of the twenty-first century is an open question.

In response to the problems of sectarian violence, and to an opinion poll in September 2002 which found that one-quarter of those Scots questioned considered themselves to be 'racist', the Scottish parliament stirred itself into action. The executive launched the 'One Scotland, Many Cultures' campaign, primarily to promote multiculturalism and tolerance of non-white minorities. Sectarian crimes were to be dealt with in the same manner as racist crimes, with tough sentences imposed and a special record kept of those convicted.[59] While this initiative is to be applauded doubts remain whether legislation in itself will remove deep-rooted prejudices, at least quickly. The proposal, even more recently mooted, to ban footballers from making the sign of the cross, arguably is less well conceived. As Gerald Seenan pointed out, 'the tradition of players blessing themselves before taking a penalty kick or after scoring a goal is ... part of the global football tradition'.[60]

Conclusion

Jim Sillars' bitter conclusion that, for many Scots, sport had long served as a surrogate for political nationalism contained a considerable degree of truth. For much of the century success on the football field, in particular victory against England, brought succour to a stateless nation unsure of its national identity. Since the 1970s rugby union, too, provided a similar platform for outbursts of nationalist sentiment. However, as the twenty-first century dawned, sport arguably had become less central to most Scots' sense of identity. In part, its loss of importance was a product of the decline of Scottish football and, more recently, of rugby union as major forces in their respective world games. Admittedly, Scots continue to take great glee in increasingly rare triumphs, especially over the English, but that is best explained, as Ian Bell argued, by a centuries-old history that 'cannot be easily erased'.[61] More critically, Sillars' misgivings about sport perpetuating a political backwardness within the Scottish nation have proved to be over-pessimistic. A clear majority of Scots did rally behind the movement for devolution, if not the total independence urged by the SNP, and convincingly voted for the creation of a Scottish parliament. Whatever its achievements and its peccadilloes, 90 per cent of Scots continue to support it, according to a recent opinion poll, and it offers a new focus of identity.[62] It would be Utopian to anticipate that it will preside over a Renaissance of Scottish football and rugby, yet to its credit it has begun to seek to redress the sectarian and racist tensions, all too evident in football, that blight the creation of a new Scottish identity.

Acknowledgements

The author is grateful to Paddy McNally and Adrian Smith for their encouragement and advice.

Notes

1 T. Nairn, *The Break-Up of Britain: Crisis and Neo-Nationalism*, London: New Left Books, 1977, pp. 129, 135, 145–6; A. Herman, *The Scottish Enlightenment: The Scots' Invention of the Modern World*, London: Fourth Estate, 2002.
2 Nairn, *Break-Up*, pp. 173–4; J. Foster, 'The twentieth century, 1914–1979', in R.A. Houston, and W.W.J. Knox (eds) *The New Penguin History of Scotland: From the Earliest Times to the Present Day*, London: Allen Lane, 2001, pp. 417–18; M. Fry, *The Scottish Empire*, Edinburgh: Tuckwell Press, 2001, p. 494; L. Colley, *Britons: Forging the Nation 1707–1837*, London: Pimlico, 1994, p. 5.
3 M. Polley, *Moving the Goalposts: A History of Sport and Society since 1945*, London: Routledge, 1998, pp. 12–13.
4 C. Harvie, *Scotland and Nationalism: Scottish Society and Politics, 1707–1977*, London: Allen and Unwin, 1977, pp. 172–4, 245–7; Foster, 'Twentieth Century', pp. 478–80; a report outlining Labour fears was leaked to the *Scotsman*, 9 February 1976; *Daily Record*, 17 May 1976.
5 T.M. Devine, *The Scottish Nation 1700–2000*, Harmondsworth: Penguin, 2000, pp. 587–90; C. Harvie, *Scotland and Nationalism: Scottish Society and Politics from 1707 to the Present*, third edition, London: Routledge, 1998, p. 197.
6 C. Harvie, 'Scotland after 1978: from referendum to Millennium', in Houston and Knox (eds) *History of Scotland*, p. 502. See also W. Keegan, *Britain Without Oil*, Harmondsworth, Penguin, 1985, *passim*.
7 Harvie, 'Scotland after 1978', pp. 514–18; Charles Kennedy cited in Devine, *Scottish Nation*, p. 605.
8 Devine, *Scottish Nation*, pp. 606–17; G. Jarvie and I.A. Reid, 'Sport, nationalism and Culture in Scotland', *The Sports Historian*, 1999 vol. 19 (1), pp. 106–7, 110.
9 Jarvie and Reid 'Sport, nationalism and culture', p. 98.
10 Polley, *Moving the Goalposts*, p. 99.
11 Harvie, *Scotland and Nationalism*, p. 38; H.F. Moorhouse, 'One state, several countries: Soccer and nationality in a "United" Kingdom', *International Journal of the History of Sport*, 1995, vol. 12, p. 58.
12 *Glasgow Herald*, 3 April 2000.
13 *Guardian*, 14 June 2002.
14 M. Cronin and D. Mayall (eds) *Sporting Nationalisms: Ethnicity, Immigration and Assimilation*, London: Frank Cass 1998, p. 2; S. Kuper, *Football against the Enemy*, London: Orion Books, 1994, pp. 85–92.
15 *Glasgow Herald*, 26 October 1991, where Brian Meek praised the Scottish rugby team's achievement.
16 J. Burnett and G. Jarvie, 'Sport, Scotland and the Scots', in G. Jarvie and J. Burnett (eds) *Sport, Scotland and the Scots*, Phantassie: Tuckwell Press, 2000, p. 18.

17 See Ian Archer in the *Glasgow Herald*, 18, 20 May 1974.
18 N. Ascherson, *Stone Voices: the Search for Scotland*, London: Granta, 2002, *passim*.
19 *Daily Record, Daily Mirror*, 17 April 1967; *Scotsman*, 20 May 1974. In an interview, Baxter later confessed that he 'just wanted to take the piss' out of the English, *Daily Record*, 13 November 1999.
20 H. McIlvanney, *McIlvanney on Football*, Edinburgh: Mainstream, 1994, pp. 17–20.
21 Jarvie and Reid, 'Sport, nationalism and culture', pp. 114–17; R. Holt, 'The king over the border: Denis Law and Scottish football', in G. Jarvie and G. Walker (eds) *Scottish Sport and the Making of the Nation: Ninety Minute Patriots*, Leicester: Leicester University Press, 1994, p. 60.
22 *Glasgow Herald, Scotsman*, 20 May 1974; For Frank McElhone's condemnation see *Glasgow Herald*, 6 June 1977.
23 *Glasgow Herald*, 18 June 1974; McIlvanney, *McIlvanney on Football*, pp. 185–9.
24 *Glasgow Herald*, 15, 20 and 22 June 1974.
25 *Sunday Post*, 16 May 1976; *Glasgow Herald*, 17 May 1976.
26 *Daily Record*, 17 May 1976.
27 *Scotsman*, 12, 30 May 1978; *Daily Record*, 20 May 1978.
28 See leading article in the *Daily Record*, 17 May 1978; *Sunday Post*, 21 May 1978.
29 *Scotsman*, 8 June 1978.
30 *Glasgow Herald*, 13 June 1978; *Scotsman*, 9, 13 June 1978.
31 McIlvanney, *McIlvanney on Football*, p. 202; *Scotsman*, 17 March 1990.
32 *Daily Mirror*, 4, 6 June 1977; *Glasgow Herald*, 13 November 1999.
33 *Scotsman*, 23 May 1988; also *Daily Record*, 23, 24 May 1988.
34 Black, *Tales of the Tartan Army*, Edinburgh: Mainstream, 1977, pp. 62, 84; I. Husband in the *Observer*, 3 June 2001; S. Walsh, *Voices of the Old Firm*, Edinburgh: Mainstream, 1995, p. 217.
35 R. Boyd and R. Haynes, *Power Play: Sport, Media and Popular Culture*, Harlow: Pearson, 2000, pp. 155–8; also R. Giulanotti and G. Armstrong in *Glasgow Herald*, 17 June 1996.
36 *Daily Record*, 9, 12, 13 November 1999; *Glasgow Herald*, 15 November 1999; *Scotsman*, 13 November 1999.
37 Joan Burnie in the *Daily Record*, 15 November 1999; *Glasgow Herald*, 18 November 1999.
38 Meek in the *Glasgow Herald*, 15 November 1999, Bell in the *Scotsman*, 13 November 1999; for Ascherson see *Independent on Sunday*, 18 May 1997.
39 R. Holt, *Sport and the British: A Modern History*, Oxford: Oxford University Press, 1989, pp. 105, 255; J.A. Mangan, 'Braveheart betrayed? Cultural cloning for colonial careers', in Cronin and Mayall (eds) *Sporting Nationalisms*, pp. 194–5, 202–5.
40 *Scotsman*, 29, 31 March 1971.
41 *Daily Record*, 21 February 1976; *Sunday Post*, 22 February 1976; *Glasgow Herald, Scotsman*, 23 February 1976.
42 *Scotsman*, 23 March 1990; *Daily Record*, 11 March 1990.
43 *Observer Sport Monthly*, March 2003.
44 *Scotsman*, 19 March 1990; *Glasgow Herald*, 17 March 1990.
45 *Scotsman*, 20, 21 March 1990.
46 Cited in J.M. Bradley, 'Sport and the contestation of cultural and ethnic identities in Scottish society', in Cronin and Mayall (eds) *Sporting Nationalisms*, pp. 143, 147.
47 *Glasgow Herald, Scotsman*, 26 October 1991.
48 *Glasgow Herald*, 1 April 2000.

49 R. Boyle, '"We are Celtic supporters …": questions of football and identity in modern Scotland', in R. Giulanotti and J. Williams (eds) *Game Without Frontiers: Football, Identity and Modernity*, Aldershot: Arena, 1994, p. 86; *The Absolute Game*, May, June, July 1994.
50 P. Dimeo and G. Finn, 'Racism, national identity and Scottish football', in B. Carrington and I. McDonald (eds) *Racism, Sport and British Identity*, London: Routledge, 2001, pp. 35–6; B. Murray, *The Old Firm: Sectarianism, Sport and Society in Scotland*, Edinburgh: John Donald, 2000, p. xi.
51 Bradley, 'Sport and the contestation of cultural and ethnic identities', pp. 143, 147.
52 Dimeo and Finn, 'Racism, national identity and Scottish football', p. 37; H.F. Moorhouse, 'On the periphery: Scotland, Scottish football and the new Europe', in J. Williams and S. Wagg (eds) *British Football and Social Change: Getting into Europe*, Leicester: Leicester University Press, 1991, p. 205; Foster, 'Twentieth century', p. 482.
53 G. Walker, 'Identity questions in contemporary Scotland: Faith, football and future prospects', *Contemporary British History*, 2001, vol. 15 (1), pp. 44, 55.
54 *The Absolute Game*, January/February 1994, no. 36, pp. 12–14.
55 For this episode see Dimeo and Finn, 'Racism, national identity and Scottish football', pp. 32–3.
56 *The Absolute Game*, March/April 1993, no. 32, pp. 2, 12.
57 Murray, *Old Firm*, pp. 285–7; Walker, 'Identity questions in contemporary Scotland', pp. 55–6.
58 *Glasgow Herald*, 16 May 1988; *Guardian*, 13 March 2002.
59 *Guardian*, 25 September, 1 December 2002.
60 *Guardian*, 7 January 2003.
61 *Scotsman*, 13 November 1999.
62 *Guardian*, 2 January 2003.

5 Who are the boys in green?

Irish identity and soccer in the Republic of Ireland

Michael Holmes and David Storey

We stand for *Amhrán na bhFiann*. I sing the anthem in Irish, having learned it phonetically ... I am proud of my country, proud of the song, proud to sing it in our native tongue in a Yorkshire brogue.[1]

Phenomena such as support for a national sporting team, or for an individual representing their country can be read as an indicator of people's identification with their nation. While many of those who support national teams might not ordinarily be seen as ardent nationalists, their support nevertheless reflects the embeddedness of national identity. The ease with which many people lend their vocal support and the expense that many people are prepared to incur in following their team to various events around the world suggests that national identity (and not just love of the sport) is very deeply ingrained. International sporting events can be viewed as occasions when members of a national grouping can truly feel they are part of a larger imagined community.[2] It has been suggested in some instances that this way of expressing national identity may act as a substitute or replacement for more overt political forms. For example, Morgan suggests that more radical forms of Welsh nationalism were kept at bay through an acceptance of rugby as a means of triumph, particularly in victories over England.[3] By the same token many international sportspeople speak of the huge pride they feel in representing their country.

Soccer is a truly global game but despite its increasing commercialisation and the trans-national nature of support for club teams, international fixtures are still seen as major events and many people behave as '90–minute nationalists' on such occasions. Performances by national teams can put countries on the map, as Senegal's progress in the 2002 World Cup finals amply demonstrates.[4] Much of what has been written about soccer and national identity relates to fans or to the broader context of the political impact of the successes or failures of national teams. This chapter focuses on international soccer players and, more specifically, players who have elected to play for a country other than the one in which they were born. It seeks to cast light on the complex senses of national identity felt by international sportspeople who are members of a diaspora.

International sportspeople are unusual in the sense that they are often forced to make a very public 'choice' of national identity. Such choices have recently engendered discussion in a variety of sports. The issue was highlighted by a number of instances occurring during the 2002 Commonwealth Games, including a Scottish squash player representing England, a wrestler from Nigeria who represented Canada and a runner from England who competed for Pakistan.[5] The focus here is on the Republic of Ireland's soccer team. In recent decades the national team has included a significant number of players born outside Ireland. This chapter explores the institutional background to player selection (in other words, the rules and regulations of soccer's governing bodies concerning player eligibility); outlines changes to the extent of the Irish 'player pool' (in other words, who was chosen, or who chose, to play for Ireland); and tentatively examines the extent to which players' national 'declarations' are linked to cultural and/or career-related factors. Before proceeding it is useful to provide a brief overview of debates surrounding sport and national identity in an Irish context.

Sport and national identity in Ireland

In Ireland, existing literature relating sport to broader political and cultural issues has tended to focus on the connections between particular sports and specific cultural groupings; Gaelic games (Gaelic football, hurling, comógie) are organised and regulated by the Gaelic Athletic Association (GAA) and the organisation's origins and ethos are closely linked to Irish national identity, both politically and culturally, in the sense of being perceived as both 'Irish' and 'Catholic'.[6] On the other hand, rugby union and, more particularly, cricket are often seen as elitist sports and tend to be more strongly associated with Protestants rather more than with Catholics and, by extension, are seen to be much less closely associated with Irishness.[7] Soccer, as elsewhere, tends to be seen as a working class sport but in Ireland the picture is complicated on account of the game's origins. It arrived in Ireland as a 'garrison game' played by the soldiers of a British colonial regime.[8] In keeping with other 'British games' it tended to be frowned upon. Rather than engaging in the recreational pursuits of the coloniser, it was felt that indigenous sports should be embraced.[9] Thus issues of class, cultural identity and politics are reflected in the playing of sport within Ireland.

The partition of Ireland into six northern counties, which remain within the United Kingdom, and a 26-county Irish Free State in 1922 (to become a republic in 1949) has, not surprisingly, added to the complex interrelationships between sport and national identity. The GAA, as might be expected, effectively ignores the border and operates on a 32–county basis as does the Irish Rugby Football Union, though in the case of the latter, this has created controversies over the flying of flags and the playing of national anthems.[10] In soccer, however, partition led to the creation of a new football authority in Dublin, detaching itself from the pre-partition Belfast-based Irish Football Association. For a number of years this led to the two associations drawing players from both parts of the island in representative games and both using the title 'Ireland'.[11]

Football in Northern Ireland has been, predictably, associated with issues surrounding identity. Thus, the sectarian nature of support for the Northern Ireland football team has led to occasional verbal abuse of Catholic players. The most recent and most notorious of these incidents was the death threat issued against the Catholic-born player Neil Lennon in 2002.[12] He has subsequently indicated that he has no wish to play for Northern Ireland again. Certain clubs, most notably Linfield in Belfast, have been seen as Protestant bastions with loyalist graffiti appearing in and around the ground warning Catholics that they are unwelcome.[13] In these circumstances it is not surprising that proportionately few Catholics follow the Northern Ireland team, preferring to support the Republic.[14]

Rules of eligibility in international football

The rules governing a footballer's international eligibility are complex and have changed considerably over time. Changes in regulations have had a profound effect on who can or cannot be selected for a particular country. This means that international sport is an interesting framework within which to study national identity. For most people, multiple identities are no more than a curiosity. The usual rule in sports is that you cannot represent more than one country. Therefore, those who have multiple identities must choose one of them. This rule has its exceptions, however, and there are examples of players representing more than one country. For example, rugby in the 1990s allowed considerable national promiscuity but this was clearly part of a special effort to promote the game (both union and league). Football went through a similar phase. A number of Argentinian internationals moved to Italy in the early 1920s and not just to Italian clubs – they played for Italy too.[15] Spain was another country that exploited such links with the notable example of Alfredo di Stefano, who moved from Argentina to Spain in the 1950s, and played for both countries.

Eventually, football's authorities decided to curtail such 'international transfers'. This meant putting in place sets of rules governing eligibility for national teams. It might be thought that general rules of nationality might be sufficient; that if you are eligible to hold a passport for a country under its national rules then you are eligible to play football for it. And certainly, holding a valid national passport is now required by FIFA (*Fédération Internationale de Football Association* – the game's international govern-ing body). In the March 2001 World Cup qualifier between Andorra and

Ireland a FIFA inspector checked that all players on both teams had appropriate passports. In April 2001 American Samoa's team in their World Cup qualifying campaign in the Oceania region was decimated because many players did not hold appropriate passports. This resulted in some crushing defeats on the pitch.

However, while holding a passport is a necessary condition, it is not a sufficient indicator of nationality. There are a number of reasons why national rules of eligibility are insufficient. First, there are no standard procedures, as can be seen by comparing France and Germany. France's approach is built around birthplace on French territory (including overseas territories) coupled with considerations of parents' citizenship. This helps explain the highly mixed origins of the current and recent team. For example, Marcel Desailly was born in Ghana, Christian Karembeu in New Caledonia, Patrick Vieira in Senegal. Germany's approach is much more restrictive and emphasizes a racial, blood link so that the large Turkish communities in Germany have struggled to gain citizenship. As a result, very few players of Turkish origin have played for the national team. Conversely, the present Turkish international team includes a number of German-born players.

Nationality can be acquired through residency or through marriage. Emmanuel Olisadebe, a Nigerian who moved to Polonia Warsaw, acquired Polish nationality through residency and now plays for the Polish national team. Roy Wegerle, although born in South Africa, played for the USA after marrying an American. Many countries allow exceptions to their rules of eligibility, in some cases specifically for individuals of sporting prowess. Moreover, a growing number of countries allow dual nationality and do not require a person to plump for one or the other, a phenomenon likely to become more common in an increasingly globalised world.

In addition to national regulations, football authorities themselves have developed their own sets of rules governing eligibility. Football first emerged and was codified in Britain in the latter half of the nineteenth century. It spread very rapidly, not through formal colonial links – cricket was the preferred sport of the British elite – but through economic contacts. The first football 'colonies' were in mainland Europe and in South America where pioneer clubs soon combined to develop the national football associations required to run the game.[16] Immediately, there was an interest in establishing a dominant body of some description to ensure that all football was played to a common set of rules and to regulate relations between national associations. FIFA was formed in 1904 by the Belgian, Danish, Dutch, French, Spanish, Swedish and Swiss football associations. It established the World Cup in 1930 and now runs a host of other international representative tournaments. There are also a number of regional associations such *Union des Associations Européennes de Football* (UEFA, 1954) which legislate on various aspects of the game and, amongst other things, play a part in codifying and harmonising rules on international eligibility.

Currently, FIFA has primary responsibility for establishing the rules but these have changed over time and a variety of new considerations have emerged. These include age qualifications – players playing for national youth teams are not always 'tied' to that country – and place of birth/parentage/grandparentage. Appearances in 'friendly' matches generally do not count: only competitive appearances tie a player to one country. In essence, place of birth and eligibility for citizenship are the key criteria. The utilisation of the parent and, more particularly, the grandparent route to attaining citizenship has led to the coining of the term 'granny rule' to describe the situation where a player represents the country in which one of their parents or grandparents was born rather than the country in which they themselves were born.

All of this suggests that some players, depending on their family background, may have more than one country for which they can opt. Overall, when it comes to choosing nationality for footballers, three features come into play: the regulatory environment, cultural connections and career or economic considerations. Having outlined the complex nature of the first of these, attention is now turned to the importance of cultural connections and career aspirations in the context of the selection of non-Irish born footballers for the Republic of Ireland national team.

The emergence of the 'anglos'

This exploration begins in 1986, the year in which Jack Charlton was appointed as manager of the Republic of Ireland national team. Charlton was a former England international player and had been a member of the 1966 World Cup winning team. His appointment was initially resented by some Irish supporters; some English observers were not exactly thrilled either.[17] The subsequent years saw a number of key changes in Irish soccer. First, the national team went through a period of unprecedented success qualifying for the finals of the European Championship in 1988 and reaching the final stages of the 1990, 1994 and 2002 World Cups. Second, team support increased, as might be expected given their success, and Irish fans acquired a reputation for being a 'jolly green army', seen as one of the best-behaved groups of international football fans. Third, there was an upsurge of interest in the team amongst the emigrant Irish and, more significantly, amongst second generation Irish people brought up in Britain and elsewhere. Fourth, the team relied heavily on changing FIFA regulations governing international eligibility.

It is this latter element which is central to this chapter. Charlton's most significant decision as Irish manager was to exploit fully FIFA rulings on national eligibility. It should be pointed out that he was by no means the first or only manager (either in Ireland or other countries) to use it. Shay Brennan, born in Manchester, had probably been the first non-Irish born player to represent the Republic back in the 1960s.[18] Charlton's policy meant, however, that many English-born (and some Scots or Welsh-born) players were selected for Ireland on the basis of where their parents or grandparents were born. In popular discourse Ireland was seen as relying heavily on the so-called 'granny rule'. On occasions this policy was criticised by those outside Ireland who felt it was unfair and against the spirit of the game and also inside Ireland by some who felt that it was diluting the Irishness of the team. Given that English-born players were the main converts to the Irish cause, criticism from England occasionally reflected an annoyance over the loss of players who might (many felt should) have played for England. Jokes about having once visited Dublin or having drunk a pint of Guinness being sufficient grounds for playing for Ireland began to circulate. During the 1994 World Cup finals the English journalist Jim White, writing in the *Independent*, referred to the former Irish international Liam Brady as 'an unusual beast … an Irish international with an Irish accent' and remarked, in relation to the England player Chris Waddle: 'The pity is that, but for an unfortunate accident in his grandparents' birth, he could have been out there playing' (for Ireland – England did not qualify).[19]

More recently, negative comments on Ireland's selection of English-born players in the 2002 World Cup finals emerged in newspaper letters pages: 'These players can claim they are Irish until the cows come home, but does anyone believe them?' asked one *Observer* letter-writer under the headline 'The Irish question: were they unlucky, plucky – or just a bunch of Englishmen?'.[20] To these stories may be added many anecdotal episodes revolving around players whose first visit to Ireland was to play for the team or who were unable to tell which was the Irish national anthem and which that of the opposition. Such stories have been used to denigrate the purity of the national team and to suggest a strongly mercenary and strategic element underlying the players' motivation. The 'mercenary' tag was also used by the then Northern Ireland manager Billy Bingham prior to a World Cup qualifying game between the Republic and Northern Ireland in 1993 – a match with special significance given Ireland's complex history and played against the backdrop of a particularly violent period in the Northern Irish conflict.

Within Ireland, attitudes towards the 'anglos' are difficult to gauge. On the basis of anecdotal evidence, it seems likely that, while many people accepted the legitimacy of their right to play for Ireland, others were sceptical. There are suggestions that some of the 'anglos' were seen as mercenaries who might have turned out for a number of countries, while others were perceived to be second-raters who would have liked to play for England but were not good enough. (Of course it might be argued that 'anglos' who performed well were less likely to be criticised than those who might be seen as under-performing.) In so far as this happened, it fits into an idea of Irishness as defined in terms of place of birth or long-term residence rather than through a blood line. In any event it can be interpreted as a reductionist attitude to national identity; one which suggests that possession of an Irish accent is the only badge of authenticity. While some may have been sceptical, others adopted a more positive viewpoint seeing the selection of 'anglo' players as a reclaiming of the offspring of Irish emigrants.

One by-product of the policy was the fact that a number of black players began to appear for Ireland. Chris Hughton, Paul McGrath, Terry Phelan, Phil Babb, Curtis Fleming, Steven Reid and Clinton Morrison were all English-born, although McGrath and Fleming could pass the 'accent' test as they grew up in Dublin. The extent to which these players may have contributed to a more racially tolerant conception of Irishness remains a matter for conjecture though it may be significant that McGrath (now retired) has remained an enduringly popular figure despite well-documented alcohol problems that occasionally impinged on his playing.

During the Charlton era (1986–1996) almost all Irish players were based outside of Ireland, the vast majority being in England. This itself is a long-standing feature of Irish teams. The majority of talented Irish footballers are snapped up as teenagers by scouts from English or Scottish clubs, a reflection of the poorly developed state of club football in Ireland and the relative economic strength of the major English and Scottish clubs. Players such as David O'Leary, Frank Stapleton and Liam Brady were all based in London and playing for Arsenal from their mid-teen years. However, the significance of the Irish teams from the mid-1980s onwards was that the majority of players were not just playing in Britain, they were also born there. Under Jack Charlton's managership a total of 56 players played for Ireland. Of these 33 were born outside Ireland. Thirty-three players obtained their first cap in this period and, of these, 21 were born outside Ireland.[21]

The extent of the 'anglo' dominance in the late 1980s and early 1990s is demonstrated by the fact that on six occasions a team started with nine non-Irish born players (once in 1987, twice in 1988 and once each in 1990, 1991 and 1992). On four occasions (three in 1990, one in 1992) Ireland ended a game with ten non-Irish-born players. On the three times this happened in 1990, the only Irish-born player was goalkeeper Packie Bonner. Between 1988 and 1995 Ireland played 79 international matches. On only six occasions were there more than five Irish-born players in the team. Ireland's squad of 20 for the European Championship finals in 1988 contained 13 players born outside Ireland; the squad of 22 for the 1990 World Cup finals had 16, while the 1994 World Cup finals squad had 15, again from a total of 22 players.

More recently, under Mick McCarthy, manager from 1996 to 2002, the reliance on non-Irish-born players has been reduced. Of 63 players selected by McCarthy, 29 (just under half) were born outside Ireland. Of more significance, however, was that of the 42 players to receive their first cap under McCarthy, 26, representing a majority, were born in Ireland. In part, at least, this perceptible shift may be due to the success of Ireland's various youth teams in the late 1990s. Many young Irish-born players have risen through the ranks to the senior team. Yet, despite this, 11 of the 23 players selected for the 2002 World Cup finals squad were born outside Ireland.

Three points are worth making here. First, although much has been made of the so-called 'granny rule', it is worth bearing in mind that the majority of non-Irish-born players selected had at least one Irish parent. Three players in this category, David O'Leary, Paul McGrath and Curtis Fleming, although born in England, grew up in Dublin. Second, it could be suggested there was a sort of 'snowballing' effect. As an increasing number of players 'declared' for Ireland, it became easier for others, who might not have previously considered it, to follow suit. Finally, it is a moot question as to whether all those who declared their allegiance to Ireland would have done so if the team had been less successful. Ireland's relative success must certainly have made 'joining up' a more attractive proposition. Of course, that success in turn drew more attention to the controversial selection policy.

Senses of Irishness

We now turn to the as yet unexplored issue of how 'Irish' these players may have felt and what factors may have influenced their decision to choose Ireland. As yet little concrete information on players' attitudes exists. Indeed, little research into professional sportspeople's attitudes to issues of national identity has been undertaken.[22] Nevertheless, in its absence, we can utilise sources such as player (auto)biographies and media interviews with players which provide some clues as to the feelings and motivations behind their decisions. A number of Irish international players have written books in recent years documenting their experiences of playing for Ireland. There are obvious limitations in using these as definitive sources. Such books are generally ghost-written and are likely to be presented in a way which will appeal to fans rather than unsettle them. Sports autobiographies in general tend to be written primarily with a view to commercial success and, as such, are likely to reflect what fans want to hear. Nevertheless, in the absence of any further information they provide some indication of a player's feelings. Players are regularly interviewed by print and broadcast media and, again, these interviews can be useful source material. Naturally, many interviews tend to focus on more immediate aspects of the game, such as the player's or the team's performance, rather than their feelings on playing for Ireland. Even when players enthuse about the team, the nature of team sport is such that this reflects a team loyalty as much as an automatic identification with Ireland. However, it is possible, utilising these various sources critically, to draw some tentative conclusions based on players' public utterances.

On their return to Dublin following the quarter-final defeat in the 1994 World Cup in Italy the team captain Mick McCarthy, Yorkshire-born with an Irish father and subsequently to become manager, declared that everyone in the team was '110 percent Irish'. More recently, he has reiterated the point that he sees himself as Irish: 'I have an emotional tie with Ireland that'll never be broken. I've just got the wrong accent!'[23] An earlier newspaper piece casts some further light on McCarthy's sense of his own identity:

> As a kid, he used watch his father hurl in fields near their home and this image was the genesis for his sense of place. Mick once recalled: 'I was aware of my Irishness, but it wasn't my country. I wasn't born there, I lived in England all my life. But to get the opportunity to represent me dad in Ireland was brilliant'.[24]

More recently, he has said that he 'discovered a sense of belonging the first time I pulled on a green shirt, a pride in my nationality that has never diminished in the eighteen years since'.[25]

Another former player, John Aldridge, was born and raised in Liverpool but played for Ireland courtesy of a great-grandmother born in Athlone. In his autobiography, Aldridge endeavours to lay to rest any doubts as to his feelings of Irishness. In an appropriate allusion to the passport rule, Aldridge, who had been angered by Billy Bingham's 'mercenary' jibe in 1993, states that 'among my proudest possessions is a small book which is of little monetary value ... it is my Republic of Ireland passport and it means everything to me'.[26] Aldridge goes on to claim that he grew up in a partly Irish background on his mother's side of the family and that his family always supported the Irish team. 'I might have been born in England but I felt as Irish as any of the five million or so who lived in the Republic'.[27]

If we accept this declaration at face value we might also wish to reflect on a slightly different view from a player whose eligibility to play for Ireland is identical to Aldridge's. Michael Robinson was born in England with a great-grandmother from Cork. Paul Rowan has documented how Robinson's Irishness only emerged when he realised he was in fact eligible to play for them. In the early stages of his career he was on record as wishing to play for England. He subsequently issued a number of what now appear quite cringe-inducing comments about his love of Ireland and things Irish.[28] Mark Lawrenson, another former Irish international, born in Preston, who qualified for Ireland on the basis of his Irish mother recently described himself on a radio programme as a 'pseudo-Irishman'.[29] This definition, however, might be more properly have been applied to Tony Cascarino.

In his controversial autobiography, Tony Cascarino, winner of a then record 89 caps for Ireland, reveals that he was never eligible to play for

Ireland. Born in London, his claim to Irishness was his mother's Irish father.

> Why did I choose the Republic of Ireland? Well, to be honest, I suppose because they chose me ... I grew up with a strong sense of 'Irishness' and got to know Michael (his Irish grandfather) quite well when he came to live with us.[30]

In the book it emerges that this man was not his grandfather, thereby indicating that Cascarino did not have an actual blood link to the country. 'My mum wasn't an O'Malley as I'd always believed. I didn't qualify for Ireland. I was a fraud. A fake Irishman'.[31] Cascarino's comments reflect his genuine belief at the time that he was partly Irish but might also be construed as symptomatic of the looseness of football's rules regarding national eligibilty.

In endeavouring to examine the complex issues of national identity amongst those who have worn Ireland's colours on the pitch, it seems highly likely that family background may be an issue here. Tony Grealish, an Irish international in the 1970s and 1980s, grew up in a close-knit Irish family in London and played Gaelic sports. Although he had trial matches with England Youth he opted to play for Ireland.[32] Another former player, the Yorkshire-born Séamus McDonagh, has spoken about his confusion over his identity. Like many second generation Irish in England, McDonagh spent childhood holidays in Ireland. Reflecting the 'neither one thing or the other' feelings of second generation Irish, McDonagh felt he was not accepted by anyone. In Ireland, his accent marked him out as English while in England his name made him Irish. Having initially been selected for the England youth team, McDonagh subsequently won 25 caps in goal for Ireland. As related in an interview, McDonagh appears to have a sense of Irishness reflected in an interest in Irish history and culture that he claims was there before he elected to play for them. His comments on anti-Irish prejudice also suggest someone who was aware of the ambiguities of his own situation.[33]

Similarly, Kevin Kilbane, a current Irish international player, grew up in Preston but appears to have had a keen sense of Irishness derived from the fact that both his parents were born in Ireland and that he grew up in an 'Irish' environment.

> All my life, I'd been supporting Ireland. I still remember how special Ray Houghton's goal against England in Stuttgart was to me ... all my friends were the same, in school there were the lads who supported Ireland and the ones who supported England. It all seemed completely normal.[34]

Thus, as he claims in another interview, though he was selected to train with the England youth squad, he never had any intention of getting picked.

My heart just wasn't in it. It's just that I always wanted to play for Ireland and no other country. My dad is from Mayo and my mum is from Waterford. So despite the way I speak I've always felt Irish.[35]

Similar tensions between cultural and career-related factors appear to have been at play in the case of Andy O'Brien who was born in Harrogate and whose grandparents are Irish:

I decided to play for Ireland because I experienced both camps (he played for both Ireland and England at under-21 level) and I thoroughly enjoyed the Ireland camp, more than the England one. In the English camp it was colder. There was just a feeling to it that didn't feel right to me … It was amazing how I felt warm in the Irish camp … on the whole the Irish lads were more pleasant towards me.

In addition to these comments reflecting particular national stereotypes, O'Brien, perhaps being mindful of the Irish newspaper's readership, goes on to add: 'I didn't sing the English national anthem, if that's anything'.[36]

For some players, however, their sense of Irishness appears to have been less natural and more instrumental. In 2000–01 a long-running saga unfolded concerning the international intentions of London-born Clinton Morrison, then playing for Crystal Palace. As well as England, Morrison was eligible to represent Jamaica, his father's country, and Ireland, by virtue of his grandmother. Newspaper comments by Morrison at the time suggest a variety of factors were at play. Initially he is quoted as saying he 'could pull on an Ireland shirt and feel passionately about it because it's international football and everyone wants to play international football'.[37] As the story developed, Morrison's agent indicated that 'as yet no approach has been made by any association … but for the last few days Clinton has been feeling very Irish'.[38] Subsequently Morrison's statements have tended to emphasise his awareness of his Irishness. When he was young he says he listened to Irish music in his grandmother's house and 'most of my family were telling me to play for Ireland'.[39] While Morrison has proved popular amongst Irish supporters, it is difficult not to conclude that there is an element of retrospective justification in some of the comments attributed to him.

This, however, is not to deny that 'Irishness' may well be an evolving thing for Morrison and for some others who have declared for Ireland. Andy Townsend, born in Maidstone, had an Irish grandmother and subsequently was Ireland's team captain at the 1994 World Cup. He later recalled that, after his initial selection, 'the thought of playing football for Ireland just didn't seem … right', adding that:

In my twenty-five years, I had never set foot in Ireland before and was feeling just a touch uncomfortable when our flight touched down in

Dublin. Technically Irish, I was never more conscious of my Englishness and my South London accent.[40]

Reflecting on this, he says that 'the wearing of a green shirt didn't suddenly make me Irish; my affinity towards the team, the nation and its
people would be a slowly evolving thing'.[41] Yet, as his international career
developed and 'the more I travelled to Dublin, the more I felt at ease with
my new identity'.[42] This suggests the awakening of a possibly hitherto
latent sense of Irishness linked to his acceptance as an integral part of a
successful team.

A more unusual case occurred in 2000 when Manchester-born Paul
Butler became the first player to declare for Ireland on the basis of
being married to an Irish woman. As well as England, he also qualified to
play for Wales and, at the time, was forced to make a choice between
Wales and Ireland. He chose the latter and his stated reasoning was as
follows:

> I have to admit that when I looked at the resources of the two teams,
> Ireland appeared to be that much better off with a lot of their players
> involved in the premiership. I mean it's exciting for me to be involved
> in the same squad as players like Roy Keane and Robbie Keane.
> The other fact which impressed me is the type of game Ireland play.
> It seemed to me that it was better suited to my strengths and so here
> I am.[43]

The then international manager, Mick McCarthy, adopted a pragmatic
response to criticisms over Butler's selection: 'according to FIFA rules, he
is eligible to represent Ireland and that is good enough for me'.[44] To date
Butler has made only one appearance for Ireland and was substituted at
half-time.

There is of course another dimension to this. There are numerous
players who qualify to play for Ireland but have not taken this option. A
well-known contemporary example is the Arsenal defender Martin
Keown. Both his parents are Irish, one from the North and one from the
Republic, and yet Keown, who was born in Oxford, was, until recently, a
regular member of the England squad. In an interview with an Irish newspaper, he spoke of his pride in playing for England

> When I play for England there is nobody more English than me. I
> don't think anybody could ever doubt my commitment. But I had a lot
> of relations, cousins and uncles who said to my father: 'You know, we
> can't believe you let him play for England'. But my dad says: 'This is
> the country you were born in and you make all your own decisions' ...
> A generation had come over and the children, like myself, adopted the
> English culture ... I think I felt Irish when I was young.[45]

Another player, David Linighan, indicated his wish to play for Ireland, though he was never actually selected, despite the fact that his brother was an England international. There are also those who momentarily expressed a desire to play for Ireland but never actually did so. One player, English-born Vinnie Jones, attempted to prove his Irish origins, but subsequently played for, and captained, Wales.

Implications

The situation discussed in this chapter is one in which some individuals, in this case international football players, are faced with a decision which effectively involves them publicly 'choosing' a national identity. On the basis of the limited evidence available from player autobiographies and media interviews, it is possible to draw some tentative conclusions. In all of this discussion, it is apparent that for some players, such as Grealish and McDonagh, the ambiguities and difficulties of growing up 'betwixt and between' two cultures creates a certain sense of exclusion, a sense of being neither fully Irish nor fully English. This phenomenon reflects broader issues within the lives of Irish people living in Britain.[46] Norman Tebbitt's infamous 'cricket test' was predicated on the view that a person must be one thing or the other. This ignores the complex reality whereby members of a diaspora may have a hybrid identity; rather than an either/or scenario, the feeling is one of possessing a little of both. Recent developments within the arena of cultural studies suggest the importance of understanding hybridity.[47] This seems particularly relevant to a country with a long history of extensive out-migration and substantial emigrant communities in Britain, the United States and elsewhere.

For our purposes, this suggests a need to move beyond a conception of national identity that is intrinsically linked to Ireland as a bounded space. It may be more appropriate to conceive of Irish identity in diasporic terms; an identity that is no longer place-bound or constrained by the actual borders of Ireland.[48] A whole host of factors have served to precipitate massive social, economic and cultural changes in Ireland in recent decades. Combined with a history of emigration it seems inappropriate to limit a consideration of Irish identity to a definitive territorial link to the island.[49] More inclusive conceptions of identity (rather than limiting chauvinistic ones) tend to suggest that the hybrid nature of international sporting teams more accurately reflects the complex nature of the relations between people and place at the start of the twenty-first century. For those players who elect to represent Ireland, it may be the only effective way in which they can lay claim to that particular part of their identity. In terms of birthplace or accent they may appear to belong elsewhere but when donning the green shirt they can assert, in a highly public manner, an Irishness otherwise denied to them. Moreover, as this chapter has shown, the current trends in player selection could be seen as a return to a somewhat more fluid situation akin to the times in the past where players' national affiliations were more flexible.

In overall terms it is possible to theorise about the nature of the 'anglo' players. It might be tentatively proposed that the factors influencing players' decisions exist on a spectrum ranging from primarily cultural affinity at one end to primarily career-related at the other. For some players, their Irishness appears always to have been a prominent part of their make-up. In general this can be seen as a consequence of family background. For some there may never have been a question in that they may have readily accepted their Irishness. Ireland's recently retired goal-keeper, Preston-born Alan Kelly, was also the son of an Irish international goalkeeper (born in Ireland) and it seems likely that, despite his English upbringing, Ireland was never a 'foreign' country to him. On the other hand, it is probably not unfair to suggest that there are some for whom the lure of international football and the prestige, money and career-enhancing opportunity were the primary motivations rather than any intrinsic sense of Irishness. In the first instance there is a deeply embedded sense of Irishness while, in the second, it is merely a matter of convenience. This binary distinction, however, obscures reality in many ways. In the case of some players, it may be that an initial opportunist motivation was overlain by feelings of Irishness or quasi-Irishness. It may also be the case that, for some, a sense of Irishness previously latent or not thought about was engendered through the process of playing for the team. A sense of family background and a latent sense of Irishness may have (re)emerged. In any event more work is clearly needed involving direct interviews with players in order to unravel the complex feelings of identity and belonging in operation here.

One final point worthy of note is the connection between the team and its supporters. It is apparent that more and more second-generation supporters emerged in recent years. Although some important work on these so-called 'plastic paddies' has emerged, the sense in which second-generation fans identify with second-generation players remains largely unexplored.[50] It seems reasonable, however, to suggest that fans born and brought up in Britain might well feel a particular sense of affinity towards those on the pitch whose backgrounds resembled their own. This second-generation support can be seen as the ultimate celebration of the Irish diaspora now that the sons and daughters of earlier 'lost generations' were turning out to watch other sons of the same diaspora representing the country that their parents or grandparents had left. While they asserted their Irishness, their sense of self was informed by their upbringing in Birmingham, Wolverhampton, Manchester, Paris, Brussels or Berlin.

This idea of the players representing the Irish diaspora has been drama-tised by the playwright Dermot Bolger who tried to capture the changing nature of Irishness using the 1988 European Championships as a back-drop. His play *In High Germany* deals with the aftermath of Ireland's exit from the tournament. The lone character is an Irish emigrant living in Germany who reflects on issues of identity and what it means to be a part of the Irish diaspora. His thoughts are shaped in part by the performance and the composition of the Irish team and the varied locations from which the supporters have travelled:

> I raised my hands and applauded, having finally ... found the only Ireland whose name I can sing, given to me by eleven men dressed in green. And the only Ireland I can pass on to the son who will carry my name and features in a foreign land.

He sees the generations of emigrants being represented by the players – 'and suddenly it seemed they had found a voice at last, that the Houghtons and McCarthys were playing for all those generations written out of history'. They were also playing for the as yet unborn children of emigrants 'who would grow up with foreign accents and Irish faces, bewildered by their fathers' lives'.[51]

Notes

1 M. McCarthy (with C. Dervan), *Ireland's World Cup 2002*, London: Simon and Schuster, 2002, p. 227. Mick McCarthy was manager of the Republic of Ireland team at the 2002 World Cup finals.
2 See B. Anderson, *Imagined Communities. Reflections on the Origin and Spread of Nationalism*, revised edition, London: Verso, 1991.
3 K.O. Morgan, *Rebirth of a Nation. Wales 1880–1980*, Oxford: Oxford University Press, 1990, pp. 134, 348. See also the chapter by Johnes in this volume.
4 *Guardian*, 14 June 2002, for 'the mouse that roared'.
5 *Guardian*, 24 July 2002.
6 M. Cronin, *Sport and Nationalism in Ireland. Gaelic Games, Soccer and Irish Identity since 1884*, Dublin: Four Courts Press, 1999, Chapter 4.
7 There are some local variations exemplified by the working class nature of rugby in Limerick.
8 D. Hannigan, *The Garrison Game. The State of Irish Football*, Edinburgh: Mainstream, 1998, p. 11.
9 J. Sugden and A. Bairner, *Sport, Sectarianism and Society in a Divided Ireland*, Leicester: Leicester University Press, 1993, Chapter 3.
10 Sugden and Bairner, *Sport, Sectarianism and Society*, pp. 52–63.
11 Sugden and Bairner, *Sport, Sectarianism and Society*; Cronin, *Sport and Nationalism in Ireland*, p. 74; S. Ryan, *The Boys in Green. The FAI International Story*, Edinburgh: Mainstream. 1997, p. 33.
12 *Guardian* 22, 23 August 2002.
13 A. Bairner and P. Shirlow, 'Loyalism, Linfield and the territorial politics of soccer fandom in Northern Ireland', *Space and Polity*, 1998, vol. 2 (2), pp. 163–77.
14 Sugden and Bairner, *Sport, Sectarianism and Society*, pp. 79–81.
15 C. Taylor, *The Beautiful Game: A Journey through Latin American Football*, London: Phoenix Books, 1998, p. 56; K. Radnedge, 'Passport to confusion', *World Soccer*, 2000, vol. 41 (3), pp. 4–5.
16 The early development of football in Brazil illustrates this process. See the

account in A. Hamilton, *An Entirely Different Game: the British Influence on Brazilian Football*, Edinburgh: Mainstream, 1998. pp. 35–66.

17 Charlton later recalled that he was 'mildly apprehensive' about the way his appointment would be received in Ireland. In general, he claims, reaction was 'remarkably enthusiastic'. See J. Charlton (with P. Byrne), *The Autobiography*, London: Corgi Books, 1997, pp. 246–47.

18 See P. Rowan, *The Team that Jack Built*, Edinburgh: Mainstream, 1994, p. 57.

19 *Independent*, 20 June 1994.

20 See *Observer* 23 June 2002

21 Biographical information on players is derived mainly from two sources: S. McGarrigle, *The Complete Who's Who of Irish International Football 1945–96*, Edinburgh: Mainstream, 1996; also A. Ward, *Republic of Ireland. Gifted in Green*, London: Hamlyn, 1999. This has been supplemented through reference to various editions of *The Rothman's Football Yearbook*.

22 For a rare example see J. Tuck and J. Maguire, 'Making sense of global patriot games: rugby players' perceptions of national identity politics', *Football Studies*, 1999, vol. 2 (1), pp. 26–54.

23 *Guardian*, 25 May 2002.

24 Mick McCarthy quoted, *Irish Independent*, 24 March 2001.

25 McCarthy, *Ireland's World Cup 2002*, p. xii.

26 J. Aldridge (with H. Jawad), *My Story*, London: Hodder & Stoughton, 1999, p. 145.

27 Aldridge, *My Story*, p. 203. Aldridge's population figure is that for the island of Ireland and not the Republic.

28 Rowan, *The Team that Jack Built*, p. 56, citing an early 1980s interview in which Robinson says his favourite music is by the Wolfe Tones and the Dublin City Ramblers and his biggest disappointment is not being born in Ireland.

29 Mark Lawrenson interviewed, *Radio 5 Live*, 1 November 2000.

30 T. Cascarino (with P. Kimmage), *Full Time: the Secret Life of Tony Cascarino*, London: Simon and Schuster, 2000, p. 16.

31 Cascarino, *Full Time*, p. 180.

32 Rowan, *The Team that Jack Built*, pp. 60–2.

33 Rowan, *The Team that Jack Built*, pp. 62–4.

34 Kevin Kilbane quoted, *Irish Times*, 13 November 1999.

35 Kevin Kilbane quoted, *Irish Examiner*, 17 November 1999.

36 Andy O'Brien quoted, *Irish Times*, 13 January 2001.

37 Clinton Morrison quoted, *Irish Times*, 27 January 2001.

38 Neil Fewings, Clinton Morrison's agent, quoted, *Irish Times*, 13 January 2001.

39 See the article headed 'Irish pretender at the Palace', *Irish Times*, 28 January 2002.

40 Townsend (with P. Kimmage), *Andy's Game: the Inside Story of the World Cup*, London: Stanley Paul, 1994, p. 74.

41 Townsend, *Andy's Game*, p. 76.

42 Townsend, *Andy's Game*, p. 78.

43 Paul Butler quoted, *Irish Times*, 22 February 2000.

44 Mick McCarthy quoted, *Irish Times*, 11 February 2000.

45 Martin Keown quoted, *Irish Times*, 13 May 2000.

46 M. Hickman, and B. Walter, *Discrimination and the Irish Community in Britain*, London: Commission for Racial Equality, 1997. See also J. MacLaughlin (ed.) *Location and Dislocation in Contemporary Irish Society: Emigration and Irish Identities*, Cork: Cork University Press, 1997. For details of an ongoing project on the Irish in Britain see: http://www.apu.ac.uk/geography/progress/irish2/index.html.

47 See H.K. Bhabha, *The Location of Culture*, London: Routledge, 1994.

48 See A. Brah, *Cartographies of Diaspora*, London: Routledge, 1996.
49 See F. O'Toole, 'The ex-isle of Erin. Emigration and Irish culture', in MacLaughlin (ed.) *Location and Dislocation in Contemporary Irish Society*, pp. 158–78.
50 M. Free, "Angels" with drunken faces? Travelling Republic of Ireland supporters and the construction of Irish migrant identity in England', in A. Brown (ed.) *Fanatics! Power, Identity and Fandom in Football*, London/New York: Routledge, 1998, pp. 219–32.
51 All quotations from D. Bolger, *In High Germany*, in D. Bolger, *Plays: 1*, London: Methuen, 2000, p. 97.

6 'One Nation, One Soul, One Dream, One Goal?'[1]

Sport and national identity in South Africa

Marc Keech

Morné du Plessis, the former captain and manager of the South African rugby team, read out 26 names live on national television in May 1995. Not ordinary names, but rugby union players who carried the hope of the nation and who gathered behind a large sign which read 'One Team, One Country'. Nobody who watched the 1995 Rugby World Cup final will forget how Joel Stransky, standing deeper than normal at fly half and slightly to the right of the posts, just outside the opposition 22-yard line, calmly slotted the winning drop goal in extra time to secure the title. But is that really what people remember about the match at Ellis Park, the citadel of Springbok rugby? More likely, the image that is imprinted in the mind is of President Nelson Mandela, wearing the green Springbok rugby shirt, the sporting symbol of apartheid, emblazoned on the back with the yellow number 6, the shirt of team captain, Francois Pienaar. And whilst the crowd chanted 'Nel-son, Nel-son' before the match, Pienaar collected the trophy as the victorious captain before being interviewed by the host broadcaster:

> 'Francois, fantastic support here today from 63,000 South Africans?' ... I replied, 'David, we didn't have the support of 63,000 South Africans today. We had the support of 42 million South Africans'.[2]

When South Africa won the Rugby World Cup, it was a seminal moment in a nation's sporting history, more noted internationally than when Mandela, a year later, attended the final of football's African Cup of Nations, as South Africa again hosted and won the tournament. With Mandela's presence, the rugby team stood as the symbol of the 'rainbow' nation, supposedly at last having come to terms with the past. Mandela, a nation's icon, was now irrevocably associated with that country's greatest sporting achievement. It was seen as a political masterstroke, although perhaps the Springboks needed Mandela more than he needed them to engender support from a divided nation. During the tournament much was made of black support for the team although its dynamics were seldom explained.

The new South Africa had opened up a wider range of possible identifications for the previously oppressed majority, for it had not been possible to identify with a team associated with the oppressors, but with apartheid officially out of the way it was less problematical to support a team that claimed to represent the whole of South Africa. Culturally, black support for the Springboks found expression in uninhibited dancing and praise singing of the 'Amabokoboko'.[3]

But to assert that the nation had achieved unity and found a new national identity masked deep-rooted legacies of discrimination and segregation that continue to mould attitudes to sport in South Africa in the post-apartheid era. According the Chester Williams, the only black player in the winning squad, that sense of unity lasted about a week, and he remained subject to abuse by team mate James Small who reminded him of his 'kaffir' status.[4] When the African National Congress (ANC) was elected in 1994 it set out to build a united, non-racial nation, based on healing the divisions and sub-identities caused by apartheid through a project of reconciliation, and to forge a new South Africanism. The term 'rainbow nation' became a metaphor for the 'new' South Africa, the imaginary nation being constructed in the post-apartheid era.[5] Tension between unity and diversity, however, has been reflected in the difficulties and debates about building a new national identity from the polarised identities of the past.

The clear attraction of sport as vehicle for nation building has meant that governments have assumed control of sport, particularly in Africa. Sport in Africa has represented one of the most visible avenues of recognition for nations in which political power has often been tenuously held and subject to one-party (or one-person) dictatorships.[6] In South Africa, sport became a cultural forum through which white identity could be both asserted and challenged. For different groups at different times, the same sport has had numerous meanings depending on the social positioning of particular individuals.[7] During recent years there has been substantial interest in the transformation of domestic politics in South Africa following the dramatic collapse of apartheid. The elections of 1994 saw South Africa emerge as a fledgling multi-party democracy with a majority government elected on the principle of universal suffrage. These developments during the 1990s stimulated much academic debate from which two schools of literature emerged. The first examined the problems inherent in the nation's transition to democracy.[8] The second was concerned with evaluating the significance of specific events, issues, organisations and movements involved in the politics of apartheid.[9]

Sporting texts have tended to straddle both spheres of study and this chapter is no different as it traces the development of the relationship between sport and national identity in South Africa. Of necessity, there is a need to articulate the development of those sporting practices within the

South African social formation prior to 1945, which shaped the practice of sport by different population groups. Closely examined is the impact of apartheid, introduced by the ruling National Party in 1948, on sporting identities, which were articulated through political domination or protest. The forging of a nascent 'one-nation' identity during the transformation to democracy is also explored. Finally, the post-apartheid period is analysed by examining the key issues raised by merit selections as opposed to affirmative action and the intentions of domestic sports policy.

The significance of sport in South Africa

South Africa is one of the most complex nations in the international community, made up of many conflicting cultures, languages (eleven are officially recognised) and spaces. The national anthem, 'N'kosi Sikele Africa', is sung in four languages (Sotho, Xhosa, Afrikaans and English). South Africa has had only one decade in which to consider its (one-nation) national identity. Whilst there has been much hyperbole around the concept of national unity, it should be stated from the outset that it is too early to define a one-nation identity in South Africa. In fact, such a definition may ultimately prove to be impossible for the term 'one-nation' assumes heterogeneity whilst South Africa has suffered centuries of racial and cultural division and currently exhibits a rich complexity of cultural sub-identities within the country. Internationally, the 'rainbow nation' has become very much an imagined community, largely perpetuated by mediated images of triumphal sporting moments.

Previously, the social, economic, geographical, political, cultural and sporting divisions that resulted from apartheid had supported numerous cultural identities based on social divisions moulded over three hundred years, and enshrined and crystallised without sentiment by the white minority and, more specifically, the National Party, which ruled from 1948 to 1994. The profile of sport within the anti-apartheid movement inside and outside of South Africa can be largely attributed to the comprehensive coverage given to it by the media in general and the sporting media in particular. Rarely can a single sporting issue have gained such coverage throughout the world, although the focus of such interest was generated by the profile of sport within South Africa itself.

> Sport is incredibly significant in South Africa and sports news is *the* news. I remember an occasion where the local news bulletin was first about a couple of leopards the police had set out after ... second, about the success of the local rugby team ... and third about the devaluation of the currency.[10]

Sport became a contested terrain in which sporting identities were formed and delineated through apartheid legislation. The popularity of sport in

South Africa was not lost on the non-white population which, according to Ncgonde Balfour, now Minister for Sport, took the view that for white people, sport, particularly rugby union, was not just a game. It was an embodiment of identity, culture, ideology and religion.[11] Rugby in particular has held a position of prominence and symbolic importance for the white South Africans who dominated society.[12] Furthermore, the widely recognised mastery of, and passion for, rugby raised its international political significance and led to an intense political struggle within the broader effort against apartheid.[13] Sport, especially rugby, was a core cultural concern not only for whites but also, in some cases, for coloured communities as well.[14] Although it is unclear precisely when rugby became the Afrikaner preserve, the game was progressively Afrikanerised during the 1920s and 1930s.[15] To former Springbok rugby captain Morné du Plessis:

> Rugby was the one thing that we could show the world that we were the best at. It embodied everything about Afrikaner culture. It showed that discipline was an important part of this culture.[16]

The elevation of sport within South African society ensured that it became a visible element in reinforcing apartheid and maintaining cultural hegemony. Consequently, rugby became a constant target for the sports based anti-apartheid movement. Sensing the value attached by Prime Minister John Vorster to maintaining rugby links with New Zealand in the late 1960s and early 1970s, protest groups in New Zealand were encouraged to try and prevent Springbok rugby tours to that country.[17] In Britain, the Stop the Seventy Tour campaign (STST), led by Peter Hain, mounted a concerted effort during the Springbok tour of 1970. Paradoxically, sport in general and rugby in particular were to become catalysts for the construction and reinforcement of the ideological consent involved in the Afrikaner identity, whilst the significance of sport to the maintenance of the status quo was recognised by the anti-apartheid campaign from the mid-1950s onward.

Sport, segregation and apartheid – shaping post-Second World War divisions

Apartheid is Afrikaans for 'separate-ness' or 'apart-ness', although the bare nature of this translation cannot do justice to the manifold consequences of its implementation. A more comprehensive definition of apartheid is required:

> First, it (was) the hierarchical ordering of the whole social, economic and political structure of South African society on the basis of statutory defined race. Second, apartheid involved systematic political and

economic discrimination against all blacks, but particularly against Africans. Thirdly, it involved segregation of the races, not only politically and economically but also socially, particularly in housing and social services, including education and health care. Fourthly, apartheid (was) the legalisation and institutionalisation of the hierarchical discriminatory and segregated system.[18]

This definition permits South Africa to be singled out from other nations that have practised discriminatory politics. South Africa differed from other states where there was evidence of discriminatory practices in terms of the intensity of the discrimination and the extent to which it permeated throughout society. As Krotee pointed out, the entire socio-cultural process within South Africa had been shaped by apartheid and sport could not have hoped to escape.[19] The historical context of racial segregation in South Africa demonstrates that the white population subjugated all aspects of the social formation to discriminatory control. Booth contends that South African history offers a rejoinder to those who idealise sport as a practice that transcends racial boundaries. South African racism developed through contradictions, ambiguities and inconsistencies that resulted from complex interplay between local and national conditions. When the Dutch East India Company established a station near the Cape of Good Hope in 1652 it instigated and maintained a correlation between legal status and race by reinforcing the inferior conditions of non-white workers. By 1806, the British had taken permanent control of the Cape with the intention of maintaining political order through 'strong support for the white farmer, some protection for the servant, and some mitigation of abuses for the slave. Sport was a method by which indigenous populations would be assimilated and incorporated as British subjects'.[20]

During the latter half of the nineteenth century political and territorial segregation of blacks increased, especially at the Cape and in Natal. Accompanying such moves, municipal authorities began to bar blacks from sports and entertainment facilities and, although South Africa was a founding member of several international federations, for example, the International Rugby Board in 1890, sport between the races did not occur due to white fears of defeat by inferiors. Two reasons account for the growth of sport: first, the migration to South Africa of large number of Europeans attracted by the discovery of the richest mineral deposits in the world; and second, the growth of sport as a mass leisure activity in the latter half of the nineteenth century. It is a truism to state that 'migrants were mirroring what was happening at "home"'.[21]

The Native Affairs Commission was established in 1903 to formulate uniform policy on blacks as an essential precondition to uniting the four Southern African colonies as one nation. The commission recommended territorial separation and proposed laws to regulate African movements and separate political institutions for Africans. Its proposals became law in

1913 (Native Land Act) and 1923 (Natives Urban Area Act) resulting in blacks only being welcome in white areas to serve white purposes. In sport notions of racial superiority were reinforced in tennis, rugby, boxing and cricket.[22] The 1930s and the 1940s marked a significant period of demographic transformation in South Africa. Not only did the pace of urbanisation increase but the rise of Afrikaner nationalism as the dominant force in white politics reflected increasingly stringent attempts to control the location and behaviour of the urban non-white population. Football, however, achieved a mass following in the 1930s, particularly in the townships of the Transvaal and Natal. By the 1940s, its popularity had grown in most townships across the country although rugby was prominent in the Eastern and Western Cape.[23]

In the 1940s apartheid was far from being a single cohesive policy although there was support among a broad cross-section of Afrikaner nationalists who perceived a need to maintain the foundation of white supremacy that had been laid in the first half of the century.[24] Achieving this required the total exclusion of the non-white population from political power. It was important that a consensus on the method to accomplish continued domination be quickly arrived at. Apartheid became the stated and intended policy of the government from 1948 until 1994. The ruling National Party formulated and implemented a set of economic, political and social practices, including sporting practices, designed to ensure white domination. Apartheid was initially characterised by a barrage of legislation that codified and extended the history of racial domination. The cornerstone of the policy was the continued racial segregation of the South African population. The Prohibition of Mixed Marriages (1949) and the Immorality Act (1950) extended the existing ban on marriages between whites and black Africans to prohibit sexual contact between whites and all other South Africans. The Population Registration Act (1950) classified people into four racial categories: Whites, Coloureds, Asiatics (Indians) and Natives (later Bantu or Africans). The Group Areas Act (also 1950) extended the principle of separate racial residence areas on a compulsory basis.[25] The Natives Resettlement Act (1954) gave the state power to forcibly remove Africans into separate townships. The Reservation of Separate Amenities Act (1953) enforced segregation in all public areas such as cinemas, beaches and sporting arenas. Educational apartheid was introduced into schools (1953), colleges (1955) and universities (1959).[26] Nauright articulates the effect of legislated segregation on the policy and ideology of separate development and social isolation:

> Under the Group Areas Act many urban areas occupied initially by black people were re-designated as areas for whites only and, during the 1950s and 1960s, this led to the demolition of old and famous townships such as Sophiatown in Johannesburg and District Six in Cape Town. Forced removals and segregationist policies impacted

heavily on social and cultural life, and disrupted sport among blacks. A broad non-racial identification through sport was made impossible by apartheid's focus on maintaining and creating differential group identities.[27]

In any historical analysis of the relationship between sport and national identity in South Africa, one must explore the extent to which ethnic identity was subsumed by a state managed national identity that promoted white supremacy at the expense of cultural diversity. In examining the roots of the anti-apartheid movement in sport, the Gramscian concept of hegemony has been identified as a particularly useful tool through which to augment one's understanding of the complex relationship between sport, culture and power.[28] In South Africa different sports became symbolic of different population groups and the white nation's battle against struggle and resistance. Non-racial sports, how and wherever practised, gradually became united through the administration of the non-racial sports movement, as a site of struggle, in order to challenge the cultural symbolism of sport for the white minority. Sport in South Africa under apartheid became defined by whether it propagated or challenged apartheid ideology.

Identity and protest in South African sport since 1945

The history of South Africa in the second half of the twentieth century has been dominated by two features: first, the imposition of apartheid policies that were 'legitimised' through legislation and, second, the growth of a resistance movement, originating within the non-white population, that grew to be a significant international social force when internal resistance was suppressed. Each decade, broadly speaking, was marked by differences in both the content and implementation of policy, as well as in the tactics and strategies employed by the protest movement.[29] To the National Party, apartheid policy meant many things: *baasskap* (domination), white leadership, separate development, parallel development, multi-nationalism and co-operative existence.[30] In essence the common denominator was the continuing control over power whilst the rest of the population remained disenfranchised.

The link between sport and political protest in South Africa is undeniable although sport was not at the forefront of Black Consciousness Movement (BCM) ideology or African National Congress (ANC) policy. South Africa was a prime example of the way states use sport as an instrument of domestic policy and it became recognised as one of the most prominent symbols of identities within the country. Much of the initiative for sports-based protest was located among sports persons and organisations that felt they could contribute to the anti-apartheid movement. Significantly those who operated outside of sporting circles, such as politicians, union members and other social movements gradually saw sport as a vehicle for protest and sought to discover more about its practice in South Africa. Apartheid created a tremendous imbalance in the development of sport. White schools were usually well equipped and pupils had an array of sports to choose from, whilst in black schools equipment and facilities were lacking or non-existent, with the range of sports limited to soccer and for some, cricket and netball.[31] One way for sports persons to identify a role in the campaign against apartheid was to join the increasingly politicised sports and community organisations (for example, the South African Council on Sport (SACOS)). The use of sport as a significant form of political opposition dated back to the 1950s, and the increasing antagonism between the white dominated network of clubs, national bodies and umbrella federations whose leaders were part of the apartheid establishment, and the anti-establishment, anti-apartheid non-racial sector.[32] The non-racial sporting movement followed a strict policy of non-collaboration, which defined the identity of apartheid resistance more generally during the 1970s and 1980s. The logic of non-collaboration was to exploit the morality of authority and shame the ruling class into granting concessions.[33]

The white population began to appropriate national sports participation in such a way that the development of white, establishment sport entailed the under-development of non-white sport. To the white minority sport was an essential element of Afrikaner culture, an embodiment of national identity and something akin to a national religion.[34] The question of why the National Party could not abandon apartheid in sport and retain it elsewhere in South African society was examined by Robert Archer, who concluded that racial integration of sport would have provoked an electoral backlash because of its cultural significance in South Africa.[35] The problem of apartheid in sport and the consequent sports boycott remained one of the most politically sensitive issues among the white minority, whose morale was gradually sapped by the steady curtailment of international sporting contacts. At the same time, because of its status within Afrikaner ideology, sport played a prominent role in propagating apartheid policies and reinforcing the notion of white supremacy:

> Defeat on the sports field is treated as national humiliation for whites ... success confirms their view of the master race; their heroic image of themselves, and justifies the position of superiority they claim to hold.[36]

Peter Hain saw sport as perhaps the most prominent cultural vehicle through which the myth of racial supremacy and the dominance of one culture over another was reinforced. Acceptance of sports teams and individuals abroad was used by the National Party to boost white morale, sapped by the lack of international competition. Furthermore, a whole layer of predominantly black sport never achieved recognition because sport, embedded in the ideology of separate development, could only represent those that enforced the policies of apartheid.[37] Grundlingh chronicled the historical development of rugby and Afrikaner nationalism throughout the period and concluded that 'Afrikaner appropriation of rugby in South Africa, coinciding with general Afrikaner nationalistic political ascendancy, was a way of demonstrating and representing a specific brand of ideological power'.[38]

The evolution of contemporary sport in South Africa can be described in terms of political strategies that were in opposition to the government or in alliance with it. Thus the struggle against apartheid through sport was not just one of race relations. Rather, it was one of identity and the domination, subordination and inequality that were directly associated with, and affected by, the infringement of non-white human rights. The government used sport to reinforce divisions in non-white population groups through the classification system of Indian, Coloured and Black population groups. The legislation surrounding the Pass Laws necessitated all non-white population groups carry their 'pass' with them at all times. Included on the pass was a section that identified the owner's population group. Moves to non-racialism attempted to challenge legislative machinery such as the Pass Laws, but such was the control of the government over apartheid legislation that anyone found not carrying their pass could be imprisoned. Pass laws restricted access to sports facilities in white areas, as many non-whites were not given freedom to enter such communities. The government initially saw little need for a sports policy since social differentiation already existed.

> By savagely curtailing black access to education, urban residence, employment, wealth and the freedom to associate, the Nationalist government necessarily stunted the development of sport and dealt a crippling blow to the attempts of black players to improve their standards of play and organisation.[39]

Through legislation, it became as illegal for whites and non-whites to mix in sporting competition as it was in every other aspect of life. White sports bodies rigidly enforced the colour bar through key legislation. The Population Registration Act of 1950 underpinned the system of apartheid by forcing all citizens to register for a racially defined population group for political and economic purposes. The Registration of Separate Amenities Act of the same year imposed racial segregation in stadia and other public places that might be used for gatherings. The Group Areas Acts of 1950 and 1965 extended the principles of the previous two acts by excluding black spectators from sporting matches or any other form of entertainment at which whites were present. The act even extended into sporting practice. When 'Papwa' Sewgolum won the Natal Open golf championship in 1963 he received his trophy in the rain as the act prevented Indians from entering the clubhouse unless they were servants. For these reasons, the origins of sports-based protest challenged the political legitimacy of apartheid and created starkly contrasting identities defined by legalised discrimination.[40]

Brothers in arms – white identity and political control of sport

In the study of the role of the state in apartheid sport, significant attention is given to the Broederbond (Brotherhood), an organisation created in 1918 to champion the cause and interests of Afrikaner nationalism. The aim of the Broederbond was to maintain and guarantee the perpetuation of Afrikaner supremacy. Acting clandestinely, the organisation refused entry to women and non-Afrikaner speaking men and was composed of some of the most significant figures in white South Africa. During the apartheid epoch, every prime minister was a member. The organisation remained shrouded in secrecy until an informer went public.[41] The Broederbond was highly involved in National Party politics and policies. Furthermore, significant sports were heavily influenced, in particular rugby union.[42] Avril Malan and Dawie DeVilliers were just two of a number of Springbok captains who were Broeders.[43] The fact that the Broederbond became involved in the politics of sport was, in hindsight, an obvious and natural extension of its spheres of influence. Henrik Verwoerd, the architect of apartheid legislation, and his successor John Vorster, retained the notion of white supremacy in policy decisions. Vorster, however, later became cognisant of the need for policy change, despite his awareness of the depth of Afrikaner nationalism in the national team. Rugby had led to splits in Afrikaner unity. The inclusion of non-whites in foreign touring teams was seen as a significant diversion from Broederbond policy, and was denounced by the more radical members of the organisation who broke away to form the 'Herstigte' (Reformed) National Party in 1969. Vorster was more concerned about rugby than cricket, a sport mainly played by the English speaking population.[44]

The government had to devise a sports policy that would satisfy both foreign opinion and also maintain the policy of separate development. The response was the introduction of the 'multi-national' sports policy in 1971. Vorster initially instructed Dr Piet Koornhof, a Broeder who was to replace Frank Waring as Sports Minister, to construct the policy with the direct aim overturning the international community's isolation of South Africa. Vorster announced that South Africa was a 'multi-national' nation, not multi-racial and therefore consisted of four separate nations. White, Indian, Coloured and Black peoples would continue to practise their sport separately but nations would be able to compete against each other provided non-South African nations took part. According to former SACOS treasurer, Reg Feldman:

> What you must remember is that the Broederbond wanted sport to help maintain white supremacy. If we were to play sport against the whites, of course they would win. The policy was designed to ensure that white people would not lose status within South Africa whilst attempting to demonstrate that they could play international sport. But cricket and rugby weren't even multi-national as the Broederbond did not want to see whites play against non-whites. In cricket, South Africa played against England, Australia and New Zealand and that was it. In rugby, it was essential for the Springbok side to have inter-national competition. When the multi-national policy was announced it was apparent that anyone who would take part in multi-national competitions would condone the policy and serve to maintain inter-national ties.[45]

The multi-national policy made no significant amendment to the impact of apartheid in sport and served to intensify racism in sport through the con-comitant approaches of maintaining a level of racial oppression whilst making a concerted effort to conceal its existence. The policy, when it was eventually formally endorsed in 1976, demonstrated the desperation of the Broederbond to regain entry to international sport, but it had taken five years to become formal policy and provided ample opportunity for protest. The grip of the Broederbond on South Africa extended to sport and cultivated the association between Afrikaner nationalism, identity and sporting performance, especially in rugby, where all bar one of the post-war managers of the Springbok rugby team were Broeders.

At the heart of competing rugby identities during apartheid was the struggle between the Broederbond and Danie Craven, president of the South African Rugby Board (SARB) from 1956. Craven never entered the Broederbond and was constantly wary of their influence. In attempting to propagate the myth of supremacist identities through rugby, however, the sport became a source of division and protest, notably in the 1970s in Britain and in New Zealand in 1981, where Errol Tobias, the only black player in the squad, was under constant scrutiny. Rugby, however, again led to a split in Afrikaner unity. The insistence that the 1980 Craven Week rugby tournament, established by Craven himself as a showcase for the best young talent, be open to all players, regardless of colour, was one reason for the formation of the Conservative Party in 1982.[46]

Changing identities in changing times

One of the most difficult issues in democratic transformation is the 'problem' of the past in which attitudes were enshrined by where one's skin colour placed an individual within the apartheid system. In South Africa, the Truth and Reconciliation Committee (TRC) provided the catharsis through which the country could begin to come to terms with the past.[47] In sport, it quickly became evident that the new dispensation would have to undergo its own form of reconciliation, a process which was epitomised with fraught negotiation as the establishment clung grimly to the legacy of its mythical sporting supremacy. The intense struggles of the 1980s led by the UDF (United Democratic Front), COSATU (Confederation of South African Trade Unions), the MDM (Mass Democratic Movement) and the ANC took place under increasingly repressive states of emergency. Whilst the ANC enjoyed popular support they lacked the resources and organisational ability to directly challenge the National Party. The resultant emphasis on the politics of power and transformation were precursors to the changing nature of the struggle and, consequently, the changing nature of the sports struggle.

The emergence of the National Sports Congress (NSC) in 1988 was attributed to those who realised the fusion between tactics and principles in the two-pronged approach of furthering non-racialism and destroying apartheid in sport.[48] A move to progressive policies and a programme stating what the NSC stood for, rather than against, was required. Whereas the NSC established itself as a non-racial sports organisation, SACOS, for so long the recognised organisation of sports protest, was seen as having been locked into a political struggle whose forms and identities had been set by the agendas of the white authorities.[49] According to then General-Secretary, Krish Naidoo, the NSC's emergence was sheer accident. A draft document on sport was prepared for circulation to interested sports persons but fell into the wrong hands and was leaked to the press. Naidoo further contends that the NSC told SACOS that it would be emerging as a national sports body in the future, it would be aligned to the MDM, and its ideology would be that of the MDM.[50] SACOS stated that it wished to restrict the NSC to working in rural areas and townships whilst it worked in urban areas.[51] Non-collaboration had posed a major problem to SACOS. It became a principle rather than a strategy and limited the flexibility of the resistance movement.[52] Throughout the period of 1988–1990, the NSC publicly acknowledged SACOS as the sports wing of the liberation struggle whilst developing a strategy of 'treading very carefully so as not to create division among the nascent identity of non-racial sports persons'. Attacking SACOS would only have created divisions along racial lines as most of SACOS's members 'are coloured or Indian.'[53] In establishing the strategy, the NSC had to consider the historical identities inherent within the existence of SACOS, the existence of establishment sports bodies and the absence of a formally constituted sports body in predominantly black areas.

More pragmatically, the lack of finance amongst black sports persons had prevented the development of sport beyond local communities but this did not prevent the establishment of significant sporting communities. Rugby had become important in many urban communities; witness the link between coloured rugby and its working class constituents from District Six and the Bo-Kaap areas located in the shadow of Table Mountain in Cape Town. Nauright has chronicled the development of soccer's emergence in the urban areas of Natal, Johannesburg and Pretoria. Current teams such as the Orlando Pirates and the Moroka Swallows developed their community base during the apartheid years but suffered from the lack of facilities available to black communities.[54] As Merrett noted in his study of Pietermaritzburg, the fabric of African lives made sporting achievement a remote possibility.[55]

The formation of the NSC was a critically significant event in that it created an identity through which a broader alliance of sporting protest could internally challenge the white identity in sport. There was a need for South African sport to isolate the South African government internally and the NSC brought sport even closer to the broader alliance against apartheid.[56] The policies of SACOS constituted a political statement which defined and delimited the identity of sporting protest without developing the practice of non-racial sport. By March 1989, SACOS acknowledged that its position as the sports wing of the liberation movement was under threat. Caught cold by the speed of change, SACOS was unable to put forward an alternative sports dispensation, and attacked the NSC's willingness to embrace new ideologies. Some of the problems confronting SACOS were largely of its own making as it did not easily discard or change its guiding principles. Its position as a point of contact for international organisations through its hegemony of non-racial sport was being challenged, and Erwin articulated the concerns of many when he proposed that components of mass action were not reflected in SACOS strategies.[57]

The NSC repeatedly acknowledged its Congress origins but refused to accept that it was dictated to by the ANC. It is clear, however, that the ANC saw sport as an instrument in precipitating social identity and structural non-racialism. The ANC's involvement in the sports question can be attributed to Steve Tshwete, a former rugby player, inmate of Robben Island, and the country's first black sports minister. Tshwete's brief was to facilitate unity. His first success culminated in the creation of the UCBSA (United Cricket Board of South Africa) on July 1, 1991. The first director of the UCBSA, Ali Bacher, believes that without Tshwete, unity would not have happened. To Bacher, it was the ANC that put cricket back into international sport and their range of influence was quite astonishing.[58] Bose chronicles the communication process that focused on Bacher and Tshwete from their first meeting through to the readmission of the UCBSA to international sport and the short but historic tour to India in November 1991. The significance of Tshwete's role cannot be underplayed, especially in his negotiations with the West Indies, Pakistan, and India.[59]

South Africa returned to the Olympic movement on 6 November 1991 when the National Olympic Committee of South Africa (NOCSA) formally accepted the IOC invitation to participate in Barcelona. Even so, whilst apartheid legislation had been abolished, majority rule still existed. In addition, unity in sport was tenuous, with many Olympic codes still to be formally constituted. The implications of the timescale imposed by the IOC had forced the NSC's hand. Mthobi Tyamzashe commented that all concessions to establishment sports codes would have to be linked to development and that these bodies could not now just run their sport as they pleased.[60] In accepting the invitation Sam Ramsamy, previously the arch-enemy of white sports administrators, and now in charge of NOCSA, announced that South Africa would compete without any symbols of apartheid national identity.[61] The replacement of the Springbok enraged the white community. Louis Pienaar, the National Party Minister for Sport, called Ramsamy's decision arbitrary and a slap in the face to all South Africans.[62] Ramsamy had established a position where, as chair of NOCSA, he could control international participation and make such decisions. He was walking a fine line between appeasing establishment sport and marginalising the effectiveness of the NSC's decision-making process. That South Africa participated in Barcelona was indeed remarkable. It was motivated by the desire of international sports administrators to readmit South Africa for commercial rewards whatever the status of negotiations and the concomitant political situation. The conditions laid down by the IOC Commission in March 1991 had still not been met by the time of Barcelona. Whilst football was readmitted by FIFA in 1992, South African Football Association chief executive, Danny Jordaan, stated that true unity was not achieved until 1996.[63]

It became obvious that national teams selected on merit would consist of a majority of players from the establishment bloc. Whilst development programmes in townships were seen as a priority, there were those in more popular sports such as cricket and rugby who saw international participation as an essential extension of development. The NSC's constituency would not be able to participate internationally and the NSC's prime focus was on developmental aspects as it was through these programmes that the Africanisation of sport could take place. The NSC's desire to link development with international participation was compromised by the lack of administrators experienced in international sporting affairs. The problem the NSC faced was that their development programmes were starting literally from nothing but many sports appointed black administrators far more quickly.

Unity talks foundered on disagreements inherent in historical and ideological differences between establishment and non-racial sport. Progress to unity was painstakingly slow although rugby seemed able to circumvent these issues in its race to reassert itself internationally. In August 1992, the ANC's support of Springbok rugby had been stretched to breaking point by the playing of the white anthem 'Die Stem van Suid Afrika' ('The Voice of South Africa') prior to a test match with New Zealand. For good measure, Louis Luyt, the domineering Afrikaner and president of the Transvaal RFU, insisted it be played again over the loudspeaker, with an even more overbearing rendition from the white crowd.[64] In November 1992, the long-running dispute between the NSC and SARFU began to acquire public interest, after arguments over the implementation of development programmes.[65] Furthermore, the readmission to international rugby needed to be carefully managed. Contrary to folklore, the Springbok team of the early 1990s, having been denied experience in international competition, was weak and required time to adjust. It was essential to ensure that the myth of Springbok supremacy did not sustain undue damage from repeated defeats, whilst not playing weaker teams too often. Rugby quickly announced that its moves toward unity were complete. In order, however, to achieve unity, quota systems were introduced to permit the participation of formerly excluded, non-racial sports persons. This severely angered establishment rugby although the issue was circumvented as national and provincial teams could be selected on merit alone. According to Denver Hendricks, the new rugby federation (SARFU) was one of the best examples of the new sports dispensation, and he added that 'white sports administrators tolerate the intrusion of non-racial sport in return for international competition, whilst paying lip service to development'.[66]

The display of unity for the Barcelona Olympics was at best premature and, at worst, a sham. Nevertheless, the lifting of sports sanctions made a small contribution to the preparations for a democratically elected government. Tyamzashe later conceded that the NSC was hindered by external constraints and admitted that international pressure had led to sport's premature readmission. 'It would have been better', he commented, 'to open the door from the inside than have it opened from outside'.[67] Non-racial administrators took advantage of the collapse of the apartheid system to proceed with what many thought was indecent haste to re-establish international sports contact. Unity talks continued after Barcelona. Non-racial and established sports administrators were supposed to unite under one power bloc and sports development programmes were to be implemented in the townships. Neither were achieved in totality.[68] Indeed, following his appointment as Chief Officer for Sport and Recreation in April 1997, Denver Hendricks commented: 'I look around the table at our meetings and little has changed since 1990'.[69]

Sporting identities under the 'rainbow'

There is still a distinct uneasiness within South Africa when the subject turns to what defines the nation's identity, and the level of (in)tolerance regarding social, cultural and political diversity makes many extremely uncomfortable. Many South Africans appear to define their country in a geographical sense and find it difficult to discuss issues of nationhood. Many groups have felt threatened by the strong identities of others. Coloured populations felt threatened by white and black identities and some Xhosa populations felt threatened by Zulu identity, emphasising the contention that identity is a vulnerable entity which can be compromised by tolerance and the resulting erosion of a group's culture.[70] According to MacDonald to be South African:

> means to be comfortable with ambiguity. A new South African nation will not be built ... until we perceive ourselves to be part of a political community that inhabits, not inhibits, ambiguity ... There are still many South Africans who do not accept and cannot cope with the concept of a nation that bestows equal rights on all its citizens. It is undoubtedly easier to accept the concept of a nation in a homogenous society, than in the heterogeneous rainbow nation that is South Africa ... Cultural clashes, rejecting and embracing are part of the painful process of coming to terms with the ambiguity of what it means to be South African and what it means to inhabit this national space with others who are different from ourselves.[71]

Whereas previously apartheid had led to the development of almost exclusive subgroup identities, there has been a growing appreciation of the sense of overarching nationhood and what it means to be South African. Subgroup identities have now become important elements in the search for a more cohesive national identity. This feeling is strongest amongst previously disadvantaged communities, who were denied the opportunity to associate with or belong to a nation under apartheid. Nevertheless, anxieties about the place of formerly exclusive communities has encouraged many, but by no means all, to seek ways in which the social fabric of the country can be rebuilt. Even so, it is clear that ethnic/cultural groups do not share any or all of the ideals of the proffered identity, which, to the ANC, has taken on the form of African renaissance. Thus a national identity will revolve primarily around the culture, values and interests of the African majority. It is also contended that Afrikaner nationalism and apartheid encouraged the ANC to dilute exclusive Africanist feelings and tendencies.[72] Reflecting developments elsewhere in the continent South Africa's transformation to democracy has been followed by a growing Africanist ideology. The ANC's document *Nation Formation and Nation Building* urges caution regarding the value of the concept and popular imagery ascribed to the rainbow nation.[73]

The profile of sport in South Africa currently reflects practices under apartheid, the transformative qualities that it possesses in the process of fostering a more cohesive identity, and the tensions inherent within a process of Africanisation. The legacies of apartheid have meant that sporting transformation is an ongoing process, characterised by the fissures of the past. It is evident that sporting successes such as the 1995 Rugby World Cup, successful test cricket performances, the 1996 African Cup of Nations, Olympic medals, and the hosting of the 7th All Africa games in Johannesburg in 1999, all provided moments of national pride and identification. Such feelings quickly dissipated as the country confronted its much greater political, social, economic and cultural challenges. A major change to the identity of South African sport was with regard to the emblems used. The Protea replaced the Springbok in most sports, although rugby union retained the symbol because of the direct intervention of President Mandela. Whilst the Springbok has been retained as a conciliatory gesture by the ANC, it is noticeable that in soccer, most closely associated with black Africans, the team is universally known by the African name 'Bafana, Bafana' ('The Boys, The Boys') whereas 'Amabokoboko' is a term used only in South Africa to describe the rugby union team.

As is the case with many other African governments, sport has become one component of broader social policy objectives. The theme of the government's first white paper on sport, published in 1994, was 'Getting the nation to play', an attempt to permit people to experience activities which are also inherent in nation-building, fostering national unity and redressing past inequalities in local communities.[74] The United Kingdom–South Africa and Australia–South Africa sports initiatives are two examples of this. The former 'targeted' black people, women in particular, in order to create a more equitable sports delivery system in accordance with government policies of affirmative action and redistribution of resources.[75] The latter, whilst similar in nature, examined how to create greater opportunities for young people, particularly in local schools, and affirmed that sport could play a key role in empowering disenfranchised communities.[76]

In 1998 the South African Sports Commission (SASC) Act was approved. The Act created the commission to administer and deliver sport and recreation programmes under the guidance of the Minister of Sport. Accordingly, the DSR was renamed as Sport and Recreation South Africa. One element of the SASC's work is the indigenous games project, launched in February 2001 to promote activities that have broader appeal, especially in rural communities, such as Jukskei and Morabaraba. The SASC is in the process of establishing a national structure for indigenous games federations to establish structures which will permit the presence of the activities within the South African Games. Elsewhere, however, transformation has been notoriously difficult. As one may expect, there have been extreme tensions within the rugby community, but it is important to examine other examples.

In cricket, the United Cricket Board of South Africa (UCBSA) looked to extend opportunities to previously disadvantaged communities through its development programme. It sought to broaden the culture of the game, democratise opportunities and assist in establishing cricket as a people's game by providing facilities in African townships and producing African coaches.[77] Black youngsters were disadvantaged by poverty, inadequate facilities and equipment, and consequently were not competing with white children on equal terms. The UCBSA decided to place talented black young people into previously white schools. Prominent black players in the current South African team, such as Makhaya Ntini and Herschelle Gibbs, are products of 'white' schools, and the eight (out of 14) black South Africans in cricket's under 15 World Cup were all attending 'white' schools.[78] Broadly speaking, the selection of sports players has resulted in a debate over the value of merit selections, where players are chosen purely on ability with no consideration of 'race', as opposed to quotas, which in many eyes has weakened the national team. The two most recent South African tours of Australia, in 1997–98 and in 2001–02, have been a focus for debates between merit and quota selections. As Odendaal noted: 'It's always seen as whites being threatened and the effect of that is to make the victims of yesterday the problems of tomorrow'.[79] Vahed contends that the changes in cricket have reflected the identities of national sporting teams, from all white teams (1991–95), to calls for the inclusion of some players of colour (1996–97), to demands for quota selections (1997–99) and finally for demands of African control (post-2000).[80]

The 1994 government sports policy aimed to further sporting unification by establishing affirmative action controls at all levels of sports administration to reflect the parties involved in the process. Affirmative action is embraced on the implicit assumption that society is discriminatory, and that to redress the historic imbalance, programmes of equality of opportunity are introduced. In sport, quota systems have been introduced as the practical manifestation of affirmative action, conforming to the important ideal of equality of result.[81] Affirmative action aims to improve the economic and social status of the disadvantaged. It embraces a number of dimensions. This includes remedies for past discriminations as well as establishing programmes, and actions to distribute to disadvantaged individuals the information and skills required to compete effectively for and to acquire desired positions.[82] The aim to achieve equality of result by selection and active participation of blacks in national teams has not been achieved in male/female white dominated sports. Enforced affirmative action programmes have been divisive. Proactive programmes promoting reconciliation, along with intercultural learning and understanding, may be essential if equality of opportunity and result are to be achieved. If affirmative action contradicts the notion of sport as a meritocracy, it is consistent with multicultural nationalism that seeks to stabilise relationships in a cultural network. Booth asserts that four decades of apartheid is more than enough moral justification for affirmative action but there is an avowed determination amongst the ANC to Africanise sport.[83]

Conclusion

There are few national societies in which the cultural centrality of sport has been more readily apparent than in South Africa. Links between rugby and white identity assumed mythical status in attempts to reinforce white supremacy before and especially during the apartheid era. Apartheid legalised a brutal system of discrimination in which sport was a prominent site of cultural contestation. Sporting identities became enshrined within strategies designed either to perpetuate apartheid or protest against it. Eventually, aligned with a broader democratic movement led by the ANC, sport was able to assume a position representative of the majority of the population. Moves toward unified sporting structures have been characterised by tense negotiations in which whites have felt threatened by the process of Africanisation, designed as it is to redress past inequities and empower previously disadvantaged communities. This is a process which has barely begun and, as a result, sport remains one of the highest profile arenas for the ongoing negotiations amongst the myriad of cultural sub-identities, enshrined during the apartheid era. For the moment, the 'rainbow nation' is little more than a myth, as South Africa's cultural fabric is defined by its struggle to come to terms with such a rich diversity that is now located within ongoing processes of transformation and reconciliation.

Notes

1 The slogan in the title is taken from a 1997 television advertisement for Castle Lager, which featured 'Bafana Bafana', the South African national football (soccer) team.
2 F. Pienaar with E. Griffiths, *Rainbow Warrior,* London: Collins Willow, 2000, p. 203.
3 A. Grundlingh, 'From redemption to recidivism? Rugby and change in South Africa during the 1995 Rugby World Cup and its aftermath', *Sporting Traditions,* 1998, vol. 14 (2), 78. When the Springboks resisted a name change, a compromise was reached. They were simply 'renamed' *amabokoboko,* which provided the illusion of Africanisation. This did not meet with much resistance because of the prominence of the 'Springbok' within rugby circles and the subsequent intervention by Mandela. The 'new' name was familiar because the meaning had not changed and was fashioned after and imitative of the soccer team, the Orlando Pirates, who have been known for many years to black South Africans as *amabakabaka* (The Buccaneers). P. Gqola, 'Defining people: Analysing power, language and representation in the new South Africa', *Transformation,* 2001, vol. 47, 102.
4 M. Keohane, *Chester: A Biography of Courage,* Cape Town: Don Nelson, 2002, pp. 45–54.
5 G. Baines, 'The rainbow nation? Identity and nation building in post-apartheid South Africa', *Mots Pluriels,* 1998, no. 7, 1.
6 R. Uwechue, 'Nation building and sport in Africa', in B. Lowe, D. Kanin and A. Strenk (eds) *Sport and International Relations,* Champaign, Illinois: Stipes, 1978, pp. 538–50.

7 J. Nauright, *Sport, Cultures and Identities in South Africa*, London: Leicester University Press, 1997, p. 1.

8 There are numerous texts that review the transition to democracy. For a review of the initial negotiations which began to establish democratic frameworks see M. Ottaway, *South Africa: The Struggle for a New Order*, Washington DC: The Brookings Institute, 1993, pp. 2–20, 157–78. The origins of the reconciliation process are articulated by urging the population to face up to the apartheid past in K. Asmal, L. Asmal and R. Roberts, *Reconciliation through Truth: A Reckoning of Apartheid's Criminal Governance*, Cape Town: David Philip, in association with Mayibuye Books: 1996, pp. 6–11, 28–40. The role of key politicians in the process has been analysed by P. Waldmeir, *Anatomy of a Miracle,* New York: Viking, 1997, pp. 169–218. Collections of journalistic writing provide snapshots of the political tensions of the period 1990–1995, see for example, K. Nyatsumba, *All Sides of the Story,* Johannesburg: Jonathan Ball, 1997, pp. 26–7, 48–50, 53, 283–291.

9 Two examples are R. Price, *Apartheid State in Crisis: Political Transformation in South Africa, 1975–1990*, Oxford: Oxford University Press, 1991 and L. Thompson, *A History of South Africa,* New Haven, Connecticut: Yale University Press, 1995.

10 Bob Watson cited in R. Archer and A. Bouillon, *The South African Game*, London: Zed Press, 1982, pp. 1–2.

11 Ncgonde Balfour, speaking on 'A Whole New Ball Game', BBC 2, 26 July 1994.

12 J. Nauright and D. Black, 'Sport at the centre of power: Rugby in South Africa during apartheid', *Sport History Review*, 1998, vol. 29, 192.

13 Nauright and Black, 'Sport at the centre of power', p. 196.

14 J. Nauright, 'Masculinity and popular culture: "Coloured" rugby's cultural symbolism in Cape Town c.1930–1970', in: F. Van der Merwe (ed.) *Sport as Symbol, Symbols in Sport:* Proceedings of the 3rd ISHPES Congress, Cape Town 1996, Sankt Augustin, Germany: Academia Verlag, pp. 1–6.

15 A. Grundlingh, 'Playing for power? Rugby, Afrikaner nationalism and masculinity in South Africa, c.1900–70', *International Journal of the History of Sport*, 1994, vol. 11 (3), 410–17.

16 Interview – Morné du Plessis, 21 August 1997.

17 J. Nauright and D. Black, 'It's rugby that really matters: New Zealand – South Africa rugby relations and the moves to isolate South Africa, 1956–1992', in R. Wilcox (ed.) *Sport in the Global Village*, Morgantown, WV: Fitness Information Technology, 1994, pp. 168–72.

18 M. Lipton, 'Reform: Destruction or modernisation of apartheid', in J. Blumenfeld (ed.) *South Africa in Crisis*, London: The Royal Institute of International Affairs in association with Croom Helm, 1987, p. 35.

19 M. Krotee, 'Apartheid and sport: South Africa revisited', *Physical Education Review*, 1988, *vol.* 11(1), 52–60.

20 D. Booth, *The Race Game: Sport and Politics in South Africa*, London: Frank Cass, 1998, pp. 10–12.

21 A. Odendaal, 'The thing is not round', in A. Grundlingh, A. Odendaal and B. Spies (eds) *Beyond the Tryline; Rugby and South African Society*, Johannesburg: Ravan, 1995, p. 27.

22 Booth, *The Race Game*, pp. 20–23.

23 Nauright, *Sport, Cultures and Identities*, pp. 11–12.

24 D. Posel, 'The meaning of apartheid before 1948: Conflicting forces within Afrikaner nationalism', *Journal of Southern African Studies*, 1987, vol. 14, 123–39.

25 A. Mabin, 'Comprehensive Segregation: The Origins of the Group Areas Act

and its Planning Apparatus', *Journal of Southern African Studies*, 1992, vol. 18, 405–29.

26 P. Christie and C. Collins, 'Bantu education: Apartheid ideology and labour reproduction', in P. Kalloway (ed.), *Apartheid and Education: The Education of Black South Africans*, Johannesburg: Ravan, 1994, p. 64.

27 Nauright, *Sport, Cultures and Identities*, p. 12.

28 G. Jarvie, *Class, Race and Sport in South Africa's Political Economy*, London: Routledge and Kegan Paul, 1985, pp. 18–24, 39–43.

29 N. Worden, *The Making of Modern South Africa: Conquest, Segregation and Apartheid*, Oxford: Blackwell, 1994, p. 95.

30 R. Omond, *The Apartheid Handbook: A Guide to South Africa's Everyday Racial Polices*, Harmondsworth: Penguin, 1985, p. 11.

31 Archer and Bouillon, *South African Game*, pp. 170–7.

32 B. Kidd, 'From quarantine to cure: The new phase of struggle against apartheid sport', in C. Roberts (ed.) *Challenges Facing South African Sport*, 1990, Cape Town: Township Publishing Co-Operative, p. 43.

33 D. Booth, 'Accommodating race to play the game: South Africa's readmission to international sport', *Sporting Traditions*, 1992, vol. 8 (2), 192.

34 C. De Broglio, *South Africa: Racism in Sport,* London: International Defence and Aid Fund, 1970, pp. 4–5, P. Hain, *Sing the Beloved Country*, London: Pluto, 1996, pp. 45–8.

35 R. Archer, 'An exceptional case: Politics and sport in South Africa's townships', in W. Baker and J.A. Mangan (eds) *Sport in Africa: Chapters in Social History*, 1987, New York: Africana Publishing Company, pp. 246–7.

36 J. Brickhill, *Race Against Race: South Africa's Multinational Sports Fraud*, London: International Defence and Aid Fund, 1976, p. 8.

37 P. Hain, 'The politics of sport and apartheid', in J. Hargreaves (ed.), *Sport, Culture and Ideology*, London: Routledge and Kegan Paul, 1982, pp. 242–4.

38 A. Grundlingh, 'The new politics of rugby', in A. Grundlingh, A. Odendaal and B. Spies (eds) *Beyond the Tryline*, p. 427.

39 Archer and Bouillon, *South African Game*, p. 44.

40 Interview – Denver Hendricks, 7 August 1997.

41 The revelations were serialised in the Johannesburg *Sunday Times* and made into a book; I. Wilkins and H. Strydom, *The Super Afrikaners*, Johannesburg: Ravan, 1978.

42 D. Woods, *Black and White,* Dublin: Ward River Press, 1981, p. 45.

43 Wilkins and Strydom, *The Super Afrikaners*, p. 242.

44 Grundlingh, 'The new politics of rugby', p. 422.

45 Interview – Reg Feldman, 12 August 1997.

46 P. Dobson, *Doc: The Life of Danie Craven*, Cape Town: Human and Rousseau, 1994, pp. 210–11.

47 The South African Truth and Reconciliation Commission was set up in 1995 by the ANC to help deal with what happened under apartheid. The conflict during this period resulted in violence and human rights abuses from all sides. The creation of the commission was identified as a necessary exercise to enable South Africans to come to terms with their past on a morally accepted basis and to advance the cause of reconciliation.

48 NSC, *Presentation to ANOCA*, Harare: 3–4 November 1990, pp. 1–2, Ramsamy Papers, Mayibuye Centre, University of the Western Cape: MCH 63–20.

49 M. Keech, 'Conflict, contest and resistance in South Africa's sport policies', in J. Sugden, and A. Tomlinson (eds) *Power Games: Theory and Method for a Critical Sociology of Sport*, London: Routledge, 2002, pp. 169–73.

50 NSC, *Progress Report*, Johannesburg, 31 May 1989, Ramsamy Papers: MCH 63–20, p. 4.

51 NSC, *Secretarial Report*, Cape Town, 1 June 1990, Ramsamy Papers: MCH 63–20, pp. 1–3.
52 Booth, 'Accommodating race to play the game', p. 185.
53 NSC *Progress Report*, Johannesburg, 31 May 1989, Ramsamy Papers: MCH 63–20, p. 5.
54 Nauright, *Sport, Cultures and Identities*, pp. 103–10.
55 C. Merrett, 'Sport, racism and urban policy in South Africa: Pietermaritzburg, a case study', *Sporting Traditions*, 1994, vol. 10 (2), p. 111.
56 Interview – Mvuso Mbebe, 5 August 1997.
57 A. Erwin, 'Sport: The turning point', in C. Roberts (ed.) *Sport and Transformation: Contemporary Debates on South African Sport*, Cape Town: Township Publishing Cooperative, pp. 45–9.
58 Interview – Ali Bacher, 5 August 1997.
59 M. Bose, *Sporting Colours: Sport and Politics in South Africa*, London: Robson, 1994, pp. 214–20, 231–8.
60 'Now deliver the goods', *South*, 11–18 November 1991.
61 M. Keech, 'At the centre of the web: The role of Sam Ramsamy in South Africa's readmission to international sport', *Culture, Sport and Society*, 3 (3), 41–62.
62 'Springbok may not be ready to die yet', *The Citizen*, 8 November 1991.
63 Danny Jordaan, speaking on 'The Soul of South African Soccer', SABC 2, 25 August 1997.
64 McRae, *Winter Colours: Changing Seasons in World Rugby*, London: Mainstream, 1998, p. 52.
65 'A tale of different strokes for different folks', *Pretoria News*, 31 October 1992.
66 Interview – Denver Hendricks, 7 August 1997.
67 NSC, *Secretarial Report*, Johannesburg, June 2, 1994, Ramsamy Papers: MCH 63–21, p. 2.
68 D. Booth, 'Elite sport is winning', *Southern Africa Report*, November 1995, 27–29, D. Booth, 'United sport: An alternative hegemony in South Africa', *International Journal of the History of Sport*, 1995, vol. 12 (3), 105–24.
69 Interview – Denver Hendricks, 7 August 1997.
70 S. DuToit, R. Biggs and A. Greyling, *Project Reconciliation, Research Report*, Rondebosch: Institute for Justice and Reconciliation, 2001, pp. 3–5.
71 H. MacDonald, 'Being comfortable with ambiguity', *Financial Mail*, 15 June 2000, published via www.ijr.org.za/art_pgs/art1/html, retrieved on 15 April 2001.
72 D. Booth, 'The antinomies of multicultural nationalism: A comparative analysis of Australia and South Africa', *International Sports Studies*, vol. 21 (2), 16–18.
73 ANC (1997) *Nation Formation and Nation Building: The National Question in South Africa*, http://www.anc.org.za/ancdocs/discussion/nation.html, retrieved May 21 2000, pp. 1–6.
74 Department of Sport and Recreation, *Getting the Nation to Play: White Paper on Sport and Recreation*, Pretoria: Department of Sport and Recreation, 1994.
75 C. Burnett and W. Hollander 'Sport development and the United Kingdom-South Africa sports initiative: A pre-evaluation report', *Journal of Sport Management*, 1999, vol. 13 (3), 241.
76 C. Burnett, 'Social impact assessment and sport development: Social spin-offs of the Australia–South Africa junior sport programme', *International Review for the Sociology of Sport*, 2001, vol. 36 (1), 41–57.
77 G. Vahed, 'What do they know of cricket whom only cricket know? Transformation in South African cricket, 1990–2000', *International Review for the Sociology of Sport*, 2001, vol. 36 (3), 322.
78 Vahed, 'What do they know of cricket?', 323.

79 A. Odendaal, 'Why "change" really isn't a dirty word', *South African Sports Illustrated*, January 2001, 60–5.
80 Vahed, 'What do they know of cricket?', 332.
81 J. Ryan, 'The Birmingham Four: Affirmative action in South African women's sports', *International Journal of the History of Sport*, 1999, vol. 16 (1), 118–19.
82 G. Moens, *Affirmative Action; The New Discrimination*, 1985, p. 8, cited in Ryan, 'The Birmingham Four', 117–18.
83 Booth, 'The Antinomies of Multicultural Nationalism', 17.

7 Cricket and a crisis of identity in the Anglophone Caribbean

Keith A.P. Sandiford

No other activity, apart from cricket, has ever managed to bring the English-speaking islands of the Caribbean and the country of Guyana together as a unity. Cricket and English, as Clive Lloyd the great cricketer from Guyana once observed, are the only two unifying forces in the region.[1] This has almost always been the case ever since the cricketers from the British West Indies, as they were then called, organized their first tour (to Canada and the United States) in 1886. Apart from CARICOM, founded in 1973 as a belated and half-hearted response to the European and other common markets that emerged after World War II, there have been only two regional institutions operating across the archipelago for any length of time: the West Indies Cricket Board of Control (WICBC) founded in 1927 and now known simply as the West Indies Cricket Board (WICB), and the University of the West Indies (UWI), first established in 1948 as the University College of the West Indies (UCWI), an affiliate of the University of London. Even the British West Indian Federation, a noble attempt at political and economic unification and integration which deserved a far better fate, came to grief in 1962 after four short and difficult years.

The tragedy of the Federation reflected the awesome power of what some analysts have called the 'many diverse island nationalisms'. Hilary Beckles, a devoted federalist himself and one of the sharpest minds produced by the islands, has often lamented the myopic commitment to 'sub-nationalism', especially in this age of increasing globalisation.[2] But as strong as the forces of insularity are, they have not always triumphed in the face of two abiding Caribbean addictions: education and cricket. The inhabitants of this region have historically put great store on these two fields of endeavour. For the multitude, cricket and education have served as the most effective means of social mobility, and for the elite, cricket and education still represent the most powerful forms of socialisation and the greatest instruments of social control. It is not altogether surprising therefore that the UWI and the WICB have been able to weather a sequence of violent storms.

It is almost impossible, in fact, to render into words the importance of cricket in the lives of West Indians. They have traditionally regarded the game as the most perfect of all kinetic activities and have worshipped their cricketing stars in a very special way. International victories are joyfully celebrated by the mass of the population and defeats invariably produce much weeping and gnashing of teeth. This curiosity is perhaps best described by Trevor McDonald, a well-known Trinidadian journalist employed for many years in Britain by Independent Television News (ITN). In his biography of Viv Richards, McDonald observed that 'To West Indians defeat by England is seen as a national disaster of incalculable proportions. The pulse of the nation stops. West Indian pride dies in a torment of self-doubt'.[3] The highly-respected Barbadian journalist and cricket commentator, Tony Cozier, was moved to describe the loss of the Frank Worrell Trophy to Australia in 1995 as 'a savage psychological blow'.[4] When the team regrouped, after having lost all five of the tests against South Africa abroad (1998–99), and played exciting cricket against Australia in the spring of 1999, Michael Holding, a former star himself, joyfully reported that 'Everyone was uplifted by the victory in Jamaica and, as I travelled around the Caribbean after that, with the big crowds everywhere, you could sense people smiling and walking with a spring in their step again'.[5]

West Indies cricket and the making of a Caribbean identity

Some inkling of the meaning of cricket to West Indians may be gleaned from two quotations, randomly chosen from among countless such examples, from two distinguished natives of Antigua: prime minister Lester Bird and Tim Hector, a journalist and political activist. In one of his regular radio addresses to the nation, Bird remarked in 1996 that 'West Indian cricket is more than just a sport for us' being 'the representation of who we are on the world stage. It is a manifestation of our self-esteem'.[6] At a dinner celebrating Viv Richards' century of centuries in 1989, Hector made the profound observation that Richards had 'immortalised himself, Antigua and Barbuda, the Caribbean. Indeed, immortalised a people and a continent'.[7] Hector himself never abandoned the conviction that cricket could mould Antigua and Barbuda into a harmonious whole and serve as the 'incubator' of West Indian nationalism.[8] Cricket remained for him, as well as for Richards, a powerful symbol of African and Caribbean excellence.

Two more interesting anecdotes should suffice to make the point. During a murder trial in Bridgetown in 1950, the Chief Justice, Sir Alan Collymore, himself an erstwhile cricketer and a former president of the Barbados Cricket Association (BCA), suddenly interrupted the formal proceedings to announce that the West Indies team had won the test match at Lord's. The entire court erupted in wild cheering, in which the accused participated with equal glee.[9] On 21 November 1996, several convicts broke out of a prison in Guyana after security guards turned off a radio which was broadcasting live coverage of a test match between Australia and the West Indies.[10]

West Indian emigrants to Britain, Canada and the United States follow the fortunes of the West Indian cricketers with an indescribable intensity. During the period 1960–90, for example, the Caribbean immigrants in Britain flocked to the test matches in thousands, sometimes in London outnumbering England supporters at Lord's and the Oval. Their boisterous and incessant cheering occasionally disturbed their neighbours, unaccustomed as they were to such noisy conduct at the cathedrals of cricket. Eventually the authorities decided to impose a ban on their music and their banter. By 1991, because of new regulations, the steady increase in admission fees, and the gradual transformation of the immigrant demography, the Caribbean cheering sections had conspicuously diminished.[11] They had been a source of inspiration to the touring cricketers. As the majority of the players have admitted, both the gladiators and the spectators had gained strength from each other. Looking around at the thousands of West Indian faces in the crowd at the Oval in 1976, the senior players (as Richards reported) were determined 'not to let these people down'.[12] Significantly, with the decline of Caribbean spectatorship in England during the 1990s, the West Indian teams performed progressively worse. In the summer of 2000 they actually lost a test series in England for the first time since 1969.[13]

The players, too, understand the role of cricket in the shaping of a Caribbean identity and have generally taken to the field like so many crusaders on behalf of a religious cause. When, for instance, the team lost a World Cup match to the lightly-regarded Kenyans in 1996, the captain, Richie Richardson, publicly admitted that the disaster was more distressing to him personally than the death of his own mother two years earlier.[14] All the biographies of the cricketers who played under Lloyd and Richards during the 'Glory Years' contain a common thread: the players were all conscious of playing not only for the West Indies but for the West Indian diaspora. There was not only a certain pride in wearing the maroon cap but a very heavy responsibility.[15] In an interview just after he had demolished England at Port-of-Spain in March 1994, Curtly Ambrose, the great Antiguan fast bowler, articulated these truths in simple but emotive words: 'I understand how important it is to play my cricket hard. I do it for the people. They expect nothing less and we're very conscious of them whenever we go on the field. Their love is strong. It is demanding on you but it also makes you strong'.[16]

West Indian governments, of whatever hue, have also pandered to this cricketing craze in numerous ways. The adulation has been unbridled. Pavilions, playing-fields and cricket tournaments have been named after several former stars including George Challenor, Learie Constantine, Gordon Greenidge, Charlie Griffith, Wesley Hall, Desmond Haynes,

George Headley, Michael Holding, Rohan Kanhai, Viv Richards, Clyde Walcott, Everton Weekes and Frank Worrell. Streets, boulevards and round-abouts have been named after many more. West Indian cricketers have been routinely awarded the most prestigious national honours. Barbados alone has thus far knighted no fewer than six (Sir Harold Austin, Sir Frank Worrell, Sir Garfield Sobers, Sir Clyde Walcott, Sir Everton Weekes and Sir Conrad Hunte). Antigua conferred a knighthood on Sir Vivian Richards, while almost every international player has been awarded a distinction of some kind and West Indian postage stamps bear the images of many a test cricketer. When Brian Lara broke the world record by scoring 375 runs in a single test innings against England in April 1994, he was showered with so many gifts and awards, including the Trinity Cross, Trinidad and Tobago's highest national honour, that he almost immediately became one of the islands' wealthiest citizens.[17]

This Caribbean treatment of successful cricketers is all the more intriguing when one considers that other heroes and heroines are seldom memorialised in such a manner. There are few biographies or statues, for instance, of non-cricketing Caribbean stars. Yet the need to worship heroes remains very strong and the tendency is to compensate for this apparent shortage of other leaders and prophets by glorifying the cricketers – especially when the latter make the region immensely proud. Such adulation, however, comes at a price. The public expects so much from its cricketers that failure is not easily understood or forgiven. When Carl Hooper, a very popular player, was showing signs of disinterest towards the end of an arduous series against Australia in 1999, he was roundly booed in Barbados where, at the height of his powers, he had previously been hailed as 'King Carl'. The great Gary Sobers, universally acclaimed the finest all-rounder the game has spawned thus far, once made an ill-judged declaration to allow England to win a test match in Trinidad that the hosts should never have lost. His effigy was publicly hanged in Port-of-Spain and it took several years before he earned the forgiveness of his Trinidadian critics.[18]

On the whole, this unnatural obsession with cricket lay at the base of West Indian successes on the field throughout most of the second half of the twentieth century. For about 50 years after World War II, the West Indies were consistently the most exciting team on the international stage. They provided the sport with some of its finest batsmen and the majority of its fastest bowlers. West Indian dominance reached a peak during the period 1975–95. Indeed, in one golden streak from 1980 to 1995, the islanders played unbeaten for 29 test series, winning 59 out of 115 matches, losing only 15 and dominating the majority of the 41 left drawn (often because of the weather). England suffered the indignity of two 'black-washes', losing 24 of 38 tests during that span and winning only four. Australia, too, could win no more than five tests, while losing 14 of 28 to the rampant West Indians. India suffered 10 defeats, while winning only two out of 22 tests. Pakistan won three out of 16 but lost six.[19] This was a truly remarkable streak, unprecedented in the history of the sport.

To appreciate the enormity of this achievement, which can arguably be described as the sociological miracle of the twentieth century, one has only to examine the demography of international cricket at that time. The population of the Anglophone Caribbean is approximately 6 million. Moreover, the region is desperately poor by western standards. To compete so successfully against 18 million Australians, 58 million Britons, 897 million Indians, 128 million Pakistanis, 41 million South Africans and 17 million Sri Lankans was an achievement of epic proportions.[20]

The Caribbean people basked in the reflected glory of their cricketers who gave them a stronger sense of pride and identity than they had ever known before. It strengthened their faith in themselves and vindicated their claims to self-determination. The victories over England in 1948 and 1950 had also given a considerable fillip to the independence movement in the days when cricketing prowess was seen (by both the imperialists and the imperialised) as a necessary prerequisite for political responsibility. The Caribbean colonial leaders of the 1950s did not think in terms of separate national entities in the region but resorted to that programme as soon as the Federation disintegrated. Their calls for independent statehood in the 1960s reflected the growing confidence that the cricketers had inspired with their triumphs in England in 1963 and over Australia in 1965. By this time they had become the acknowledged (albeit unofficial) champions of the cricket world.

Cricket became (and remained) a most important symbol. It did so because there was no other activity at which the territories could shine so brightly. It also remained the only area in which the diverse islands could find a common ground. In addition, the importance of presenting a cohesive and united front on the cricket field was consistently emphasised by such captains as Frank Worrell, Clive Lloyd and Viv Richards. It was Worrell, in fact, who stressed a 'West Indian' brand of nationalism in a way in which previous captains had never been able to do. He insisted that the best players ought to be selected, irrespective of their territory of origin. He also compelled the WICB to pay more attention to the cricketers from the Leewards and the Windwards who had hitherto been given rather short shrift by the Board. He made bold to predict that Antigua, Dominica, Grenada and St Vincent, if given a fair opportunity, could shortly supply the West Indies with some of their greatest stars.[21] In reflecting some years later on Worrell's outstanding contribution, Sir Conrad Hunte (his vice-captain), remarked that 'Frank transformed the West Indies team from a collection of talented individuals into a talented team. The synergy of our collective output was considerably greater than the total of our performances as individuals'.[22]

Worrell's legacy was a most significant one. His tenure of the captaincy marked an end to the stifling system of quotas which had long formed the basis of selecting teams to represent the West Indies abroad. The idea that each of the so-called 'Big Four' (Barbados, British Guiana, Jamaica and Trinidad) should have a roughly equal number of representatives had left many a West Indian squad unnecessarily weak and unbalanced. As the first black man to lead a West Indian team abroad, Worrell also served as a source of considerable inspiration to the vast majority of West Indians. His prophecy about the smaller islands was shortly fulfilled. Within 30 years, Antigua alone had produced such dominant players as Curtly Ambrose, Viv Richards, Richie Richardson and Andy Roberts.[23]

If it did nothing else, the policy of including the 'Combined Islands' in the territorial competitions significantly expanded the catchment area in the search for talent. Even the small island of Nevis, with a population of roughly 10,000, has thus far provided the West Indies with such test stars as Keith Arthurton, Derrick Parry, Elquemedo Willett and Stuart Williams.[24] The programme did much more. It certainly removed a sense of frustration that had strangled most forms of development in such places as Anguilla, Montserrat, St Lucia and St Kitts.[25]

Countervailing tendencies – insularity and ethnicity

The ideal of a West Indian nationalism prospered for a generation or two, not least because of the impressive string of victories that the cricketers enjoyed. But a strong sense of nationalism cannot be nurtured on cricket alone. In the case of the West Indies, there are simply too many obstacles to the kind of Caribbean nationalism promoted by such federalists as Dr Hilary Beckles, Sir Conrad Hunte, C.L.R. James, Clive Lloyd, Michael Manley, Sir Vivian Richards, Sir Clyde Walcott and Sir Frank Worrell.

By far the greatest obstacle in this respect is insularity, once described by Reverend Wesley Hall, the former West Indian fast bowler of renown, as 'the scourge of West Indies cricket'.[26] So powerful and deep-rooted are these divisive forces that it is almost impossible to eradicate them. The fact is that the small Caribbean islands are spread out over a vast area. The distance from Barbados in the south-east to Jamaica in the north-west is more than 1,200 miles. There was consequently very little contact between Jamaica and the Eastern Antilles prior to the development of aviation. Transportation presented such a huge problem that some of the English cricket teams touring the islands in the early twentieth century could not include both Barbados and Jamaica in the same expedition. As A.W.F. Somerset, the captain of the MCC squad who toured the West Indies in 1913 observed, it was impractical to visit Jamaica on this occasion because that meant an additional nine-day voyage for which they could not easily plan.[27]

This problem of distance meant that the territories developed, during the colonial period, more or less as separate cocoons; each with its own politics, heroes, traditions, speech patterns, customs and conventions.

There was never any attempt at cooperation between one island and another, and the 'mother country' added to the problem by systematically pursuing a policy of 'divide and rule'. Even the systems of governance differed from one territory to another. In Barbados, for instance, there was a rudimentary form of representative government, with a largely white House of Assembly elected by a largely white electorate in the midst of a largely black population. In the majority of the other Caribbean islands, Crown Colony rule was the norm, with all important decisions being made by a colonial governor, appointed by the metropolis and advised by a local (hand-picked) legislative council.

Although English was the official language, the idioms and accents differed all across the Caribbean. Whereas Barbados had remained a British colony from the time of its settlement by Europeans early in the seventeenth century, the other colonies changed hands regularly before falling under British sway. Trinidad, for example, knew a variety of European owners before finally being brought under British dominion in 1797.[28] It had for years been controlled by the crowns of Spain and France. Jamaica, too, had been a Spanish colony before the British captured it in 1655. So the extent of the British influence has not been equal everywhere in the Caribbean. All kinds of differences still prevail. While the majority of Trinidadian Christians, for instance, have remained staunchly Catholic to this day, the majority of the Barbadians are Protestants. While the Barbadian dialect is largely a mixture of English and African sounds and words, the dialects in such islands as Grenada, St Lucia and Trinidad are based on African, English, French, Indian and Spanish forms.

These marked cultural and linguistic differences help to keep the Anglophone Caribbean divided. The division is deepened by very powerful parochialisms. The Barbadians, even in the diaspora, remain fiercely loyal to their native roots. They have a pride in Barbados that is very difficult to explain or to describe. They have always seen themselves as Barbadians first and West Indians afterwards. To make matters worse, they have traditionally played what they consider the best cricket in the world and are always critical of the West Indian selectors when their own local heroes are bypassed. Hence the furore when Richie Richardson was elevated to the captaincy over Desmond Haynes in 1991 and when Anderson Cummins was omitted from the Test XI that played at Bridgetown against South Africa in 1992. On that occasion, bristling from what they regarded as a sequence of slights and insults, the Barbadians organised the most successful boycott in the history of the game. They refused to attend. The West Indians won that match while playing before a conspicuously empty house, despite the fact that the test itself was particularly exciting.[29]

So strong are the insular prejudices that the threat of a similar boycott is never far from the surface. The Trinidadians have also been keen on boycotting a test match or two, to protest at the exclusion of local heroes, although such threats have not yet been carried out successfully. They did, however, make a very strong official protest on 28 April 1994 through the Trinidad and Tobago Cricket Board of Control (TTCBC). This organization expressed its grave concern over what it perceived as 'an organized and calculated plot ... to deny Trinidad and Tobago and its cricketers their just due'. The TTCBC listed four specific grievances, mainly having to do with West Indian team selections, and allowed the WICBC to know that it was quite dissatisfied with the manner in which such Trinidadian players as Brian Lara and Phil Simmons had recently been treated. Predictably, the WICBC regarded the public complaints as 'totally without merit', while Tony Cozier, writing for the Barbados *Sunday Sun*, dismissed the charges as 'irrelevant negativity (that) is an unfortunate, but not unusual reflection of the parochialism that continues to plague us'.[30]

To this insoluble problem of insularity is added the thorny issue of race and ethnicity. The Anglophone Caribbean is a multi-ethnic synthesis of almost every conceivable race and colour. Although the bulk of the population have African roots, there are sizeable minorities of Indians and Chinese, especially in Guyana, Jamaica and Trinidad. The descendants of indentured Indian labourers, transplanted to the Caribbean during the nineteenth century after the abolition of negro slavery, are particularly numerous in Guyana and Trinidad. In Guyana, they form almost 50 per cent of the population, which has found itself facing the prospect of racial polarisation in politics. The majority of the Afro-Guyanans support the People's National Congress (PNC), founded by Forbes Burnham in 1957, while the Indo-Guyanans tend to support the People's Progressive Party (PPP), founded by Cheddi Jagan in 1950. This has led to bitter political squabbles over the past 40 years and there has been considerable racial tension and discord in every aspect of Guyana's life. Needless to say, such attitudes have infiltrated Guyana's cricket and the Indo-Guyanans have often expressed the belief that their cricketers have traditionally been the victims of racial discrimination.

A similar situation prevails in Trinidad, where the Indians form over 40 per cent of the population and tend to vote for prime minister Basdeo Panday's United National Congress, while the Afro-Trinidadians in the main are still supporting the People's National Movement, founded by Dr Eric Williams in 1955. There is racial rivalry in many features of Trinidadian life and many Indo-Trinidadian cricketers have felt victimised by a system that, in their judgement, recognises only blacks and whites.

There is no doubt that cricketers of Indian descent have generally fared ill in the Caribbean, despite the standard of their play. Chatterpaul Persaud, one of the finest batsmen ever produced by Guyana, was never once selected to play for the West Indies, and it took a particular brand of oriental magic to allow Sonny Ramadhin, that magnificent spin bowler, to break the racial barrier in 1950. Indians in Guyana and Trinidad have consequently been less supportive of West Indian efforts than their counterparts. They have even gone so far as to cheer openly for Indian and

Pakistani touring sides when they visit the Caribbean. Two of the most popular cricketers in Trinidad and Guyana over the years have been Subhash Gupte, the wily leg-spinner who captured 149 wickets in 36 tests for India, and Sunil Gavaskar, the great Indian batsman who became the first cricketer ever to exceed 10,000 runs at international level.[31]

Such racial tensions may occasionally have led to selectorial error but they do not appear to have negatively impacted on the West Indian performance on the field. The various races have played cooperatively together and certainly Shivnarine Chanderpaul was one of the most popular members of the side in the late 1990s (just as Ramadhin had been in the 1950s). But there have been hiccups. The Indo-Caribbean community was always suspicious of Viv Richards who was so committed to Pan-Africanism and so eager to boast about the exclusively African ethnic background of his victorious team. Writing in the Antiguan newspaper, *Outlet*, on 9 February 1990, Richards asserted (rather injudiciously) that 'the West Indies cricket team ... is the only sporting team of African descent that has been able to win repeatedly against all international opposition, bringing joy and recognition to our people'. This naturally provoked an indignant reaction, especially from Basdeo Panday in Trinidad, and Richards had to offer an explanation and an apology.[32]

It is truly astonishing that, in the face of such difficulties, the West Indies were able to perform as well as they did on the cricket field. Even during their periods of triumph, racism and insular politics intervened. In 1966, for example, when Gary Sobers led his victorious squad to a 3–1 triumph in a test series in England, he took a side which he himself regarded as not the best one available. He never ceased to regret that he failed to convince his fellow-selectors to include Robin Bynoe and Clive Lloyd in the party. The politics of insularity, to his everlasting chagrin, were allowed to prevail. Lloyd later gathered that there had been much 'selectorial bartering' based on insular considerations rather than merit.[33]

Insular prejudices are markedly less dangerous during periods of boom. Even the most rabid of Barbadians, as parochial as they are, tend to be less critical of selectorial decisions so long as the West Indians are winning. They understand the need to keep a successful combination intact. Hence they could resign themselves to the consistent exclusion of Carlisle Best, one of their very finest batsmen and fielders in the 1980s, when the regional team was so consistently triumphant. But much harder for them to digest was the persistent neglect of such local heroes as Vasbert Drakes, Ottis Gibson and Roland Holder when the West Indies were losing in the late 1990s.

Current problems confronting West Indian cricket

This is one of the most pressing dangers facing cricket and the West Indies now. A prolonged and devastating slump has done untold damage to the regional psyche. The selectors face dissension and complaints from every conceivable quarter. Reverend Wesley Hall, who is now the president of the WICB, once found life as a selector 'uncomfortable, not physically yet but uncomfortable all the same, travelling to some areas in the Caribbean ... It's a mental discomfiture'. He warned, in 1997, that this 'constant, uninformed criticism and pressure [will] discourage good people from coming forward for the Board or to be selectors and that will be to the detriment of our cricket'.[34]

There are other developments that have the potential to be equally detrimental to West Indian cricket. Consider, for instance, the spectacular explosion of the black and brown bourgeoisie in the Caribbean during the 'Age of Independence'. This phenomenon has created a totally different context from the one in which such superstars as George Headley, Rohan Kanhai, Gary Sobers, and the 'Three Terrible Ws' existed. This class is active, acquisitive and ambitious and does not attach as much importance to cricket as its ancestors once did. Its sharp focus is on family and profession and other matters are secondary. Its brighter sons also appear to be more anxious to acquire certificates than to score runs. The scholar-athlete of bygone days has thus virtually disappeared from the Caribbean social landscape.

Drug abuse, which was certainly not a burning issue during the 1940s and 1950s, has now become a very serious matter throughout the West Indies. The increasing popularity of illegal substances has clearly hindered cricket's growth and will continue to do so until the unfortunate craze has run its course.

Inexorable urbanisation has also taken its toll. Where once there were wide open spaces and pastures for youngsters to play cricket cheerfully throughout the year, there are now paved roads and palatial homes, guarded by vicious dogs and sophisticated security systems. Such capital cities as Bridgetown, Castries, Georgetown, Kingston, Kingstown, Port-of-Spain, Roseau and St John's, have expanded in leaps and bounds, and the volume of traffic also makes street cricket, a very popular pastime in a previous age, an almost impossible activity now. What was an excellent training ground for budding test match players is no longer available. It was via these forms of cricket that such Barbadian superstars as Wes Hall, Conrad Hunte, Seymour Nurse and Gary Sobers had initially honed their skills.

Nor is Caribbean education what it once was. Whereas the genders were strictly separated in the leading elementary and secondary schools until about the 1970s, co-education has become the norm and seems to have hindered the development of cricket (particularly in Barbados). The whole approach to physical education has been revolutionised. Older secondary schools once appointed cricket masters and set great store by the games as a character-building exercise. Thus such institutions as the Antigua Grammar School, Combermere School, Harrison College and the Lodge School in Barbados; Queen's College in Guyana; Queen's

Royal College in Trinidad; and Jamaica College, Kingston College and Wolmer's in Jamaica served for years as productive cricket nurseries. But the vast majority of secondary schools now appoint physical education graduates who have mainly been trained in the United States. As they promote a variety of sports with an American bias, the monolithic production of cricketers has come to an end.

This is largely in keeping with the steady Americanisation of Caribbean culture. There is considerable (and increasing) exposure to the North American media. Daily access to such cities as Miami, New York and San Juan has significantly reduced the previous dependence on the United Kingdom and Europe for the provision of social and cultural models. Hence such sports as basketball, American football and golf receive almost as much television coverage as cricket. As a result, Caribbean youngsters among the middling and upper classes have a much wider range of sporting heroes to emulate than did their parents and grandparents.[35]

The steady diversification of Caribbean sports during the 'Age of Independence' has led to marked and obvious improvements in such disciplines as athletics, basketball, golf, hockey, soccer and swimming. But these advances have been made at cricket's expense. A portion of the youthful energy that had previously made the West Indies so powerful on the cricket field has gone into the production, for instance, of the celebrated 'Reggae Boyz', who brought such immense pride and joy to the Jamaican people during the football World Cup in 1998. It has also produced a number of exceptional sprinters, such as Ato Boldon and Obadele Thompson.

In the midst of these fundamental changes, a very powerful spirit of individualism has emerged, especially among the younger cricketers. In his brilliant analysis of the situation, Beckles considers this almost as important (and potentially as dangerous) as the pervasive and ebullient 'subnationalisms' that so often undermine the cohesiveness of the region.[36] Armed with contracts far more lucrative than those enjoyed by their predecessors, and employing an entourage of agents, accountants and lawyers, the modern cricketers are less governable than the old. No longer can the WICB treat the Test XI shabbily as so many hirelings. The players made this point, with crystal and painful clarity, when they went on a memorable strike just before embarking on the ill-fated tour of South Africa in November 1998. Beckles analysed these developments in the following words:

> [Courtney] Walsh is clearly the last standing hero of the age when national pride more than anything else was the motivation for performance on the field. [Brian] Lara is the first hero of the new paradigm that is characterized by the privatization, commodification, and global liberalization of cricket ... Those coming behind him will

see his corporate style and connections as the global norm, and will articulate their entrepreneurial interests in ways that transcend the WICB's notion of what is good for West Indies cricket.[37]

The WICB is particularly worried because even though it has managed to attract more generous sponsors than previously, the region simply cannot compete in commercial and economic terms with the other Test-playing countries. As Tony Cozier ruefully observed in 1982, 'Against the international giants which have become associated with Australian and English cricket – Benson & Hedges, Prudential Insurance, the National Westminster Bank, McDonald's and Schweppes among them – prospective West Indian sponsors are small fry ... The economies in which they operate are small and fragile, and the markets they service numerically insignificant'. He went on to lament that, despite all the efforts of CARICOM, there was a lack, in any case, of truly regional companies since most of the major business concerns tended to be restricted to individual islands.[38]

On the other hand, the superstars have generally prospered in the age of globalisation. This is especially true in the case of Brian Lara. According to reports in West Indian newspapers, Lara's annual earnings in the late 1990s included £100,000 from the WICB, £250,000 from computer games, £250,000 from bats and gear, £220,000 from a sunglasses manufacturer, £80,000 from a drinks company and £150,000 from miscellaneous deals in the Caribbean, not to mention the £120,000 he received from Warwickshire in 1998.[39] Such individual deals help to explain why it is becoming more and more difficult for the WICB to wield an absolute authority over the cricketers and why, in fact, the WICBC decided to discard the final C from its official designation in 1996.

West Indies cricket and post-colonial identity

Not surprisingly then, there is a profound fear, felt especially by the older members of the Caribbean community, that the continuing failure of the Test XI to distinguish itself on the international stage might lead inevitably to the end of cricket as a key cultural element in the Anglophone islands' collective post-colonial identity. But there are too many encouraging signs to support such pessimism. Apart from the fact that well-established traditions die but a lingering death if they ever die at all, it will take a major revolution in some competing field of endeavour to supersede cricket in the Caribbean pantheon of symbols. Had the 'Reggae Boyz' won the 1998 World Cup, or had several Caribbean athletes destroyed the competition at the Sydney Olympics, then the supremacy of cricket would have been in greater danger. In other words, it takes more than the defeat of an important cultural symbol to bring it to its knees. It usually requires the ascendancy of a suitable alternative.

In fact, cricket is still the only field in which the English-speaking West

Indians work as a collective whole on the international stage, and they have done so for more than a hundred years. All along the way, Caribbean cricket has surmounted a series of pitfalls, many of them potentially more devastating than those by which it is currently threatened. It has survived the pernicious quota system (which has only recently been abandoned), and the paralysing stupidity of white captaincy (which endured until 1960). It is also useful to remember that there was no annual and regular territorial competition prior to 1965. This meant that local cricketers remained largely unknown outside their native heath and could not therefore expect the automatic support of sister colonies. Older West Indian stars had to prove their worth to critical neighbours or suffer ridicule. As great a batsman as George Headley was, he never performed for Jamaica in the presence of Barbadians. He made in fact only three appearances at Bridgetown (on behalf of the West Indies) throughout his stellar first-class career.[40] The dreaded scourge of insularity, encouraged by the pernicious quota system and the paucity of first-class cricket in the region, was consequently much more vicious in the earlier days than it is now.

The pessimists must also remember that sporting fortunes tend to be cyclical. When the West Indies cricket team suffered a lengthy drought during 1967–73, there were very gloomy forebodings similar to those which are currently heard. Tony Cozier, in a doleful editorial, entitled 'Testing times for West Indies cricket' outlined a litany of unsavoury embarrassments and controversies that seemed to threaten the very fabric of the sport in the Caribbean. Writing in 1973, Cozier feared for the game's survival in a healthy state.[41] It was in response to such acute alarmism that E.W. Swanton, that celebrated 'sort of a cricket person', sagely observed that the West Indies still had many blessings to be thankful for and that their resurgence was only a matter of time.[42] Two years before that, Berry Sarbadhikary, a noted Indian cricket writer, had offered the same advice. Given the cyclical nature of cricket supremacy, there was no need for the West Indies to panic, and their turn would surely come again.[43] The words of Sarbadhikary and Swanton proved uncannily prophetic. The resurgence began in the summer of 1973 with a surprising demolition of England's best on English soil.

That resurgence took place, almost miraculously, without any intervention on the part of regional governments, commercial sponsors, or the WICBC itself. There suddenly appeared, as if dispensed like manna from heaven, a galaxy of gifted stars without the benefit of coaches, trainers or cricket academies. A similar resurgence in the twenty-first century is all the more possible because of very positive changes in the Caribbean cricket infrastructure. With Reverend Wesley Hall at the helm, there is a greater awareness of the need to pacify the various stakeholders, whether administrators, players, or the general public. The WICB has succeeded in attracting much more lucrative sponsorships than anything contemplated in the 1980s. The various CARICOM governments have come to the conclusion that cricket is too vital a feature of Caribbean life to be treated any longer with benign neglect, and have agreed in principle to work in closer collaboration with the WICB than ever before. The UWI has also shown a firm determination to play a leading role in cricket's resurgence. Indeed in October 2000 CARICOM, the WICB and the UWI jointly sponsored an inclusive conference in Antigua to discuss the interests of all the stake-holders of West Indian cricket and to put forward positive recommenda-tions. This was the sequel to a less formal symposium organized in May 2000 by the UWI and the CARICOM governments.[44]

A great deal of good, that is to say, has come directly out of the embar-rassment caused by the protracted slump. Keith Mitchell, the prime minis-ter of Grenada and a former captain of the island side, played a key role in the establishment of a cricket academy at St George's University in 1998 as well as the brand new Queen's Park Stadium complex in 2001.[45] Like most keen cricketers past and present, he is determined to keep the cricket tradition alive in the Caribbean, and to convince other prime ministers in the region to do likewise. Basdeo Panday, the prime minister of Trinidad and Tobago, also called, in 1999, for more vigorous CARICOM inter-vention in support of West Indies cricket.[46] The Barbados Labour Party Government, under Owen Arthur, another former player and keen cricket fan, has also been very generous in its treatment of the Barbados Cricket Association over the years, recently offering that organisation a guarantee on a loan of more than US$5 million from the government for the devel-opment of the Kensington Oval in Bridgetown. These funds were needed for the erection of a comfortable media stand that had long been lacking.[47]

In short, more recently most CARICOM governments have expressed a greater willingness to cooperate with the WICB than they had evinced earlier. In 1996, for instance, they had promised to assist the WICB by contributing generously to the cost of 'retainer contracts' to ensure the availability of the leading West Indian professionals. The idea of the scheme was to retain contracted players in the Caribbean, allowing them to coach and play for local clubs, rather than playing professionally abroad. But so many of the regional governments had been delinquent in their payments that the WICB had no choice but to abandon the pro-gramme in 1998.[48] Their attitude is much more positive and sympathetic now.

The UWI has been so determined to keep alive the tradition of cricket-ing excellence in the Caribbean that in the early 1990s it established a Centre for Cricket Research (CCR) at the Cave Hill Campus in Barbados. This was the brainchild of Professor Hilary Beckles, who was then the Dean of Arts. He is now the Principal and retains a healthy interest in Caribbean cricket research, encouraging students to write papers and theses on the development of the sport in the region. Beckles instituted the annual Sir Frank Worrell Memorial Lecture at Cave Hill in 1993. He also organised the highly successful Sir Garfield Sobers Lecture Series at the Queen's Park Steel Shed in Bridgetown in 1994, and the Viv Richards Lectures Series at the same venue in 1995. These public lectures, eventually reproduced in book form, were intended to prevent the younger generation losing sight of the principal plank in the Caribbean cultural heritage.[49] Another scholarly anthology, edited by Beckles and Brian Stoddart, was intended to serve as one of the basic texts for the fledgling CCR.[50] Institutions such as the CCR, and texts such as those edited and written by Beckles, represent tangible evidence of the abiding influence of cricket in Caribbean life and are deliberately geared to perpetuate that influence.

Another important institution, the Caribbean Cricket Centre (CCC), has recently been established in Antigua. It is a facility intended to provide high quality practice, coaching and playing facilities for players and teams at every conceivable level. Plans were immediately set in place for expansion to include such amenities as a pavilion, a media centre, fitness rooms, a library and a video room. The WICB wisely associated itself with the project from the very start and is using the CCC as a practice facility for test teams.[51] The WICB also initiated a programme which called for a series of personal development seminars to provide players 'with a new perspective on life while enhancing their careers'. Several promising test and first-class cricketers attended the inaugural seminar at Port-of-Spain in July 1996.[52]

Some of the secondary schools, too, have begun to respond positively to the challenge issued by the WIBC, urging them to restore cricket to the curriculum. Just before his sudden and unfortunate death in December 1999, Sir Conrad Hunte was pleased to note, for example, that Combermere School had employed a cricket teacher, and that two other Barbadian schools, Harrison College and Foundation, were planning to do the same.[53] This new concentration on cricket nurseries is another promising sign.

On the whole, then, the signs are propitious even if the results on the field have not altogether been satisfactory since 1995. For too long, the Caribbean Achilles heel has been an absence of world-class batsman other than Brian Lara. But the sudden emergence of highly talented young batsmen such as Darren Ganga, Christopher Gayle, Wavell Hinds, Marlon Samuels and Ramnaresh Sarwan gives the region a realistic gleam of hope. It is unlikely that cricket will soon cease to be the most significant of all West Indian cultural symbols. Had the end been in sight, the society would not have found the will or mustered the energy to cast around so frantically for programmes, systems and structures to right the Caribbean ship.

Notes

1 C. Lloyd (with T. Cozier), *Living For Cricket*, London: Stanley Paul, 1980, p. 13.
2 For example, H. McD. Beckles, *The Development of West Indies Cricket*, Vols. 1 and 2, Kingston: University of West Indies Press, 1998, *passim*.

3 T. McDonald, *Viv Richards: The Authorised Biography*, London: Pelham Books, 1984, p. 91.
4 *Red Stripe Caribbean Cricket Quarterly*, October/December 1995, 3.
5 Michael Holding, 'Off the long run', *Red Stripe Caribbean Cricket Quarterly*, April/June 1999, 23.
6 Quoted in *Red Stripe Caribbean Cricket Quarterly*, April/June 1996, 15.
7 Quoted in T. Cozier (ed.) *West Indies Cricket Annual 1989*, Bridgetown: Cozier Publishing, 1989, p. 10.
8 T. Hector, 'Pan-Africanism, West Indies cricket, and Viv Richards', in H. McD. Beckles (ed.), *A Spirit of Dominance: Cricket and Nationalism in the West Indies*, Kingston: Press University of the West Indies, 1998, p. 59.
9 Sir C.A. Burton, R.G. Hughes and K.A.P. Sandiford (eds), *100 Years of Organised Cricket in Barbados 1892–1992*, Bridgetown: Barbados Cricket Association, 1992, p. 25.
10 *Red Stripe Caribbean Cricket Quarterly*, January/March 1997, 4.
11 S. Berry, 'The West Indians in England, 1991', *Wisden Cricketers' Almanack 1992*, London: John Wisden & Co., 1992, p. 296.
12 McDonald, *Viv Richards*, p. 99.
13 T. Cozier, 'The West Indians in England, 2000', *Wisden Cricketers' Almanack 2001*, London: John Wisden & Co., 2001, pp. 421–454.
14 *Caribbean Cricket Quarterly*, April/June 1996, 8.
15 See, for example, J. Garner, *'Big Bird' Flying High*, London: George Weidenfeld & Nicolson, 1988; M. Holding (with T. Cozier), *Whispering Death: The Life and Times of Michael Holding*, London: Andre Deutsch, 1993; C. Lloyd, *Living For Cricket*, London: Stanley Paul, 1980; M. Marshall (with P. Symes), *Marshall Arts: The Autobiography of Malcolm Marshall*, London: Queen Anne Press, 1987; V. Richards, *Hitting Across the Line: An Autobiography*, London: Headline Books, 1991; R. Steen, *Desmond Haynes: Lion of Barbados*, London: H.F. and G. Witherby, 1993.
16 Quoted by T. Marshall, 'The professionalization of West Indies cricket', in H. McD. Beckles (ed.) *A Spirit of Dominance*, pp. 79–80.
17 *Red Stripe Caribbean Cricket Quarterly*, July/September 1994, 26.
18 T. Cozier, *The West Indies: Fifty Years of Test Cricket*, Newton Abbott: Readers Union, 1978, p. 52.
19 T. Cozier, 'The wonder years', *Red Stripe Caribbean Cricket Quarterly*, July/September 1995, 8–9.
20 K.A.P. Sandiford, 'Cricket in the West Indies: The rocky road to test status', in Beckles (ed.) *A Spirit of Dominance*, p. 36.
21 K.A.P. Sandiford, *Frank Worrell: His Record Innings-by-Innings*, Nottingham: Association of Cricket Statisticians and Historians, 1997, pp. 8–9.
22 Sir C. Hunte, 'A question of leadership', *Red Stripe Caribbean Cricket Quarterly*, January/March 2000, 8.
23 K.A.P. Sandiford, 'The contribution of the smaller islands to West Indies cricket', *The Journal of the Cricket Society*, 1998, vol. 19, 29–37.
24 *Red Stripe Caribbean Cricket Quarterly*, January/March 1993, 24.
25 T. Hector, 'Acceptance at last after years of frustration', *The West Indies Cricket Annual 1977*, pp. 13–14.
26 *Red Stripe Caribbean Cricket Quarterly*, October/December 1997, 23.
27 P. Wynne-Thomas, *The Complete History of Cricket Tours At Home and Abroad*, London: Guild Publishing, 1989, pp. 69–70.
28 J. Millette, *The Genesis of Crown Colony Government: Trinidad 1783–1810*, Trinidad: Moko Enterprises, 1970, pp. 1–34.
29 *Wisden Cricketers' Almanack 1993*, London: John Wisden & Co., 1994, p. 1039.
30 Quoted in *Red Stripe Caribbean Cricket Quarterly*, July/September 1994, 12.

31 C. Martin-Jenkins, *World Cricketers: A Biographical Dictionary*, Oxford: Oxford University Press, 1996, pp. 429–30, 433–34.
32 T. Cozier (ed.), *West Indies Cricket Annual 1990*, Bridgetown: Cozier Publishing, 1990, p. 33.
33 Sir G. Sobers (with B. Scovell), *Sobers: Twenty Years at the Top*, London: Macmillan, 1988, p. 167; Lloyd, *Living for Cricket*, pp. 19–20.
34 Quoted in *Red Stripe Caribbean Cricket Quarterly*, October/December 1997, 23.
35 See, for example, K.A.P. Sandiford and P. Lashley, 'The rise and fall of Barbadian cricket', *Cricket Lore*, 2001, Vol. 4, 8–11.
36 Beckles, *Development of West Indies Cricket*. See especially vol. 2: *The Age of Globalization*, pp. 131–34.
37 Beckles, *Development of West Indies Cricket*, vol. 2, pp. 131–2.
38 T. Cozier (ed.) *West Indies Cricket Annual 1982*, Bridgetown: Cozier Publishing, 1982, p. 3.
39 *Red Stripe Caribbean Cricket Quarterly*, April/June 1998, 4.
40 R.K. Whitham, *George A. Headley: His Record Innings-by-Innings*, Nottingham: Association of Cricket Statisticians, undated, p. 29.
41 T. Cozier (ed.) *The West Indies Cricket Annual 1973*, Bridgetown: Cozier Publishing, 1973, pp. 2–3.
42 Cozier (ed.) *The West Indies Cricket Annual 1973*, p. 5.
43 B. Sarbadhikary, 'West Indies cricket: Then and now', *The West Indies Cricket Annual 1971*, pp. 18–20.
44 *Red Stripe Caribbean Cricket Quarterly*, February/April 2001, 3, 8.
45 *Caribbean Cricket Quarterly*, May/July 2001, 51–52.
46 *Red Stripe Caribbean Cricket Quarterly*, July/September 1999, 48.
47 *Red Stripe Caribbean Cricket Quarterly*, October/December 1997, 6. See also *Red Stripe Caribbean Cricket Quarterly*, January/March 1998, 4.
48 *Red Stripe Caribbean Cricket Quarterly*, July/September 1998, 10.
49 H. Beckles (ed.) *An Area of Conquest: Popular Democracy and West Indies Cricket Supremacy*: Kingston: Ian Randle Publishers, 1994; Beckles (ed.) *A Spirit of Dominance*.
50 H. McD. Beckles and B. Stoddart (eds) *Liberation Cricket: West Indies Cricket Culture*, Manchester: Manchester University Press, 1995.
51 *Red Stripe Caribbean Cricket Quarterly*, January/March 1998, 4.
52 *Red Stripe Caribbean Cricket Quarterly*, October/December 1996, 4.
53 Sir C. Hunte, 'A question of leadership', *Red Stripe Caribbean Cricket Quarterly*, January/March 2000, 8–9.

8 Baseball and American exceptionalism

Francis D. Cogliano

> Come, base ball players all and listen to the song
> About our manly Yankee game and pardon what is wrong;
> If the verses do not suit you, I hope the chorus will,
> So join with us, one and all, and sing it with a will.
>   CHORUS
> Then shout, shout for joy, and let the welkin ring,
> In praises of our noble game, for health 'tis sure to bring;
> Come, my brave Yankee boys, there's room enough for all,
> So join in Uncle Samuel's sport – the pastime of base ball.
>   'Ball Days' in the Year A.D. 1858[1]

In 1911 Albert Goodwill Spalding, one of the founders of the National League and an ardent American nationalist declared in a best-selling history of baseball:

> I claim that Base Ball owes its prestige as our National Game to the fact that as no other form of sport it is the exponent of American Courage, Confidence, Combativeness; American Dash, Discipline, Determination; Pluck, Persistency, Performance; American Spirit, Sagacity, Success; American Vim, Vigor, Virility.
>
> Base Ball is the American game par excellence, because its playing demands Brain and Brawn, and American manhood supplies these ingredients in quantity sufficient to spread over the entire continent.[2]

Spalding believed that baseball shared an egalitarian ethos with other American institutions:

> The genius of our institutions is democratic; Base Ball is a democratic game. The spirit of our national life is combative; Base Ball is a combative game. We are a cosmopolitan people, knowing no arbitrary class distinctions, acknowledging none. The son of a President of the United States would as soon play ball with Patsy Flannigan as with

Lawrence Lionel Livingstone, provided only that Patsy could put up the right article. Whether Patsy's dad was a banker or a boiler-maker would never enter the mind of the White House lad. It would be quite enough for him to know that Patsy was up in the game.[3]

Two assumptions lay behind Spalding's comments. The first was that there was a close relationship between baseball and American nationalism. Second, he assumed that the history of the United States and the development of its institutions were the result of unique circumstances. This view of American national distinctiveness, which found wide currency during the late nineteenth and early twentieth centuries and has persisted since then, is often termed 'American exceptionalism'. Spalding's book suggests that it is possible to test the concept of American exceptionalism by considering the history of baseball and the evolution of its place in American life. Although, at first sight, baseball's origins and early history would seem to substantiate American exceptionalism, closer inspection suggests that exceptionalism, and its place in American national identity is a concept in need of revision.

American exceptionalism and sport

'The notion', in Michael Kammen's words, 'that the United States has had a unique destiny and history, or more modestly, a history with highly distinctive features or an unusual trajectory', has a long and distinguished pedigree.[4] Indeed the concept antedates the United States. From John Winthrop's assertion in 1630 that America would be a 'city on a hill' to the explorations of Crevecoeur and Tocqueville in the eighteenth and nineteenth centuries, political and religious leaders and cultural commentators have sought to explain the ways in which America differed from the rest of the world, especially Europe. During the nineteenth century the religious origins of exceptionalism, as articulated by Winthrop, gave way to a nationalism which found expression in the foreign policy of the new republic in Washington's farewell address, the Monroe Doctrine and the westward expansion of the United States under the banner of 'Manifest Destiny'.

At the turn of the twentieth century, American exceptionalism remained important for scholars on both sides of the Atlantic. In 1892, the American historian, Frederick Jackson Turner, asserted that the process of westward expansion and settlement, particularly access to vast amounts of 'free' land, made the United States uniquely democratic, free of the rigid class distinctions and lack of social mobility which characterised Europe during the period.[5] A few years later, the German sociologist Werner Sombart, identified a major preoccupation of twentieth-century students of America when he famously asked: 'Why is there no socialism in the United States?' Like Turner, Sombart believed that American political, social and environmental conditions produced a society that was different from that to be found in the industrialised countries of western Europe.[6] Thereafter, thoughout the twentieth century, American excep- tionalism proved a remarkably durable theme in comparative history.[7]

As it has evolved and been expressed by scholars (both advocates and critics) in the twentieth century, American exceptionalism can be summar- ised as the view that 'the United States avoided the class conflicts, revolu- tionary upheaval, and authoritarian governments of "Europe" and presented the world an example for others to emulate'.[8] In other words, despite the common experience of industrialisation and a shared cultural inheritance, American cultural, social and political development was dis- tinct from that of the other western industrialised democracies. Admirers of the United States often see the product of this exceptionalism as the world's most free society, characterised by social mobility, meritocracy and egalitarianism unimpeded by barriers of class. Because of its global reach and wealth the United States is the world's foremost proponent of democracy and liberal economics which are seen as the keys to expanding human freedom. Often, critics of the contemporary United States also see the country as the product of its unique circumstances. For them the United States is exceptional in its materialism, its willingness to tolerate (and encourage) extremes of wealth and poverty, and its unwillingness to recognise or address its social problems. Its supposed championing of democratic and liberal values is a sham whereby the United States extends a neo-colonial power around the globe. Each of these views takes as given the unique nature of the United States, its history, social organisation and the evolution of its political institutions.[9]

The notion of American exceptionalism is not confined to scholars. Implicitly, the concept is at the heart of American national identity. As a relatively young nation whose borders have changed dramatically over the course of two centuries, and whose citizens are mainly descended from migrants, both voluntary and involuntary, the United States cannot draw on the traditional sources of national identity, such as geography, ethnicity and a long common history. Instead, American identity is closely associ- ated with values, notably independence, self-government, and social mobility. This cluster of ideas at the heart of American national identity is very similar to those derived from the positive interpretation of American exceptionalism delineated above.

The history of sport in America seems to embody the concept of American exceptionalism. The sports which predominate in the other English-speaking countries (except Canada) – football, cricket, and rugby (both codes) – are marginal activities in the United States. In their recent book, *Offside: Soccer and American Exceptionalism*, two American schol- ars, Andrei S. Markovits and Steven L. Hellerman, modify Werner Sombart's classic question and ask: 'Why is there no soccer in the United States?' According to Markovits and Hellerman, the United States has an exceptional sporting culture in that its major sports – baseball, American football, basketball and, to a lesser extent, ice hockey – developed in relative isolation from external influence. They were self-consciously American, completely filling the nation's 'sporting space'. They developed, moreover, in close conjunction with the nation's colleges and universities; were run as 'overtly capitalist' enterprises; and were not subject to external governance by international bodies. Under such circumstances it has been impossible for soccer to find a place within the American sporting culture except as a marginal, recreational activity, despite its popularity as a sport for women and children. Just as in politics, economics and other cultural activities, sport in the United States has developed in a way which is radically different from the sporting cultures which prevail in other parts of the world. Given the importance of sport in mass culture, they insist this sporting exceptionalism has reinforced the place of American distinctiveness in the national identity of the United States.[10]

Baseball is a perfect test for Markovits's and Hellerman's thesis. In the first place, it evolved in relative isolation and developed its unique characteristics in the absence of external influence, seeming to mirror broader American development as articulated by the exponents of exceptionalism, among whom Markovits and Hellerman are the most recent. Put another way, baseball seems the most exceptional of American sports. Second, to a greater degree than any other sporting or cultural activity, the game is intimately associated with the United States and American national identity.

Baseball exceptionalism

Perhaps the greatest proponent of the view that both baseball and the United States are unique was Albert Goodwill Spalding. Born in Byron, Illinois, in September 1850, the teenage Spalding emerged as star pitcher for his local baseball team, Forest City, in Rockford. In 1871 he became a professional, joining the Boston Red Stockings in the National Association. Over the next several years he was the dominant pitcher in professional baseball, leading the National Association in wins for five straight seasons. Behind Spalding's pitching the Red Stockings won four consecutive National Association championships between 1872 and 1875. In 1876 Spalding returned to Illinois to join the Chicago White Stockings of the new National League as a player-manager. Spalding led the National League in victories in 1876 and his White Stockings won the inaugural National League championship. Spalding translated his success on the field into financial success off it. As an administrator he dominated the councils of the National League, just as he had dominated its batters on the field. In 1876, he opened a sporting-goods store which served as the foundation for the fortune Spalding earned by manufacturing and selling equipment for baseball and other sports. In 1878, he began publishing *Spalding's Official Base Ball Guide* which, for 63 years, was the most important baseball annual containing statistics, records, league rules and articles which reflected its founder's views on the state of the game.[11]

In the 1905 edition of his *Base Ball Guide* Spalding called for the creation of a special commission to look into the origins of baseball. Spalding sought to disprove the theory of Henry Chadwick, his friend and fellow baseball pioneer, that baseball had evolved from rounders, the English children's game. Spalding implied that the English-born Chadwick had promoted his 'rounders theory' so as to deny the American origins of baseball. Spalding appointed the members of the commission, all of whom were public figures associated with baseball, himself included. The commissioners conducted their research mainly by corresponding with and interviewing men who could remember how baseball was played in the 1830s and 1840s. Basing its findings on a letter it received from a man named Abner Graves, the commission concluded in 1908 that baseball had been invented at Cooperstown, New York, in 1839, by a schoolboy, Abner Doubleday.[12]

Abner Doubleday did not invent baseball. There is no evidence that Doubleday, a native of Ballston Spa, New York ever attended school in Cooperstown. In 1839 Doubleday was a cadet at West Point. Moreover, a nineteenth-century history of Cooperstown makes no mention of the community's alleged involvement with development of baseball.[13] Nevertheless, the commission's verdict gave the national pastime its own creation myth. According to this view, a schoolboy had crafted the rules of the game for his mates amidst the arcadian splendour to be found along the shores of Lake Otsego. In this Eden-like, setting baseball came to Doubleday, giving the game roots in a rural, idealised America that was becoming a distant memory in the urban, industrial nation where the game flourished by the early twentieth century. Not only did the game's supposed origins connect the nation to its rural past but its origins were uniquely American. If an American schoolboy invented the game in a moment of creative genius then the national pastime was a uniquely American institution.

For Albert Spalding there was a direct correlation between baseball's origins, American national identity, and the game's place in American life. He explained:

> To enter upon a deliberate argument to prove that Base Ball is our National Game, that *it has all the attributes of American origin*, American character and unbounded public favor in America, seems a work of supererogation. It is to undertake the elucidation of patent fact; the sober demonstration of an axiom; it is like a solemn declaration that two plus two equal four.[14]

In 1939 Major League Baseball gave its approval to the Doubleday story when it dedicated the Baseball Hall of Fame in Cooperstown to commemorate the centennial of Doubleday's supposed invention of the game.

Despite Spalding's efforts to disprove the 'rounders theory' in order to claim an American pedigree for baseball the roots of the game lay in Britain. The antecedents of baseball came to North America with British colonists during the seventeenth and eighteenth centuries. The two major British bat and ball games, cricket and rounders, were widely played in eighteenth-century America. The latter game evolved in several forms, mainly in New England, and was very popular. The American variations of rounders were known by a variety of names: 'old cat', 'barn ball', 'sting ball', 'stick ball', 'town ball', 'base' and 'base ball' and 'the New England game'. During the War of Independence, Washington's soldiers played the New England game at Valley Forge and American captives in Britain played the game in prison. During their journey to the Pacific members of the Lewis and Clark expedition sought to teach the game to the Nez Percé Indians in 1806. Each version of the game involved hitting a ball with a bat and running around fixed positions.[15]

Town ball spread throughout New England and beyond during the early years of the nineteenth century. By the 1820s the game had been taken by Yankee immigrants throughout the northeast and into the Midwest. As a consequence, the game's centre of gravity shifted from New England to New York City and its environs. Despite the game's mythical pastoral origins, it was in the industrialising towns and cities of Jacksonian America that baseball developed. In the 1830s clubs sprang up in New York and New Jersey and the 'New England game' of town ball began to evolve into the 'New York game' – baseball. The impact of the game was dramatic. Indeed, David S. Copeland, a nineteenth-century historian, complained that 'weekly winter dances in the Town Hall and the craze over base ball' had 'nearly overthrown' the public education system in Clarendon, New York during the 1830s.[16]

Sometime in the spring and summer of 1842 a group of young New Yorkers began to gather for weekly baseball games at the Elysian Fields in Hoboken, New Jersey.[17] After several years the group formally constituted themselves as the New York Knickerbocker Base Ball Club. One of its leaders, a shipping clerk named Alexander Cartwright, codified the rules for the New York game in 1846. Although local variants remained, the New York version of the game spread throughout the northeast and beyond. Indeed, in 1856 a New York newspaper referred to baseball, as played by the New York rules as 'the national pastime'.[18]

Originally, baseball had an elitist orientation. Its earliest practitioners were often urban professionals. One of the original New York Knickerbockers, a doctor named Daniel Adams, recalled that the team 'included merchants, lawyers, Union bank clerks, insurance clerks and others who were at liberty after 3 o'clock in the afternoon'. Adams provided a list of such men, adding:

Many others were members at one time or another. Besides those named in the list I remember two brothers named O'Brien, who were brokers and afterward became very wealthy. There was also a man named Morgan, who was very successful in business. Henry T. Anthony is the photographic supply dealer who is well-known all over the country through his large New York establishment. Duncan F. Curry was an insurance man, and James Moncrief became, I think, a judge of the Superior Court.

The original members of the Knickerbockers and other New York-area clubs espoused an amateur ethos. Adams recalled: 'They went into it just for exercise and enjoyment, and I think they used to get a good deal more solid fun out of it than the players in the big games do nowadays'. That may have been the case, but Dr Adams also noted that it was difficult to attract club members to training sessions and, owing to the summer holidays which took New York professionals away from the city, the playing season for the team was relatively short.[19]

As the game spread geographically, it also spread down the social scale as teams comprising bankers and other professionals were joined by barkeepers, policemen, firefighters and industrial workers. As the game became more socially inclusive the amateur ethic declined and greater emphasis was placed on competition and winning. By the eve of the Civil War baseball was a well-established activity in urban America. By 1857 there were around 50 clubs in the New York area, 14 of which formed the National Association of Base Ball Players (NABBP) at the behest of the Knickerbocker club. Dr Daniel Adams was elected the first president of the Association which sought to promote the standardisation of playing rules and to regulate inter-club cooperation. The Association had 74 members, mainly in the northeast and Midwest, by the time the Civil War began. By 1866, when the NABBP held its tenth annual convention, its membership had increased to 202 clubs from 17 states and the District of Columbia.[20]

As in so many other areas of American life the Civil War marked a turning point in the history of baseball. The conflict did much to spread the game as it was played by soldiers in both armies and in prison camps. When soldiers returned from the war they spread the game throughout the country.[21] Industrialisation and urbanisation, as well as railroads, facilitated dissemination. Baseball boomed after the war and a conflict developed between those who thought the game should be played by amateurs and those, usually players, who felt that some players should be remunerated for their efforts. Following the 1868 season the NABBP bowed to reality and voted to accept limited professionalism acknowledging that 'nearly all the leading clubs – certainly all the prominent aspirants for the championship – employed professional players, and the fact that the rules prohibiting the custom were mere dead letters'.[22]

In 1869 the Cincinnati Red Stockings became the game's first fully professional team, winning 56 straight games in 1869 and 1870, including victories over the top teams from New York and Brooklyn. Following a continued debate over the role of professionals in the game, a split occurred in the NABBP in 1870 when the advocates of full-fledged professionalism broke away to form the National Association of Professional Base-ball Players (NAPBBP), soon to be shortened to the National Association, (NA).[23] During the first half of the 1870s professionalism in baseball emerged triumphant as the game embraced the cut-throat capitalism which characterised business in Gilded Age America. In 1876, Spalding and a Chicago businessman, William Hulbert, brought leading teams together to create the National League of Professional Baseball Teams, with franchises in the major cities of the northeast and Midwest. Under the National League, the oldest active professional sports league in the world, and its rivals, baseball would be run as a business to provide mass entertainment in America's cities.[24]

In its rise from amateur activity to professional mass entertainment baseball did not go unchallenged. In the 1850s American cricket received more newspaper coverage than baseball and it had more clubs, matches, and followers. When Americans during the mid-nineteenth century listed their sports and games cricket usually featured. As late as 1885 the *New York Sportsman* boasted that it was the 'recognized authority upon all matters of news and opinion in the arena of the turf, the baseball, cricket and athletic fields, and in aquatics'. This suggested that a popular interest in cricket persisted well after the advent of professional baseball. Cricket had been played in America since colonial times and continued to find favour among the large number of British immigrants to the United States during the mid-nineteenth century.[25]

Although cricket, like baseball, was played in the urban northeast, most of its players and followers were British-born. They played the game as a means of maintaining a cultural connection with Britain during a period of growing nativism and xenophobia in the United States. American cricket clubs provided venues for British immigrants to gather and socialise. In terms of class and ethnicity American cricket clubs were exclusive and sought to remain that way. They did not seek nor promote membership or following among native-born Americans. The connection between cricket and Britain, both perceived and real, in American minds undermined the game's attraction as a sport with mass appeal for native-born Americans. In 1857 the New York *Clipper* sought to undermine the prejudice against cricket. The paper argued that it was un-American to reject cricket because of its English origins:

> We recognise no such distinctions as Englishmen, Irishmen, &c., &c., in this country, more especially in sporting circles. We are all Americans, enjoying the same privileges, and looking up to the constitution

of our country as our beacon of light. Setting aside the subject of our nationality, however we cannot conceive what objection there can be in our adoption of whatever is for the good of the community, let it come from whence it may; and that Cricket has that tendency we have evidence sufficient.

The *Clipper* concluded: 'What objection there can be to making cricket an American pastime, we are at a loss to discover'.[26]

The English origins of baseball – via rounders – were lost in the mist of time and conveniently forgotten. By 1859 the editorial page of the New York *Clipper* had given up the attempt to promote cricket as a national game for the United States. 'Cricket has its admirers', noted the paper, 'but it is evident that it will never have the universality that baseball will'. The editor presciently wrote of cricket in the present tense but baseball in the future. Baseball swept cricket aside in the sporting life of nineteenth-century America because it was seen as more inclusive, democratic, and American.[27] Albert Spalding confessed admiration for cricket, which he had played while touring in England with a baseball team in 1874. For Spalding the differences between cricket and baseball were the differences between Britain and America. 'Cricket is a splendid game', conceded Spalding, 'for Britons. It is a genteel game, a conventional game – and our cousins across the Atlantic are nothing if not conventional'. Spalding continued, 'Cricket is a gentle pastime. Base Ball is War! Cricket is an Athletic Sociable, played and applauded in a conventional, decorous and English manner. Base Ball is an Athletic Turmoil, played and applauded in an unconventional, enthusiastic and American manner'. The two games were so rooted in their respective cultures that they could not be transplanted and thus:

> It would be impossible for a Briton, who had not breathed the air of this free land as a naturalized American citizen; for one who had no part or heritage in the hopes and achievements of our country, to play Base Ball, as it would for an American, free from the trammels of English traditions, customs, conventionalities, to play the national game of Great Britain.

Cricket, despite its lineage in America, was seen as English, and hence foreign. Baseball, on the other hand, was viewed as a characteristically American game. Nationalism and national identity explain why baseball flourished and cricket withered in the United States.[28]

By the turn of the twentieth century professional baseball was firmly established at the centre of American sporting life. Its place at the heart of American sporting and popular culture was unchallenged until after the Second World War. Because of the game's importance in American life President Franklin Roosevelt urged in 1942 that professional baseball continue during the war in order to provide recreation and diversion for servicemen and wartime workers.[29] The game's stars, especially those associated with the New York Yankees, such as Babe Ruth, Lou Gehrig, Joe DiMaggio, and Mickey Mantle, were iconic figures whose celebrity was rivalled only by Hollywood's leading lights. The professional game had been racially segregated from the 1880s until Jackie Robinson and the Brooklyn Dodgers integrated the Major Leagues in 1947. Robinson's arrival made professional baseball, long played by African Americans in the Negro Leagues, truly national and opened up new sources of players; African Americans and Latin Americans, just as the Major Leagues expanded the number of franchises and spread to the west coast.[30]

Baseball remained the nation's dominant sport until the 1970s when it was superseded in popularity and mass appeal by American football. Since the 1970s baseball's popularity has declined. This decline is relative when compared to the game's complete domination of the nation's sporting culture in the early twentieth century. The increased popularity of American football, basketball, ice hockey and, latterly, stock car racing, as well as the proliferation of new forms of mass entertainment and cable television channels, not to mention the sport's horrendous labour problems, have led to a decline in attendance at games and television ratings.[31]

Despite its recent travails, many of them self-inflicted, baseball retains an important place in American sporting life and American culture at large. Indeed the history of baseball's origins and evolution seems to embody, in cultural terms, American exceptionalism. The game meets the standards for sporting exceptionalism identified by Markovits and Hellerman – it developed in relative isolation from external influence; it is self-consciously American; it has been run along overtly capitalist lines (complete with franchises going bankrupt, relocating and tortured labour relations); and it is free of the governance of an internationally-recognised body. The apotheosis of baseball's exceptionalism is the sport's championship in America, called the World Series since 1903, although the competition is limited to the 30 North American clubs which are members of Major League Baseball.[32] Viewed another way, baseball is exceptional because it conquered America while football conquered much of the rest of the world.

Baseball represents more than sporting exceptionalism. Its close association with American national identity gives it a place and importance within American culture far in excess of the number of people who attend matches or watch them on television. As Jacques Barzun wrote in 1954: 'Whoever would understand the heart and mind of America had better learn baseball'.[33] More than forty years later the documentary filmmaker, Ken Burns asked:

> What encodes and stores the genetic material of our civilization – passing down to the next generation the best of us, what we hope will

mutate into betterness for our children and our posterity? Baseball provides one answer. Nothing in our daily life offers more of the comfort of continuity, the generational connection of belonging to a vast and complicated American family, the powerful sense of home, the freedom from time's constraints, and the great gift of accumulated memory than does our National Pastime.[34]

Recent events suggest the special place that baseball occupies in American life. In the immediate aftermath of the terrorist attacks on the United States on 11 September, 2001, Bud Selig, the baseball commissioner, called off the night's Major League games. Selig then faced the tricky question as to when the games should resume. With two Major League teams in New York City, the question was particularly difficult. Selig, mindful that Franklin Roosevelt had authorised and encouraged Major League Baseball during the Second World War, was inclined to start the games again on September 15 but he met with criticism from players, fans and some government officials. Eventually Major League games resumed on 18 September. Meanwhile Minor League play was suspended and the Minor League playoffs cancelled. In defending his decision to resume play Selig appealed to the connection between baseball and America. 'I feel it was helpful for us to play again', he explained. 'Baseball is woven so deeply into the national fabric. It means so much to so many people, though what happened Sept. 11 certainly trivializes it'. On the first anniversary of the attacks, Major League Baseball and the broadcaster ESPN arranged to play and broadcast 12 hours of games from 1 pm to 1 am Eastern Standard Time on the grounds that baseball plays a special role in American life. A letter from President George W. Bush was read at each Major League game. 'During the past year', he wrote, 'baseball helped to bring Americans together. In the aftermath of the attacks, an exciting pennant race and World Series were an important part of the healing process'. At Yankee Stadium in New York, a flag recovered from the ruins of the World Trade Center was unfurled and the Yankees dedicated a monument beyond the centre field fence inscribed 'We Remember'. After the singing of the 'Star Spangled Banner' and 'God Bless America' fans spontaneously chanted 'U-S-A, U-S-A'.[35]

Baseball, exceptionalism and American national identity seem to go hand in hand. As the writer Gerald Early declared in 1994, 'there are only three things that America will be known for 2,000 years from now when they study this civilization: the Constitution, jazz music, and baseball. They're the three most beautifully designed things this culture has ever produced'. Early linked baseball and the constitution as expressions of American distinctiveness – sources of its exceptionalism.[36] The same unique circumstances which produced American democracy, also produced its national pastime. Viewed in this way, it is not surprising that America's national game is different from the international game –

football – which dominates global sport. Indeed it must be so because America is different, a product of unique circumstances, as are its institutions, including baseball. The country without socialism almost inevitably would be a country without football. This view, however, is not sustainable. America's baseball exceptionalism is problematic, calling the concept of American exceptionalism into question.

Unexceptional baseball

Implicit in American exceptionalism, whether in its scholarly or popular form, is a comparative approach to the United States. America, after all, can only be exceptional in comparison with someplace else. While many proponents of exceptionalism take comparisons as given and are happy to let them remain implicit, its more sophisticated advocates are interested in making such comparisons. In this they find common ground with practitioners of international and comparative history who frequently dissent from the notion of national exceptionalism. Although scholars have profitably compared the histories and cultures of the United States and Canada, the most common comparison has been across the Atlantic. Winthrop's city on a hill was meant to be seen in Europe and the unspoken addendum to Sombart's question, 'Why is there no socialism in the United States?' is 'as there is in Europe?' Similarly the premise that baseball is exceptional rests on a comparison with Europe. The American attachment to baseball appears to be exceptional when viewed from a transatlantic perspective of a continent dominated by football. However, when viewed from a hemispheric or a transpacific perspective, baseball does not appear to be quite so unique.[37]

Baseball is *not* a uniquely American game. Even Albert Spalding, the great advocate of baseball and American nationalism, who had doubted whether Britons who had not been naturalised Americans and breathed American air could play the game properly, was active in attempts to promote the game outside of the United States. In July and August 1874 he led the Boston Red Stockings and Philadelphia Athletics on a tour of Britain. Although it lost money and failed to convert the British, Spalding was undeterred and led an all-star team on a global tour during 1888 and 1889. The Americans departed San Francisco in November 1888 and visited Hawaii, New Zealand, Australia, Ceylon, Egypt, Italy, France, Britain and Ireland, playing exhibition matches at each stop before returning to New York in April 1889. The tour attracted curiosity but few converts to the American game. Nevertheless, when he wrote his history of the game in 1911, Spalding was keen to note the game's spread to the Caribbean and Asia.[38]

Spalding did not exaggerate in noting the game's international dimension. A survey of players who appeared on Major League rosters during the 2002 season reveals that 73.5 per cent of players were born in the United

States. The remaining 26.5 per cent were born in 18 different countries. Of these, the overwhelming majority were born in the Caribbean basin. No less than 257, or 87.7 per cent, of the foreign-born players and 23.2 per cent of the total number of Major League players were born in the Caribbean with the Dominican Republic (106), Venezuela (51), Puerto Rico (49) and Mexico (20) providing the majority. Below the Major Leagues baseball becomes even more international. For example, in 2001 the Los Angeles Dodgers' team in Florida's Gulf Coast League featured 18 foreign-born players and 29 US-born players. The foreign-born players came primarily from the Caribbean but also included players from Canada, Taiwan and Australia.[39] When one looks beyond the American major and minor leagues the international dimension of baseball becomes even more apparent. Professional leagues exist in the Dominican Republic, Mexico, Cuba, Puerto Rico, and Venezuela, as well as Australia, Japan, Korea and Taiwan, Italy and the Netherlands.[40] From the perspective of the Caribbean basin, rather than the Atlantic, baseball's international dimension is clear.

Table 8.1 Places of birth of 2002 Major League baseball players

Place of birth	Total	%
USA	812	73.5
Non-USA	293	26.5

Table 8.2 Places of birth of foreign-born 2002 Major League baseball players

	Number	Percentage of total	Percentage of foreign-born
Aruba	3	0.27	1.0
Australia	3	0.27	1.0
Belgium	1	0.1	0.3
Colombia	3	0.27	1.0
Canada	11	1.0	3.8
Cuba	14	1.3	4.8
Curacao	2	0.2	0.7
Dominican Republic	106	9.6	36.1
Germany	1	0.1	0.3
Japan	12	1.1	4.1
Mexico	20	1.9	6.8
Nicaragua	3	0.27	1.0
Panama	6	0.5	2.0
Puerto Rico	49	4.4	16.7
South Korea	6	0.5	2.0
Taiwan	1	0.1	0.3
Venezuela	51	4.6	17.4
Vietnam	1	0.1	0.3

Source: The tables are based on information from Tony Nistler and David Walton (eds), *Sporting News Baseball Register: 2003 Edition* (St. Louis: Sporting News, 2002).

The hub of baseball in the Caribbean has been Cuba. As the game spread in the mid-nineteenth century it was brought to the island by Cubans who had travelled in the United States as well as by American sailors and businessmen. In June 1866, American sailors from a sugar freighter played a game against a team of Cuban longshoremen. Two years later the first game between two Cuban clubs, Havana and Matanzas, took place. In Cuba, as in the United States, nationalism was part of the its appeal. Just as Americans adopted baseball as an 'American' game in contrast to the foreign influence of cricket, Cubans also embraced baseball, at least in part, for nationalistic reasons. Many Cubans adopted the game *because* it was of American origin – and hence associated with modernism and self-government – and they played it as a means of resisting Spanish rule. Emilio Sabourín, one of the founders of the Cuban Professional Baseball League, was also active in the independence movement, using the profits from his baseball team to help fund the nationalist cause. When the Cuban War of Independence began in 1895 Sabourín was captured by the Spanish and exiled to North Africa where he died in captivity. During the latter years of Spanish rule in Cuba the colonial authorities periodically attempted to ban baseball as a subversive activity. Playing the game had political implications which were well understood by both the Cubans and the Spanish.[41]

As in the early days of baseball in the United States, baseball in Cuba was first played by affluent, urban professionals, many of whom had American connections. Baseball soon spread throughout Cuban society and Cubans in turn helped to spread the game throughout the Caribbean. Fleeing discord in their own country during the Ten Years' War (1868–1878), Cubans brought the game to the Dominican Republic where the Cuban pattern was replicated – urban professionals adopted the game, established the first teams and leagues, and the sport soon spread throughout society. A Cuban entrepreneur, Emilio Cramer, organized the first teams in Venezuela and Cuban émigrés brought the game to Mexico's Yucatán peninsula.[42] The early history of baseball in the Caribbean suggests parallels with the development of the game in the United States. In the Caribbean, as in the United States, baseball and nationalism went hand in hand.

If middle-class urban professionals laid the foundation for the game in the Caribbean, however, it was American imperialism, both economic and military, which caused the game to flourish there. At the turn of the twentieth century American business interests, especially in the oil, sugar, tobacco, fruit and distilling industries, came to dominate the economic life of the non-Anglophone Caribbean. American businesses sponsored and promoted baseball for their workers as a matter of policy. Many of the most important teams in the various Caribbean leagues were associated with American-sponsored industries and corporations. These were intended to provide entertainment for employees, their families and communities as well as cementing the bonds between workers and their companies. During these years of 'Dollar Diplomacy', as American economic interests in the region increased, so too did American political and diplomatic interests – and interference – in the Caribbean. The result was a much more aggressive and interventionist American policy toward the region and this, in turn, impacted on the development of baseball.

The history of baseball and American military history occasionally intersect with important consequences for the former. The Civil War did much to spread the game beyond the northeast and to make it a truly national game played in all regions of the United States. Similarly, American military intervention in the Caribbean during the early twentieth century helped to foster and promote the game. Between 1898 and 1933 the United States marines landed 34 times in ten different countries – often staying for months or years – in order to protect American economic, political and diplomatic interests in the region. American soldiers and sailors played their national game when they occupied Cuba, the Dominican Republic, Nicaragua, Mexico, Puerto Rico (which became an American colony), Haiti, and Mexico. They often played with and against local players and teams.[43]

American imperialists believed that they could promote baseball, already well established in the region, as means of imposing order and control over people who might resent American military intervention. As James Sullivan, the American ambassador in Santo Domingo, explained in 1913:

> The American national game of baseball is being played and supported here with great enthusiasm. The remarkable effect of this outlet for the animal spirits of the young men, is that they are leaving the plazas where they were in the habit of congregating and talking revolution and resorting to the ball fields where they become wildly partisan each for his favorite team. The importance of this new interest to the young men in a little country ... should not be minimized. It satisfies a craving in the nature of the people for exciting conflict and is a real substitute for the contest in the hill-sides with rifles, if it could be fostered and made important by a league of teams in the various towns in the country.[44]

For local teams, playing against the American occupiers had political significance, especially if they could beat the Americans at their 'national pastime'. If baseball prevented young men from taking to the hills with their rifles, it also served as a less dangerous way to offer symbolic resistance to the United States. Just as Cubans embraced baseball in the 1870s as a means of resisting Spanish imperialism, during the early decades of the twentieth century, Cubans, Puerto Ricans, Nicaraguans, Mexicans, and Dominicans played the game to resist American imperialism. Paradoxically American imperialism and military activity helped to stimulate and encourage baseball in the Caribbean as a means of opposing American influence. In Cuba, after the communist revolution, baseball became especially important in this respect. Since 1959, the Cuban government, at the behest of Fidel Castro, himself a devoted player and fan of the game, has actively promoted the country's national team in international competitions where defeating the United States has been the highest priority. Indeed, for a while the Cubans enjoyed great success, dominating competition at the Pan Am Games and winning gold medals at the 1992 and the 1996 Olympics. By the late 1990s, however, many of Cuba's top players had defected to the United States, tempted by the multimillion dollar contracts to be had in the Major Leagues. The Cuban national team declined and in the 2000 Olympic Games the United States, with a team comprised of college and Minor League players, upset the Cubans to win the gold medal.[45]

The correlation between the development of baseball in the Caribbean and American imperialism suggests that America may not be exceptional. On the contrary there is a striking similarity between the history of baseball and American imperialism and that of cricket and British imperialism. American entrepreneurs, soldiers and diplomats helped to spread baseball through the Spanish-speaking countries of the Caribbean basin in much the same way as their British counterparts had encouraged the growth of cricket in the British Empire during the latter half of the nineteenth century. Just as Cubans, Dominicans, Nicaraguans and Mexicans embraced baseball as a means of resisting American imperialism, so their neighbours in the British West Indies (and beyond) played the English game of cricket as a way of offering cultural resistance to British imperialism.[46]

Conclusion

Baseball has, for 150 years, been closely indentified with American national identity. Its early history reveals that America may be no more unique than other nations. Moreover, its later development is the story of cultural exchange and interaction between regions and nations. Where does the early history of baseball leave the concept of American exceptionalism? When viewed solely from the United States, or from a transatlantic perspective, then the idea of baseball as a unique feature of the American identity seems valid. However, when viewed from the perspective of the Caribbean or the Pacific, then the history of baseball reveals, not American uniqueness, but the similarity between American cultural development and that of its neighbours, as well as the similarity between American and British imperialism. This comparative approach calls into question the centrality of American exceptionalism to American identity.

Baseball may well be central to the national identity of the United States and its citizens and, indeed, a strong argument can be made that such is the case. However, it is important to acknowledge that the game has played an equally important and similar role in the cultures of Cuba, the Dominican Republic and Japan. In those countries, as in the United States, the game played a role in helping to forge national identities during crucial historic periods. In each country the game helped its followers to assert a degree of cultural independence in the face of imperialism. In the American context, the game, complete with a fabricated history of its origins, allowed Americans to assert cultural and sporting independence from its former colonial master. In Cuba, baseball played a direct role in the formation of the independence movement against Spain. In both Cuba and the Dominican Republic, the game helped citizens of relatively poor countries resist American domination, a role which it still plays. The correlation between baseball, national identity and resistance in such disparate cultures suggests that the roots of American identity lie not in the nation's supposed exceptionalism but in what it has in common with other nations. There is little room for exceptionalism in an age of globalisation, nor is there in the history of baseball in America. Albert Spalding's successors will need to write a history of the game which includes Cuban, Dominican and Japanese players as well as legends about New York schoolboys. The rich, complicated history of baseball in the Americas suggests that in their quest to define themselves Americans should not stress the ways in which they are different from Europeans. Rather they should turn away from Europe and consider the common history, including cultural exchange as well as military conflict and economic domination, which binds them to their neighbours.

Acknowledgements

I wish to thank Arnar Arnarson, Owen Dudley Edwards, Mi Källman, Robert Mason, Dil Porter, Adrian Smith and Alan Taylor for their guidance, advice and assistance. The Faculty of Arts at the University of Edinburgh provided financial support which made the completion of this study possible.

Notes

1 H. Chadwick, *The Game of Base Ball,* New York: George Munro, 1868; repr. Columbia, S.C.: Camden House, 1983, p. 178.
2 A.G. Spalding, *America's National Game: Historic Facts Concerning the Beginning, Evolution, Development and Popularity of Base Ball with Personal Reminiscences of its Vicissitudes, Its Victories and Its Votaries*, New York: American Sports Publishing, 1911; repr. Lincoln: University of Nebraska Press, 1992, pp. 4–5.
3 Spalding, *America's National Game*, p. 6.
4 M. Kammen, 'The Problem of American Exceptionalism: A Reconsideration', *American Quarterly*, 1993, vol. 45, 1–43. For recent examples of the huge

literature on this subject see I. Tyrrell, 'American Exceptionalism in an Age of International History', *American Historical Review*, 1991, vol. 96, 1031–55; Byron E. Shafer (ed.) *Is America Different?: A New Look at American Exceptionalism*, New York: Oxford University Press, 1991; J.P. Greene, *The Intellectual Construction of America: Exceptionalism and Identity from 1492 to 1800*, Chapel Hill: University of North Carolina Press, 1993; D.K. Adams and C.A. van Minnen, *Reflections on American Exceptionalism*, Keele: Keele University Press, 1994; G.M. Frederickson, 'From Exceptionalism to Variability: Recent Developments in Cross-National Comparative History', *Journal of American History*, 1995, vol. 82, 587–604; S.M. Lipset, *American Exceptionalism: A Double-Edged Sword*, New York: Norton, 1996; H. V. Nelles *et al.*, 'Review Chapters: American Exceptionalism', *American Historical Review*, 1997, vol. 102, 748–74.

5 See F.J. Turner, *The Frontier in American History*, New York: Henry Holt, 1925. Turner's essay was originally delivered as a conference paper for American Historical Association in 1892. See also D.M. Wrobel, *The End of American Exceptionalism: Frontier Anxiety from the Old West to the New Deal*, Lawrence, Kansas: University of Kansas Press, 1993.

6 W. Sombart, *Why is There No Socialism in the United States?*, London: Macmillan, 1976, originally published as *Warum gibt es in den Vereinigten Staaten keinen Sozialismus?*, Tübingen: 1906. Also see K. Voss, *The Making of American Exceptionalism: The Knights of Labor and Class Formation in the Nineteenth Century*, Ithaca: Cornell University Press, 1993; S.M. Lipset and G. Marks, *It Didn't Happen Here: Why Socialism Failed in the United States*, New York: Norton, 2000.

7 During the Cold War, Louis Hartz suggested that the absence of a feudal past had made America uniquely free. See L. Hartz, *The Liberal Tradition in America*, New York: Harcourt Brace, 1955; 'Comment', *Comparative Studies in Society and History*, 1963, vol. 5, 279–84, 'American Historiography and Comparative Analysis: Further Reflections', *Comparative Studies in Society and History,* 1963, vol. 5, 365–77; M. Meyers, 'Louis Hartz, the Liberal Tradition in America: An Appraisal', *Comparative Studies in Society and History*, 1963, vol. 5, 261–68.

8 As quoted in Tyrell, 'American Exceptionalism', p. 1031.

9 For a recent examples of the exceptionalist interpretation which presents the United States in a favourable light see D. D'Souza, *What's So Great about America*, Washington: Regnery Publishing, 2002. For interpretations unfavourable to the United States see, W. Hutton, *The World We're In*, London: Little Brown, 2002: also G. Vidal, *The Last Empire*, New York: Doubleday, 2002.

10 A.S. Markovits and S.L. Hellerman, *Offside: Soccer and American Exceptionalism*, Princeton: Princeton University Press, 2001.

11 P. Levine, *A.G. Spalding and the Rise of Baseball*, New York: Oxford University Press, 1985; A. Bartlett, *Baseball and Mr. Spalding*, New York: Farrar, Strauss & Young, 1951.

12 *Spalding's Official Base Ball Guide, 1905*, New York: American Sports Publishing, 1905; repr. St. Louis: Horton, 1992, pp. 3–13; *and* 1906, p. 6; *also* 1908, pp. 35–49. All of the relevant documents relating to the Commission can be found in D.A. Sullivan (ed.) *Early Innings: A Documentary History of Baseball, 1825–1908*, Lincoln: University of Nebraska Press, 1995, pp. 279–95.

13 S.M. Shaw and I.N. Arnold, *A Centennial Offering: Being a Brief History of Cooperstown with Other Interesting Local Facts and Data*, Cooperstown: Freeman's Journal, 1886. Shaw and Arnold make only one mention of baseball, noting that, in 1877, 'a famous game of old-fashioned base ball was played here' (p. 105).

14 Spalding, *America's National Game*, pp. 3–4, emphasis added. That the game was created at the same time and place that James Fenimore Cooper was 'creating' American literature and its first national hero, Natty Bumpo, who inhabited a literary frontier as mythic as Doubleday's playing field, reinforced the national distinctiveness of Doubleday's game. See A. Taylor, *William Cooper's Town: Power and Persuasion on the Frontier of the Early American Republic*, New York: Knopf, 1995.

15 For one version of the rules of town ball see R. Carver, 'A Description of "Base, or Goal Ball"', *The Book of Sports*, Boston: Lily, Wait, Colman and Holden, 1834; repr. in Sullivan, *Early Innings*, p. 3. The best source for the early history of baseball is H. Seymour, *Baseball: The Early Years*, New York: Oxford University Press, 1960. Also see G.C. Ward and K. Burns, *Baseball: An Illustrated History*, New York: Knopf, 1994, pp. 3–4; J. Thorn, 'Our Game', in J. Thorn, P. Palmer and M. Gershman, (eds) *Total Baseball: The Official Encyclopedia of Major League Baseball*, seventh edition, Kingston, New York: Total Sports, 2001, pp. 1–10. For rounders and its relationship with baseball see D.H. Fischer, *Albion's Seed: Four British Folkways in America*, New York: Oxford University Press, 1989, pp. 148–51.

16 D.S. Copeland, *History of Clarendon from 1810 to 1888*, Buffalo: Courier Co., 1889, p. 68. For evidence of the spread of Town Ball see *The Constitution of the Olympic Ball Club of Philadelphia*, Philadelphia: Private Printing, 1838. Other local histories trace the progress and development of baseball in New York during the 1830s. See E. Briggs, *History of the Original Town of Concord*, Rochester: Union and Advertiser Co., 1883, pp. 526, 839; A.H. Masten, *The History of Cohoes, New York from its Earliest Settlement to the Present*, Albany: J. Munsell, 1877, p. 141; W.P. Boyd, *History of the Town of Conesus, Livingston, Co., N. Y.: From Its First Settlement in 1793 to 1887*, Conesus, N.Y.: Boyd's Job Print, 1887, p. 132. For a description of the game as played in Rochester, New York, during the Jacksonian period see T. Weed, *Autobiography of Thurlow Weed*, Boston: Houghton Mifflin, 1884, p. 203.

17 Accounts of matches played between New York-area teams can be found in the *New York Morning News*, 22, 25 October 1845, reprinted in Sullivan, *Early Innings*, pp. 11–13. See also 'Baseball's Disputed Origin is Traced Back, Back, Back', *New York Times*, 8 July 2001.

18 *New York Mercury*, 5 December 1856; Seymour, *Baseball: The Early Years*; Ward and Burns, *Baseball*, pp. 4–20. Cartwright's rules were revised in 1854. See C. Peverelly, *The Book of American Pastimes*, New York: 1866, pp. 346–48. For developments in New York see M. Adelman, *A Sporting Time: New York City and the Rise of Modern Athletics, 1820–1870*, Chicago: University of Illinois Press, 1986; also S. Wilentz, *Chants Democratic: New York City and the Rise of the American Working Class, 1788–1850*, New York, Oxford University Press, 1984.

19 For Adams see 'Memoirs of the Father of Base Ball', *The Sporting News*, 29 February 1896, reprinted in Sullivan, *Early Innings*, pp. 13–18.

20 *The Spirit of the Times* (New York), 31 January 1857; Peverelly, *Book of American Pastimes*, p. 508. Seymour, *Baseball: The Early Years*, p. 68. For baseball prior to professionalism see D. Voigt, *American Baseball from Gentleman's Sport to the Commissioner System*, Norman: University of Oklahoma Press, 1966; I. Tyrell, 'The Emergence of Modern American Baseball, *c.*1850–80', in R. Cashman and M. McKernan (eds) *Sport in History: The Making of Modern Sporting History*, Brisbane: Queensland University Press, 1979; T. Melville, *Early Baseball and the Rise of the National League*, Jefferson, N.C., McFarland, 2002, Chapters 1–2; W. Goldstein, *Playing for Keeps: A History of Early Baseball*, Ithaca; Cornell University Press, 1991; J. Tygiel, 'The National Game:

Reflections on the Rise of Baseball in the 1850s and 1860s', in J..Tygiel (ed.), *Past Time: Baseball as History*, New York: Oxford University Press, 2000, pp. 3–12; J.L. Terry, *Long Before the Dodgers: Baseball in Brooklyn, 1855–1884*, Jefferson, N.C.: McFarland, 2002.

21 For the Civil War see P.E. Millen, *From Pastime to Passion: Baseball and the Civil War*, Bowie, Md., 2001; G.B. Kirsch, *Baseball in Blue and Gray: The National Pastime during the Civil War*, Princeton: Princeton University Press, 2003; W.J. Ryczek, *When Johnny Came Sliding Home: The Post-Civil War Baseball Boom, 1865–1870*, Jefferson, N.C.: McFarland, 1998.

22 H. Chadwick, *DeWitt's Base Ball Guide*, New York: R. M. Dewitt, 1869, p. 24.

23 For the continued debate over professionalism see the *New York Clipper*, 18 December 1869; also J.H. Hainie, *1871 – Baseball Rules and Regulations*, Chicago: J.W.O. Kelly, 1871, pp. 12–13.

24 For the rise of professionalism and the National League see Seymour, *Baseball: The Early Years*; Melville, *Early Baseball*; S. D. Guschov, *The Red Stockings of Cincinnati: Base Ball's First All-Professional Team and Its Historic 1869 and 1870 Seasons*, Jefferson, N.C.: McFarland, 1998; Spalding, *America's National Game*, Chapters 14–16.

25 *New York's Great Industries*, Chicago: Historical Publishing, 1885, p. 180. Also see S.R. Cathrop, *A Lecture on Physical Development*, Boston: Ticknor and Fields, 1859, p. 23; also N. Sands, *The Philosophy of Teaching*, New York: Harper and Brothers, 1869, p. 19. For the place of cricket in nineteenth-century America see G. Kirsch, *The Creation of American Team Sports: Baseball and Cricket, 1838–1872*, Chicago: University of Illinois Press, 1989 and T. Melville, *The Tented Field: A History of Cricket in America*, Bowling Green, Ohio: Bowling Green University Press, 1998. Between 1820 and 1914 2.6 million English immigrants arrived in the United States. R. Daniels, *Coming to America: A History of Immigration and Ethnicity in American Life*, New York: Harper Perennial, 1991, p. 123.

26 *New York Clipper*, 16 May 1857, reprinted in Sullivan, *Early Innings*, p. 25.

27 *New York Clipper* as quoted in Markovits and Hellerman, *Offside*, p. 60; see pages 58–60 for a discussion of cricket and baseball in nineteenth-century America.

28 Spalding, *America's National Game*, pp. 5, 7, 9. In the first history of baseball published in 1888 Jacob Morse declared: 'No, the American would not sacrifice a morning for a cricket game. He is quick and active, nervous and energetic, and he wants his sport to answer the requirements of his temperament. Base ball has answered his purpose admirably'. J. Morse, *Sphere and Ash: History of Base Ball*, Boston: J.F. Spofford, 1888; repr. Columbia S.C., Camden House, 1984, p. iii.

29 Most professional players as able-bodied young men were subject to military service – many volunteered and others were drafted. For most of the war Major League baseball was played by older players and men unfit for military service.

30 For baseball during the early twentieth century see H. Seymour, *Baseball: The Golden Age*, New York: Oxford University Press, 1971; L.S. Ritter (ed.) *The Glory of Their Times: The Story of the Early Days of Baseball, Told by the Men who Played It*, New York: Random House, 1966. D. Halberstam, *Summer of '49*, New York: William Morrow, 1989, and *October 1964*, New York: Villard Books, 1994, provide an analysis of baseball's place in post-war America from the perspective of the New York Yankee teams which dominated the game during the period. The definitive work on desegration is J. Tygiel, *Baseball's Great Experiment: Jackie Robinson and His Legacy*, New York: Oxford University Press, 1983.

31 Since 1972 there have been eight work stoppages in Major League baseball

including a prolonged strike in 1994–95. For a discussion of baseball's development since the 1960s see Thorn, 'Our Game', pp. 7–10.

32 Baseball has a long history at the international level. The first international match was held on 15 July 1912, at the Stockholm Olympics, when a team of Swedes was defeated by a team of Americans drawn from the United States track and field athletes. Baseball featured intermittently as an exhibition sport at the Olympics in 1936, 1964, 1984 and 1988; and as a medal sport in 1992, 1996 and 2000. In 1938 the United States and Britain competed for the 'World Championship', hosted by Britain. Perhaps the most important international baseball competition has been at the Pan Am Games, which has been dominated by Cuba. Most revealing is that these international competitions of America's 'national pastime' have attracted little interest in the United States. See D. Osinski, 'Baseball and the Olympics', in J. Thorn, P. Palmer and M. Gershman (eds) *Total Baseball: The Official Encyclopedia of Major League Baseball*, fourth edition, New York: Viking, 1995, pp. 582–3 and 'Going Global' in A. Simpson (ed.) *Baseball America 2001 Almanac*, Durham, N.C.: Baseball America, p. 23.

33 J. Barzun, *God's Country and Mine,* Boston: Little Brown, 1954, cited in N. Dawidoff, *Baseball: A Literary Anthology*, New York: Library of America, 2002, p. 254.

34 K. Burns and L. Novick, 'Preface' in Ward, *Baseball: An Illustrated History*, p. xviii. This best-selling book accompanied Burns's eighteen-hour documentary history, *Baseball*, shown on Public Television in the United States in 1994.

35 Selig quoted in A. Simpson, (ed.) *Baseball America: 2002 Almanac*, Durham, N. C.: Baseball America, 2002, pp. 5–6. For the commemorations on 11 September 2002 see *New York Times*, 12 September 2002 and 'Baseball Reflects on Sept. 11 Anniversary', http://espn.go.com/gen/news/2002/0910/1429932.html. Throughout the 2002 season 'God Bless America' replaced 'Take Me Out to the Ballgame' as the song played during the seventh-inning stretch at major league games.

36 As quoted in Ward and Burns, *Baseball: An Illustrated History*, p. 463. There are myriad other examples linking baseball with American identity and, implicitly, an exceptionalist interpretation of the United States. In film and literature baseball is associated with America to a degree which does not pertain to the other American sports. For baseball and literature see Dawidoff, *Baseball: A Literary Anthology*. 'More good baseball books appear in a single year than have been written about [American] football in the past fifty years'. T. Boswell, *The Heart of the Order*, New York: Doubleday, 1989, p. 31. For baseball films see Bob Carroll, 'Reel Baseball: The Movies', in *Total Baseball*, fourth edition, pp. 633–40.

37 For a superb critique of exceptionalism from the perspective of international history see Tyrrell, 'American Exceptionalism'. For exceptionalists who embrace the comparative approach see S.M. Lipset, *Continental Divide: The Value and Institutions of the United States and Canada*, New York: Routledge, 1989 and *American Exceptionalism: Double-Edged Sword*; G.M. Frederickson, 'From Exceptionalism to Variability: Recent Developments in Cross-National Comparative History', *Journal of American History*, 1995, vol. 82, 587–604.

38 Spalding, *America's National Game*, Chapters 13, 18, 26–8. 'The American Baseball Players', *The Times* (London), 13 March 1889, *New York Clipper*, 13 April 1889, reprinted in Sullivan, *Early Innings*, pp. 173–8.

39 Simpson, *Baseball America: 2002 Almanac*, p. 160.

40 Simpson, *Baseball America: 2002 Almanac*, pp. 359–74; 'International Baseball Results', *Total Baseball*, seventh edition, pp. 2481–4.

41 For an analysis of the relationship between baseball and the Cuban independence movement see L.A. Pérez, Jr., 'Between Baseball and Bullfighting: The Quest for Nationality in Cuba, 1868–1898', *Journal of American History*, 1994, vol. 81. 493–517. The definitive work on Cuban baseball is R.G. Echevarría, *The Pride of Havana: A History of Cuban Baseball*, New York: Oxford University Press, 1999. R. Ruck, 'Baseball in the Caribbean', in *Total Baseball*, fourth edition, pp. 560–8 is a very concise overview. See also S. Fainaru and R. Sanchez, *The Duke of Havana: Baseball, Cuba and the Search for the American Dream*, New York: Villard Books, 2001; J.S. Figueredo, *Cuban Baseball: A Statistical History, 1878–1961*, Henderson, N.C.: McFarland, 2002; M.H. Jamail, *Full Count: Inside Cuban Baseball*, Carbondale, Ill.: Southern Illinois University Press, 2000.

42 On the Cuban role in dispersing baseball in the Caribbean see Pérez, 'Between Baseball and Bullfighting', p. 514 and Ruck, 'Baseball in the Caribbean', p. 561. On baseball in the Dominican Republic see A.M. Klein, *Sugarball: The American Game, the Dominican Dream*, New Haven: Yale University Press, 1991; and 'Culture, Politics, and Baseball in the Dominican Republic', *Latin American Perspectives*, 1995, vol. 22, 111–30; and R. Ruck, *The Tropic of Baseball: Baseball in the Dominican Republic*, Lincoln: University of Nebraska Press, 1999. For Mexico see G. Joseph, 'Forging a Regional Pastime: Class and Baseball in the Yucatán', in J. Arbena, (ed.) *Sport and Society in Latin America*, Westport, Conn.: Greenwood, 1987, pp. 29–62 and A.M. Klein, *Baseball on the Border: A Tale of Two Laredos*, Princeton: Princeton University Press, 1997.

43 For baseball and the armed forces see E.M. Coffman, 'Army Life on the Frontier, 1865–1898', *Military Affairs*, 1956, vol. 20, 193–201; also S.W. Pope, 'An Army of Athletes: Playing Fields, Battlefields, and the American Military Sporting Experience, 1890–1929', *Journal of Military History*, 1995, vol. 59, 435–56. Later a similar pattern whereby American military occupation encouraged previous indigenous development occurred in Japan and Korea. The Philippines are an exception to this pattern. J.E. Reeves, *Taking in a Game: A History of Baseball in Asia*, Lincoln: University of Nebraska Press, 2002; Y. Nagata and J.B. Holway, 'Japanese Baseball', in *Total Baseball*, fourth edition, pp. 547–59. In Japan baseball was embraced after the 1890s as a team sport which could be used to resist western domination. In this the Japanese example parallels developments in Cuba. See D. Roden, 'Baseball and the Quest for National Dignity in Meiji Japan', *American Historical Review*, 1985, vol. 85, 511–34.

44 James M. Sullivan to William Jennings Bryan, 1 November 1913, cited in Pérez, 'Between Baseball and Bullfighting', p. 517.

45 For baseball as resistance to American imperialism see Pérez, 'Between Baseball and Bullfighting', pp. 515–17. For American expansion in the Caribbean and Latin America see, B.R. Beede, (ed.) *The War of 1898 and U.S. Interventions, 1898–1934*, New York: Garland, 1994; M. Boot, *The Savage Wars of Peace: Small Wars and the Rise of American Power*, New York: Basic Books, 2002; G. M. Joseph *et al.* (eds) *Close Encounters of Empire: Writing the Cultural History of U.S.–Latin American Relations*, Durham: N.C., Duke University Press, 1999; P.H. Smith, *Talons of the Eagle: Dynamics of United States-Latin American Relations*, New York: Oxford University Press, 1999; L. Schoultz, *Beneath the United States: A History of U.S. Policy Toward Latin America*, Cambridge, Mass.: Harvard University Press, 1998; M.A. Renda, *Taking Haiti: Military Occupation and the Culture of U.S. Imperialism, 1915–1940*: Chapel Hill: University of North Carolina Press, 2001; A. Iriye, *The Cambridge History of American Foreign Relations*, vol. 3: *Globalizing America, 1913–1945*, Cambridge: Cambridge University Press, 1993.

46 See B. Stoddart and K.A.P. Sandiford (eds) *The Imperial Game: Cricket, Culture and Society*, Manchester: Manchester University Press, 1998. For an instructive comparison between American and British imperialism at the turn of the twentieth century see P.A. Kramer, 'Empires, Exceptions, and Anglo-Saxons: Race and Rule between the British and United States Empres, 1880–1910', *Journal of American History*, 2002, vol. 88, 1315–53.

9   Black against gold

New Zealand–Australia sporting rivalry in the modern era

Adrian Smith

A sceptic might start by asking whether there is in fact a history of sporting rivalry between Australia and New Zealand. From the 'Australasian' Olympians and Davis Cup winners at the start of the twentieth century to the joint coaching initiatives at the end, there exists a strong tradition of collaboration. Looking beyond sport, current historiography has rediscovered common interests and a shared history while still acknowledging the markedly different paths that Australia and New Zealand trod from the late nineteenth century through to the mid-1980s.[1] This prompts the question, do the two countries share a mutual interest in beating a common foe (or foes) rather than each other? Ask Australian sports fans what they derive most satisfaction from, and the answer is predictable – beating the Poms. The Ashes remains the most visible symbol of a historic antagonism between the one-time 'mother country' and a young nation for too long handicapped by an unnecessary sense of cultural cringe. The surprising resilience of the latter reinforced the significance of sport as an affirmation of Australia's capacity to take on the world, and win.[2] Anglo-Australian sporting rivalry across the past 130 years or so has been characterised by fierce antagonism, with cricket embodying a range of emotions, from grudging respect through to mutual loathing.[3] The notorious 1932–33 'bodyline' tour provoked a genuine crisis in relations between London and Canberra, far outweighing the diplomatic spat sparked off in 1981 when Trevor Chappell's underarm bowling left New Zealand batsmen incandescent.[4]

The Ashes contest, from its earliest days, has never been marked by Australian deference, in sharp contrast to so many other facets of the imperial relationship before and even after the pivotal date of February 1942 (the British surrender of Singapore to Japan saw Canberra look to Washington as its future guarantor of national security). Arguably, a marked feature of the postcolonial relationship is *English* deference, evidenced by the winter exodus of young talent to Adelaide's cricket academy in the forlorn hope that they can acquire a level of physical and mental fitness unattainable at home. The assumption that most British – for which read English – sportsmen, and more latterly sportswomen, lack the physique and mental toughness of their Antipodean counterparts has a long history. The superior fitness of colonial yeomanry in the Boer War and the all-conquering rugby tours of 1905 and 1906 confirmed the worst fears of Whitehall policy-makers and their eugenicist advisers concerning the degenerative consequences of urban industrialisation upon the 'Anglo-Saxon mother race'.[5] For most of the twentieth century administrators and coaches in Britain were happy to concede that conditions below the Equator advantaged athletes in terms of physical prowess; but they were reluctant to concede that facilities and training methods were demonstrably superior to existing arrangements at home. It is difficult to identify a sport, and cricket would be the most obvious contender, where comprehensive defeat prompted root and branch reform. Profound shifts in the global economy from the 1980s, and the financial consequences of failure in those sports still coming to terms with the harsh realities of professionalism, saw a marked shift in attitude. The remarkable record of the Australian Institute of Sport (AIS) after 1992 confirmed what had long been obvious out on the park or in the pool, namely the superiority of southern hemisphere methods in enhancing the performance of elite athletes.[6]

By 2001 the trickle of Australian and Kiwi coaches in to Britain and Ireland had become a flood. Nor was their presence restricted to rugby. The evident success of Australia's academy system across such a wide range of sports prompted governing bodies in Britain to recruit proven administrators as their CEOs, witness the chief executives of both Sport England and the new English Institute of Sport. One factor in the success of the 2002 Commonwealth Games was the recruitment of thirty officials from the team that had planned the Olympics two years earlier. Australia's impressive medal haul in Sydney, repeated in Manchester, vindicated the aggressive, top-down strategy adopted over a decade earlier. The success of the AIS, and its parent body, the Australian Sports Commission, warrants close attention in any discussion of sport and national identity in the South Pacific. Thus, a major part of this chapter will examine the impact of Australian sporting success upon policy making in New Zealand. How did successive governments in Wellington endeavour to emulate the much grander initiatives emanating out of Canberra? With only a fifth of its neighbour's population, and an economy still reeling from the 1984 Labour Government's enthusiastic embrace of the free market, could – and can – New Zealand ever hope to compete? Notwithstanding the argument that, given the comparative size of populations, and the levels of funding for elite athletes, New Zealand's record in the Olympics is superior to Australia's, how can a small nation in a harsh economic climate continue to punch so far above its weight?[7]

New Zealand's 2003 humbling in the America's Cup exposed the tension between national ambition and commercial reality. Unlike their Tasman neighbours, too many Kiwis naively assumed that professional sportsmen and women would still be motivated by pure patriotism, indifferent to the lucrative rewards of an overarching corporate loyalty. Arguably Australia remains more comfortable with the demands as well as the rewards of globalisation, not least because of its pivotal role in the telecommunications revolution of the past 25 years. Satellite/cable TV is identified as the key factor in ensuring that today's sporting rivalry is far more visible than at any time in the past. Competition between the two countries is intense, and it is in the interest of the broadcasters that this be the case.[8] The notion of invented tradition, enthusiastically embraced by the marketing managers of Sky, Foxtel and Channel Nine, also extends to iconography. Hence location, dress, and personality are all considered as constructions of nationhood, with New Zealand the pioneer in forging a global identity, albeit at the expense of gender and/or ethnic sensibilities.[9]

Inventing a rivalry

As suggested at the outset, for the average Australian sports buff no victory is sweeter than a triumph at Lords. Similarly, over the past two decades even the most diehard Australian rules football or rugby league fan wallows in the euphoria of a Wallaby win at Twickenham. Retaining rugby union's Bledisloe Cup at Eden Park undoubtedly gives cause for national rejoicing, but winning a test series on the other side of the Tasman has always ranked low on any Australian cricketer's CV – the Kiwis were not accorded senior status until 1946 and have remained very much the junior partner ever since.[10] In contrast, any cricket contests between the two countries have always been viewed differently in New Zealand. David and Goliath would be an exaggeration; it was more a case of a younger brother taking on his big brother. This quasi-sibling rivalry is not new, though it has recently become more intense.[11]

Until the 1980s the potential for intense rivalry between the Antipodean neighbours was in fact very limited, with netball and sailing often providing the fiercest competition. The Australians simply did not take New Zealand seriously as a cricketing nation, notwithstanding a healthy respect for players like Richard Hadlee and Martin Crowe. Rugby league had increasingly been downgraded to a minority sport for Maori, ignoring the fact that honours were even between both countries up until the late 1950s. There were no great Kiwi swimmers or tennis players capable of challenging postwar giants like Dawn Fraser or Ken Rosewall.[12] On the track New Zealand's golden age of middle-distance running arrived just as Australia's came to an end.[13] The New Zealand sports fan will undoubtedly find any victory over Australia especially satisfying, but historically the greatest cause for celebration has been if the All Blacks beat the British Lions or the Springboks. Thus, far more attention has been given to South Africa than Australia as the supreme test of the nation's sporting mettle.[14]

It is often forgotten that, until the Ella brothers provided a much needed spark of inspiration in the late 1970s, rugby union in Australia had been in the doldrums since the establishment of league before the First World War. Union was seen as a predominantly white Protestant middle-class game confined largely to affluent suburbs in Queensland and New South Wales. As a consequence the All Blacks placed the Wallabies firmly in the second division – for Lions touring sides Sydney provided a warm-up match en route to the serious stuff.[15] Spurred on by the likes of Mark Ella and David Campese, the Wallabies became equal partners with their two southern hemisphere rivals by 1984. Ella was Native Australian and Campese of Italian descent. Their success went a long way to transforming rugby's image among 'ordinary' Australians, even if the popularity and strength in depth of league and football thwarted any credible attempt to establish union as a genuinely national sport.[16] The importance of this development for the All Blacks, however, was that the Wallabies emerged as a major force in world rugby at precisely the moment when South Africa, the traditional enemy, had been forced back inside the *laager*.

The traumatic yet perhaps cathartic experience of the Springboks' 1981 tour had ensured that the South Africans would never again visit New Zealand so long as Apartheid survived intact. Any All Black tour would be so mired in controversy that the chances of its actually taking place would be remote, as proved to be the case.[17] With the Springboks literally out of the game, a now rampant Wallabies side filled the gap, their victory in the 1991 World Cup confirming their new status. The Bledisloe Cup in the 1980s became far more evenly contested and a serious focal point for Australian-New Zealand rivalry. As far as that rivalry was concerned sport could now be taken seriously as symbolising both nations' complex political, commercial, cultural and emotional inter-relationship, the origins of which could be traced back to before Federation in 1901 or even the Treaty of Waitangi in 1840. The All Blacks were playing to defend national pride, and that was enough. The Australians, with one eye always on the Poms, found it hard to place this sibling rivalry on a similar pedestal.

By the late 1980s there was growing recognition that rugby league in its Auckland heartland was no longer a Maori preserve (if it ever was): New Zealand would have to play a key role in convincing rival media moguls Rupert Murdoch and Kerry Packer that here was a genuinely global sport. At the same time both the terrestial and emerging satellite/cable stations had begun to appreciate that southern hemisphere netball was a remark-ably telegenic sport. Audiences, particularly in New Zealand, confirmed netball's appeal to viewers of both sexes, with a consequent benefit in attracting fresh advertising revenue. Netball in Australia and New Zealand is so superior to the sport as played on any other continent that every contest between the two nations is tantamount to a world champi-onship.[18]

By the mid-1990s it was clearly in the interest of transnational TV stations to play up the significance and the intensity of Australia and New Zealand going head to head. Not surprisingly, cricket had led the way here, with the inauguration of the Trans-Tasman Trophy in 1985 intended to convince Channel Nine viewers that the fifth day of the Wellington test was an important date in the sporting calendar. Murdoch's News Corp looked to southern hemisphere competition as a major element in its regional and even global sports coverage.[19] In rugby league, News Corp, with its plans for a Super League in both hemispheres, took legal action against the sport's official body, which favoured a deal with Kerry Packer. After a particularly bloody struggle the outcome was today's National Rugby League (NRL). As in Britain, where the Super League's international credentials rested on a token French presence, the Auckland Warriors ensured News Corp's heavy promotion of the NRL across the Tasman divide. The Paris experiment failed miserably, and the same might have been true in New Zealand had the Warriors not belatedly emerged as winners, prompting a substantial boost to viewing figures. Television was also the agent of fundamental changes in union, notably the International Rugby Board's decision in 1995 that the game could go open. That year's World Cup had culminated in the $564 million deal to create the Super 12 and the Tri-Nations competitions. The Bledisloe Cup was effortlessly integrated in to the new structure, and sold to an expanded audience of armchair spectators as the continuation of a historic struggle waged relentlessly by successive generations of Wallabies and All Blacks.[20] The banality of the tournament for much of its history was conveniently forgotten as audience ratings became a prime driver in establishing the centrality of Tasman rivalry to the sporting calendar. The success of Super 12's Auckland Blues impacted upon gates for their league rivals, but the pendulum swung back when the renamed *New Zealand* Warriors reached the NLR grand final in October 2002. A clever marketing ploy had been vindicated in that both Maori and Pakeha were encouraged to unite behind a club posing as the national side, and with far greater potential for success in Australia than the real national side could anticipate in any future test series.

Losing that old *Black Magic* – the cautionary tale of the America's Cup

A further focus for rivalry is of course sailing, and races such as the Sydney-Hobart or Trans Tasman have often been portrayed as the ultimate test of Australasia's premier yachtsmen. Australia's 1983 triumph in the America's Cup encouraged Auckland boatbuilders, adventure capitalists, and 12 metre crews to build on Kiwi victories in ocean-going races. Sailing was the one sport other than rugby union where New Zealand could legitimately claim to be a major global player. Alan Bond's crew had broken the spell, and capturing the America's Cup from Australia was a further incentive to investors already aware that defending the title would mean an enormous commercial boost to Auckland's ambitious plans for waterfront development.[21] The success of *Australia II* had highlighted the importance of technological innovation in a competition where the crews were evenly matched, while demonstrating the extent to which beating the Americans could raise national morale. New Zealand had the technical expertise *and* the incentive: only 1 per cent of Australians sailed, so if the trophy was to remain in the South Pacific then its natural home should be Auckland.[22] Furthermore, the growing strain on relations with Washington, culminating in New Zealand's 1987 exclusion from the ANZUS Treaty over its non-nuclear policy, reinforced the case for keeping the trophy in home waters.

In fact Dennis Conner regained the America's Cup at the first attempt, and New Zealand crews experienced mixed fortunes over succeeding years. The 1988 challenge ended up in court, with judgement found in favour of the Americans. Kiwis felt cheated but a crucial outcome was replacement of the 12 metre with a new class of boat. The other key development was Peter Blake's appointment as head of the Team New Zealand challenge. By the time *Black Magic* arrived in San Diego in 1995, Kiwi crews had won the Admiral's Cup, dominated the Whitbread Round the World Race, and smashed the record for sailing nonstop around the globe. Skippers and helmsmen such as Russell Coutts, Brad Butterworth, and Blake himself were in a class of their own, and proved it by trouncing Conner's crew 5–0, repeating the feat against Italy in 2000.[23] As signalled by the name of the syndicate, winning and then retaining the America's Cup was seen as a national achievement, and celebrated as such. New Zealanders remained adamant that theirs was the world's greatest rugby nation. Yet since 1987 they had lacked demonstrable proof (and what was worse Australia had twice usurped their title). However, the America's Cup confirmed what even the most landlocked Kiwi had known all along, that when it came to sailing they were simply the best.

The bubble soon burst: Blake was murdered in Brasil, and the skippers and strategists who plotted victory in 1995 and 2000 were recruited by overseas syndicates intent on victory in 2003. One of Team New Zealand's great strengths had been its ability to raise money, not just from corporate investors but from the population at large. Now, however unfairly, it looked as if those who had benefited most from public generosity were lining their pockets by competing on behalf of foreign multi-millionaires against their fellow countrymen. Heroes became villains overnight, and a national sense of betrayal left an already debt-ridden Team New Zealand unable to match the sums raised by the ten challengers: despite an outlay of £24 million an inexperienced defending crew were reliant upon an untested new yacht which in the event twice failed to finish. By February 2003 the Alinghi syndicate had spent a staggering £34 million in order to win the America's Cup: Coutts, Butterworth and four other Kiwis led a

Swiss team to a 5–0 humiliation of Team New Zealand. It seemed, in the words of one member of the Royal Auckland Yacht Squadron, that the America's Cup had become 'nothing more than a stage for sailing mercenaries and far, far removed from anything "national"'. While the rest of the world has acclaimed Russell Coutts as arguably the greatest America's Cup skipper of all time, at home he remains a national pariah.[24]

New Zealand had been humiliated by a land-locked nation: a heroic tale of a small nation coming together to take on the world had seemingly given way to a grubby story of mercenary yachtsmen and unscrupulous property developers each making enormous amounts of money. One suspects that not many Australians would harbour such an outdated, and frankly naïve, view of what motivates professional sportsmen and women. Does this suggest that there remains a residue of innocence in New Zealand, or that Australia is unduly worldly-wise, for which read cynical? Certainly the level of anger and unashamed xenophobia generated by the America's Cup suggested anything but innocence – there was a singular absence of generosity and sportsmanship, notwithstanding an understandable annoyance that so many of the nation's leading yachtsmen clearly saw nothing wrong in competing against their own country.

Iconography – places, panoply, and people

The America's Cup aptly illustrates how national rivalry can extend to iconography; witness the centrality of location, ritual, and even dress to the respective sporting cultures. The importance of sporting symbols in making explicit a keen sense of loyalty and identification has been well documented. In demonstrating the importance of 'invented tradition' to the construction of the modern nation-state, Eric Hobsbawm singled out sport's capacity for strengthening the social cohesion and collective identity of Benedict Anderson's 'imagined communities'. While Hobsbawm focused on late nineteenth century Europe the concept of invented tradition remains valid a century later on the other side of the world. Thus E.P. Thompson argued that the greater the impact of global forces upon local, regional or national communities the tighter the grip on their indigenous symbols and traditions. Crucial to a community's cultural capital and collective identity are sporting traditions, with their capacity for relentless reaffirmation and reinvention. Maguire has similarly depicted communities responding to globalisation processes by 'wilfully clinging tighter to the mythology, nostalgia and tradition which underpin their identity'. Sports may thus become important 'anchors of meaning' for a nation's people.[25]

Familiarity breeds contempt, and nowhere more so than in sport, but even today both Australia and New Zealand foster a fortress image.[26] Thus, touring sides are expected to view a visit to the MCG or Eden Park with awe and apprehension. Sledging on and off the pitch may give Australia the edge here, notwithstanding hoary stories of Lions or Springbok hard men trembling with trepidation long before the boat laid anchor in Auckland harbour. However, New Zealand understood the significance of branding over 80 years before copywriters and semioticians made us all familiar with the concept. Tom Ellinson, pioneering tactician and Maori captain of the first national side, is accredited with the idea of a uniform black kit and a silver fern as early as 1893.[27]

Black as an athletic uniform combined menace (*big* men), mystery (from a *long* way away), and mystique (who convey an aura of invincibility). For European crowds, happy to accept the popular myth that here was a uniquely harmonious inter-racial society, the presence of Maori players simply added to the All Black aura. (For white South Africans they remained an embarrassment, conveniently airbrushed out of the picture from 1928 to 1970, when four 'Honorary Whites' were allowed to tour.) The 'otherness' of New Zealand from the rest of the Empire, especially Australia, was reinforced by an early assimilation of indigenous cultural symbols. Ironically, this 'cultural appropriation' reflected Maori players' subordination to their white team mates' dominant codes of power, control, and behaviour. Yet the *ka mate* haka, performed by *all* the team irrespective of colour, reinforced a popular, albeit mythical, image of common struggle transcending ethnic differences. Only the most informed spectator would be aware that the *ka mate* was tainted in the eyes of many Maori.[28] Television and increased touring has clearly undermined the effect of the haka on both spectators and opposing sides. Emerging rugby nations eager to perform Polynesian variants may similarly dilute the impact of the original. Nevertheless, for anyone seeing the haka 'live' for the first time it remains a spectacular restatement of a powerful and remarkably resilient representation of New Zealand nationality. Jack Lovelock, and later Peter Snell, demonstrated that black could project an image of individual frailty and solitary endeavour just as effectively as one of collective strength and team effort. On monochrome TV in the early 1960s Snell stood out in a sea of white running vests. The silver fern on uniform black background proved a simple but memorable motif, and it is noticeable even today how little the sponsors' logos attract attention away from the national badge.[29]

The apotheosis of Kiwi branding must be the netball team where a giant silver fern is spread across the front of the players' black tunics. From facepaint to footwear spectators cheering on the Silver Ferns at the 2002 Commonwealth Games displayed every possible combination of black and silver. Visual support embraced national colours to a degree matched only by Dutch soccer fans (does orange play a similarly iconic role in another small nation synonymous with a single sport?). Woe betide anybody seen as abusing the national colour; witness the failure of Blackheart, the fundraising campaign launched in September 2002 to rehabilitate the cause of Team New Zealand when aggressive advertising simply compounded an all-pervasive cynicism. The contrast with everything that

Black Magic represented ('old fashioned Kiwi sporting virtues – team-work, modesty, hard work, physical strength, love of country') could not have been more striking.[30]

Australian fans are not averse to gold and green cosmetic enhancement, but the predominance of cricket and to a lesser degree tennis as the only genuinely trans-continental sports has perhaps acted as a constraint upon iconographic innovation. White is a universal colour (not that it stopped New Zealand soccer from the canny notion of christening its national side the All Whites), hence the lack of invention prior to Channel Nine's repackaging of one-day cricket; and yet, despite the growing influence of baseball on the game, the 'baggy green cap' remains an object of tradition and reverence. By definition icons are rooted in success, hence the Kanga-roos and the Wallabies could only acquire the same monolithic connota-tions as the Springboks and the All Blacks once Australia had established itself as a dominant force in both rugby league and rugby union, and this is a relatively recent phenomenon.

Commercial exploitation and globalisation have seriously eroded the power of the sporting icon – how fearsome is an All Black shirt when Adidas market it in every shopping mall from Buenos Aires to Brisbane?[31] Notwithstanding the gracious dignity displayed by the New Zealand Seven at Manchester 2002 when upstaged by Niu's home-grown haka, most attempts to invent tradition fail. Thus the All Whites retreated into a sporting ghetto once the euphoria of qualifying for the 1982 World Cup died down. The violence surrounding the Springboks' 1981 tour had left the 'national game' seriously discredited, but as memories faded so too did soccer's challenge to the status quo. In Australia, from the commencement of non-British European immigration in the 1950s right through to the late 1990s, soccer remained an ethnic preserve. This was not the case in New Zealand where, across the whole of the twentieth century, less than half a million people have settled in the country. Thus the number of immigrants from continental Europe has been very small, with the level of cultural assimilation therefore that much greater than in Australian centres of manufacturing industry such as Geelong or the feeder towns surrounding Sydney. Add to this an early bias against Irish Catholics, and it is scarcely surprising that New Zealand has relied so heavily on the detritus of the British game. The lamentable record of Auckland's Football Kings, recruited by Sky to contest Australia's National Soccer League, became – and remains – a national embarrassment.[32] The emergence in the late 1990s of genuinely world-class Australian players confirmed the New Zealand FA's continuing inability to foster home-grown talent. The All Whites could boast a great name but little else.

Nostalgia and iconic status are clearly inseparable. Australians may be more streetwise than their Tasman neighbours about the commercial real-ities of sport at the start of the twenty-first century, but they still revere their sporting heroes (at least one of which was originally from New

Zealand – the legendary racehorse Phar Lap). If only as a consequence of its size and past success, Australia can boast a larger and more diverse pantheon. Yet how many of these heroes have acquired genuinely iconic status à la Bradman (dead, establishment, country) or Dawn Fraser (alive, maverick, city)? With notable exceptions such as the three knights – Edmund Hillary, Richard Hadlee and Peter Blake – most Kiwi sporting icons are rugby players, the likes of Colin Meads embodying a totemic stereotype of Pakeha masculinity as well as an increasingly obsolete set of patriarchal, rural, conservative values.[33] Inside the New Zealand pantheon at the start of a new millenium there is at least an acknowledgement of ethnicity and gender (who could be more literally totemic than Jonah Lomu?); whereas across the Tasman there remains a striking absence of Native Australian role models other than Evonne Goolagong, Mark Ella, Mal Meninga, and now Cathy Freeman.[34]

Kiwis catching up – national governments and the search for sporting excellence

The role of the two national governments in the search for sporting excellence offers an interesting if unexpected insight into Antipodean sporting relations. Contrary to what one might expect, the past thirty years has seen a surprising degree of collaboration, with Canberra only too happy to advise Wellington on institutional support for its elite athletes. An ungenerous view would be that Australians find smugly satisfying any evidence of humble Kiwis seeking their advice on how to take on the world, and win. However, the real answer seems to be that in the 1990s Australian administrators and coaches became generous with their time and expertise simply because, other than in a few key sports, they did not see New Zealand as a serious threat. Nor did they share their Kiwi counterparts' keen sense of Tasman rivalry. Australia was intent on conquering the world rather than its own backyard, and the paternalistic, even patronising, attitude adopted towards New Zealand spoke volumes. Nevertheless, in those sports where competition remained razor sharp – notably netball, hockey, sailing, and both codes of rugby – any exchange of ideas was rarely bilateral.[35]

Australia's quest over the past quarter of a century to become a major sporting nation is now a familiar story. Not surprisingly, New Zealand's less happy experience has been all but ignored; and yet it aptly illustrates a historic tension between ambition and reality: at the start of the twenty-first century can a population of 3.9 million support a sporting infrastructure capable of producing world champions? Unlike Australia after 1982, New Zealand for too long tacitly assumed that success on the world stage could be facilitated via a strategy where the main priority was mass participation. Naturally there was support for elite athletes, but nothing comparable to the Australian Institute of Sport (AIS). The 1990s was marked by good intentions, but New Zealand's poor medal count in Sydney forced central government to adopt a far more interventionist role than had previously been the case. At Barcelona in 1996 the Federal Sports Minister insisted that, 'we have re-established Australia as a world sporting power'.[36] New Zealand has no such grandiose ambition for the centenary Games in Athens, but there needs to be some vindication of the belated decision to adopt an academy system. National pride took a fierce hammering in the face of Sydney's obvious success as a global event, and Australia's remarkable haul of 58 medals – over ten times the number won in 1976.

Australia's failure to secure a single gold medal at Montreal was followed four years later by a similarly dismal performance in Moscow, despite the absence of the Americans. The power of the state governments, the local and regional authorities, and the national sports organisations (NSOs), together with a strong tradition of amateurism and voluntarism, had previously negated the capacity of the Federal Government to exercise a decisive influence upon the future direction of Australian sport.[37] While national politicians harnessed sport for electoral purposes, they rarely intervened, the most notable exception being in advance of the Melbourne Games in 1956. The first 'Friendly Games' are now firmly established in popular mythology as a triumph, embodying and exemplifying all the values that made [white Anglophone] Australia the 'Lucky Country'.[38] Thirty-five medals were won, including 13 golds, with swimmer Dawn Fraser securing half her career total of eight. The maverick Fraser, selected in 1988 as Australia's greatest ever sportswoman, came to symbolise a remarkable era in the nation's sporting history. The sixteenth Olympiad was seen as Australia coming of age, with success in the pool and on the track ensuring worldwide acclaim for what appeared to be a uniquely endowed sporting nation.[39] For older Australians the 1950s and early 1960s soon came to be seen as a golden age. Lawn tennis was deemed *the* sport which more than any other had demonstrated to non-Commonwealth nations, not least the United States, the depth of native-born Australian talent: inspired by Frank Sedgman, in the 1950s Laver, Hoad, and Rosewall remoulded singles play, with Margaret Court making a similar contribution to the women's game.[40] Succeeding decades saw mixed fortunes in the Davis Cup and only one Wimbledon winner (Pat Cash). By the early 1980s a perceived decline in Australian tennis was seen, along with the fallout of the 'Packer Revolution' in cricket, as clear evidence of national decline, reinforcing the case for action by central government. Those nostalgic for the pure amateur spirit of the Melbourne Games conveniently forgot the role of the Federal Government in resolving planning and budgetary disputes.

Appeasing the IOC in 1956 was a rare instance of government intervention until Labor's election in 1972. Although a constitutional crisis saw Gough Whitlam leave office only two years later, his administration set a precedent for federal intervention in tourism and sport. Federal governments of both left and right slowly came to see the promotion of sporting excellence as a potential votewinner, but the Liberal-led coalition in power from 1975 to 1983 was notable for its tardiness in responding to the twin disasters of Montreal and Moscow. In 1981 the AIS was at last established at the National Sports Centre in Canberra, providing world-class facilities and elite coaching for 150 athletes in eight sports. This marked a major shift in federal government priorities while still operating within a relatively modest budget. Major investment across the board followed Labor's return to power in 1983, with the Australian Sports Commission (ASC) established in 1985. The ASC was granted financial autonomy four years later, albeit with a remit to match public with private funding wherever possible. Success in Sydney vindicated the decision to concentrate power in a federally funded quango, even if the Commission's success in raising participation levels falls far short of its track record in enhancing elite performance. Thus, by 1991 only around 15 per cent of the adult population was rated 'highly physically active'; but the AIS had already grown to over 300 resident athletes in 17 sports and over 2000 athletes involved part-time in over 30 sports.[41] While Canberra remains the focal point for policy planning, individual sports have been relocated to more appropriate locations in Perth, Brisbane, and Adelaide.

Australia's sporting success in the 1990s and into the new century has been remarkable. At the 2002 Commonwealth Games in Manchester Ian Thorpe and his fellow swimmers helped Australia amass an astonishing total of 206 medals, including 82 gold. The netball and men's hockey teams beat New Zealand on the same day that on the other side of the world the Wallabies overcame All Black resistance to retain the Bledisloe Cup. New Zealand ultimately won the Tri-Nations tournament, as well as the Sevens competition in Manchester, but for the moment Australia remains world champion in both codes of rugby. At the same time the team moulded by Mark Taylor and Steve Waugh over the past decade is arguably the finest cricket side since the war. In all these sports, and in so many others, the role of the AIS has been critical; and, in maintaining and expanding the work of the Institute, sustained, targeted investment has proved crucial.[42]

Unlike Australia, where changes of government witnessed clear policy shifts, New Zealand's pursuit of sporting excellence from the mid-1980s was largely bipartisan. Thus the National Government implemented reforms initiated by its Labour predecessor, most notably the establishment in 1987 of the Hillary Commission for Recreation and Sport.[43] Labour's election victory three years earlier had seen the appointment of a future party leader, Mike Moore, as Minister of Recreation and Sport. The presence of a political heavyweight in a previously low-ranking ministry ensured a rapid response to two key reports, each of which recommended radical reform of administration and funding, as well as the more aggressive promotion of sport and recreation's 'community and social value'.

Sport on the Move pointed out that participation levels needed to rise significantly, hence the Commission's remit to 'enhance the mental and physical well-being of the nation by encouraging more healthy and active lifestyles'. *Recreation and Government in New Zealand* insisted that planning and delivery had to be better managed, hence the Commission's statutory authority as the principal funding agency. Establishment of the new body coincided with the introduction of a state lottery, and more critically, a programme of economic liberalisation intended to mark a sharp break with New Zealand's welfarist, interventionist tradition. With Labour shrinking the public sector, phasing out state subsidies, and reining in government expenditure, it was little wonder that the Hillary Commission endeavoured to portray itself as a lean and efficient budget-holder. Somehow it would balance the books *and* inaugurate a new era in New Zealand sport: 'one in which recreation and sport are seen not merely as Saturday afternoon "play" but rather as an important element of personal growth and cultural expression that in the long term pays worthwhile dividends to the entire community'.[44]

With a nod to tradition (the centrality of Saturday afternoon to both rural and urban lifestyles as late as the 1950s), the Commission set out to develop a 'sport for all' policy. Facilitating elite achievement was clearly not seen as a priority, the intention being 'to make excellence possible at all levels'. In this respect New Zealand's focus on grassroots initiatives was not that different from Australia's principal aim in the late 1980s, namely to maximise participation; indeed the ASC's considerable influence was openly acknowledged in the Hillary Commission's first report.[45] Thus in its first two years the Commission set up a raft of community and educational programmes, but in terms of elite sport did little more than allocate around $NZ1.1 million to the New Zealand Sports Foundation and the Olympic and Commonwealth Games Association. There appeared to be little accountability, minimal prioritising, and a complete absence of strategy and vision; witness the complacency of the chief executive's second report when he described his country's performance at the Seoul Olympics as 'quite exceptional' – he omitted to mention that all 13 medals were won in or on the water, the bulk of them sailing.[46]

The Hillary Commission was thus a very worthy body, but in terms of raising New Zealand's profile on the global sporting stage it was scarcely pro-active, delegating responsibility to the non-sporting organizations (NSOs) and playing no more than a 'supportive' role in advance of major international competitions. To be fair, this was an organisation which, according to its 1990 mission statement, was 'dedicated to helping all New Zealanders participate and achieve in recreation and sport', and in this role the Commission appeared to be genuinely pre-emptive, innovative, and inclusive.[47] The National Party's return to power in 1990 saw the new prime minister, Jim Bolger, calling for fresh initiatives to raise levels of physical fitness, particularly among schoolchildren, but at the same time reaffirming the importance of delegation and decentralisation. Thus NSOs and clubs continued to benefit from increased lottery funding, but invariably there was an absence of forward thinking by the Commission when it came to allocating individual grants. The 1992 *Life in New Zealand Survey* suggested that up to 60 per cent of the population still did not regularly participate in physical activity. That estimate was later slimmed down to 49 per cent, with one in three New Zealanders wholly inactive – a proportion that rose dramatically depending upon gender, age, income, and location. Thus the Commission's 1998 *Sport and Physical Activity Survey* concluded that, as in Australia, too many city-dwellers, whether Pakeha or Maori, were only interested in spectator sport, and even then courtesy of the television. In other words, New Zealand had an international reputation for active participation (often courtesy of tourist promotion) and for sporting excellence which belied the reality of the situation.[48]

1992 had seen ten medals at Barcelona, and predictably the solitary gold was in sailing. In 1996 three golds on the water and over the jumps saw New Zealand play to its strengths, but the final tally of five was consistent with the country's dismal Olympics record.[49] Throughout the 1980s and 1990s, the odd swimmer might enjoy modest success but, on track or field, New Zealand athletes were never among the medal winners at the Olympics and fared little better at the Commonwealth Games. What made repeated failure especially hard to swallow was that New Zealand had prided itself on producing great 800 and 1500 metres runners, such as the legendary Jack Lovelock who set a new world record in prewar Berlin, and Peter Snell repeating his Rome win in Tokyo before adding a further gold. In the 1960s Kiwi coaches matched Percy Cerruty's success on the other side of the Tasman. Indeed, whereas Australia produced no obvious successor to Herb Elliott, New Zealand could boast a new generation of runners more than capable of beating East Africa's post-independence track stars. The 1500 metres at Munich in 1972 saw Rod Dixon come third, and four years later John Walker took the gold in Montreal. With hindsight the 1970s was a golden age for Kiwi middle-distance running, making the lack of track success over the next two decades that much harder to bear.

The Hillary Commission's 1993 strategic plan *Moving the Nation* signalled a shift in thinking, not least because funding had grown significantly as a result of major sponsorship deals and guaranteed lottery revenue. The principal aim remained maximum participation by acknowledging a gender imbalance, enhancing disabled access to sport, and improving Maori facilities; but priority was now given to planning for Sydney 2000 and funding the New Zealand Sports Foundation's programme for elite athletes ($NZ2.5 million, matched by commercial sponsors). The Commission recognised that, in sharp contrast to Australia, there was a dearth of full-time elite coaches, but the sums allocated to improve the situation were paltry (18 grants of up to $NZ10,000).[50]

A limited budget forced the Commission and the NSOs to prioritise ruthlessly, resulting in a team of just 14 at the 1994 Winter Olympics (a silver in 1992 remains New Zealand's single winter sports medal), and the support of only seven coaching academies. The sports awarded academy status (cricket, netball, yachting, swimming, tennis, squash, and golf) saw New Zealand identifying where it had a genuine global presence. Regrettably, major investment in track and field support could no longer be justified given Kiwi athletes' current world rankings.[51] Unlike Australia, both codes of rugby were deemed sufficiently well-off to maintain their own elite programmes, while soccer qualification for the 1982 World Cup was presumably seen as the exception that proves the rule.[52] Comparison with Australia can be misleading as New Zealand's promotion of elite sport throughout the 1990s was so very different. The nation's premier sport (both codes) was omitted, the funding was small, the coaching academies were autonomous (and excluded the world's two biggest sports: soccer and athletics), and the degree of central direction and control was finite.[53]

The IOC's choice of Sydney to stage the 2000 Games clearly influenced the New Zealand Government's thinking on how to improve international competitiveness off the water and beyond the park. Early success for the swimmers enhanced the credibility of the coaching academies, but having the Olympics 'on our own back doorstep' prompted serious long-term planning and a further injection of lottery funding. An extra $NZ3.6 million was set aside each year for Olympic and Commonwealth Games preparation, but from now on the three major sports bodies were accountable to a government task force. The second half of the 1990s witnessed dramatic changes in New Zealand politics, with the predominantly two-party system breaking up and a complex system of proportional representation replacing 'first past the post'. With a plethora of new parties and both National and Labour in the process of reinventing themselves, the latter by way of rediscovering its social democratic roots, ministers needed to demonstrate their ability to deliver. The 'New Zealand 2000 Task Force' offered tangible evidence that Wellington had its eye on the ball, even if a general election would be called in the year prior to the Sydney Games taking place. Further evidence of fresh thinking came with the belated establishment of the NZ Sports Drug Agency in 1994, and the publication a year later of *The Winning Way* inquiry into the needs of elite athletes. National pride was at stake, and yet New Zealand sports administrators were clearly realists. Just as the creators of the Hillary Commission had looked to Canberra for inspiration, Kiwi coaches were now encouraged to tap in to the latest thinking among their Australian counterparts. The latter's readiness in the late 1990s to support a Tasman exchange programme demonstrated how seriously they took New Zealand. Even in keenly competitive sports such as swimming and athletics the Australians were happy to demonstrate just how far they had progressed.[54] In so doing they simply highlighted New Zealand's failure – or, given the size of the population and the economy, its inability – to sustain those levels of investment necessary to foster world-class talent.

While success at Atlanta and Kuala Lumpur would have been welcome, Sydney was the big one. Unfortunately, after saddle and sail again secured six medals in 1996, including three golds, the 2000 Games proved a disaster. While Australians basked in the reflected glory of their 58 medal winners, Kiwis relived Melbourne 1956. At least on that occasion their two medals were both gold. Sydney 2000 brought only one victory, in the single sculls, along with three thirds. The official explanation was that 'injury and bad luck conspired against the New Zealand team', particularly its medal-hungry showjumpers, cyclists, and yachtsmen, the latter having to contend with 'a lack of wind on the usually blustery Sydney harbour'.[55] Weak excuses could not disguise the fact that New Zealand had become an Olympic irrelevance, failing to perform even in those events where it was still a world-beater. To rub salt into the wounds Australia had hosted the most successful Olympics in modern times, and with 16 gold medals had gained three more than at Melbourne (thanks to the outstanding personality of the Games, swimmer Ian Thorpe. The real measure of progress, however, was securing three times as many silvers as in 1956).[56]

After seven years of preparation, during which time both major parties had been in power, New Zealand came away from Sydney with a surprise result in the rowing, and precious little else. The Labour-led coalition had already questioned the Hillary Commission as to why participation rates remained stubbornly low. In an interesting parallel with the West Indies, ministers voiced concern that 'American basketball, boxing, and track stars' were enjoying an unhealthy level of media attention at the expense of home-bred sporting heroes. In office from 1999 was a generation which had served its political apprenticeship in the 1980s, challenging the USA's perceived hegemonic presence in the South Pacific, not least its right to sail nuclear armed and/or powered vessels in New Zealand waters.[57] After 1984 Wellington had endured the wrath of Washington (and Paris, with the sinking of Greenpeace's *Rainbow Warrior*), and survived. Environmentalists and traditional Labour supporters, now again in the ascendancy within Helen Clark's administration, remained wary of American influence, even if the reality was that globalisation rendered such fears irrelevant: the New Zealand RFU, for example, had long since sold its soul to Rupert Murdoch. Nevertheless, there was a recognition that 'some sporting organisations are now at a crossroads where they must determine how to progress without ceding control to commercial third parties'.[58]

Even before Sydney 2000 rendered fresh thinking imperative, Labour had established a new taskforce. 'Despite the pervasive nature of recreation and sporting activities in New Zealand society', it was argued, 'it is still rare for this sport oriented nation to critically consider the beliefs and values that sustain and shape our recreation and sport'. Four months after Kiwi Olympians returned home to a summer of national soul-searching,

Getting Set – For an Active Nation recommended a more pro-active national agency to succeed the Hillary Commission. The Government needed to respond quickly, and by the time Labour strengthened its electoral position in July 2002 a powerful new body, Sport and Recreation New Zealand/ihi Aotearoa (SPARC), had already been charged with creating 'a healthier and more socially cohesive nation'. The *Getting Set* taskforce had been adamant that at the heart of its vision for enhancing the quality of Kiwi life was sporting excellence. Elite athletes were positive role models, not least because of the keen 'sense of national identity New Zealanders get through recreation and sport' and 'the feel-good factor that follows international success'.[59]

Among its many and diverse functions SPARC had to produce winners, working closely with the New Zealand Academy of Sport. Established by the NZ Sports Foundation on the eve of the Sydney Games, the Academy followed a British rather than an Australian model not least because a decentralised system based in regional centres involved far less initial investment. Also, it was important that the Academy should not be seen by partner NSOs as a threat to their central or local control. New Zealand, with its compact land mass, unitary constitutional framework, and cohesive sporting identity, was ideally suited to a single Wellington-based sports institute; and yet budgetary considerations and island/provincial sensitivity prevented a Canberra-style model. Ironically, it was precisely because the Commonwealth constitution is so protective of the states' rights and individual identities, and the sporting culture so fractured, that the academy structure in federal Australia was so highly centralised. Though run on a shoestring compared to the AIS, the New Zealand Academy of Sport posted a modest early success for its 'Kiwi Support Base' at Manchester in 2002. Notwithstanding disappointment on the hockey pitch and the netball court, New Zealand nudged ahead of South Africa to secure fifth place in the final medals table, albeit a long way adrift of the big four.[60]

Conclusion

While accepting his reservations regarding the concept of 'imagined communities', few would question Grant Jarvie's insistence that sport, 'whether it be through nostalgia, mythology, invented or selected traditions, contributes to a quest for identity'. For both Australia and New Zealand the 'cultural marker of nationalism' remains above all sport.[61] The past quarter century has seen confirmation of a keen sporting rivalry, although New Zealanders bestow upon it a significance not always apparent to their neighbours.[62] For Australians nothing can replace beating the English, but putting the Kiwis in their place remains a highly pleasurable experience. For New Zealanders any win is a triumph over adversity, with the obvious exceptions of rugby, sailing, and possibly netball. Victory for the All Blacks is not viewed as a win but simply as a re-establishment of the natural order. There is simply nowhere else in the world where a nation is so closely identified with one particular team in one particular sport. Naturally within that nation there are large sections of society who reject any such association, and as in Australia local/community/ethnic loyalties can rival or outweigh national identity. Across the Tasman sports nationalism remains a largely Anglo-Celtic phenomenon, hence 'intercolonial and intercommunity rivalry have often caused sport to divide rather than unite Australians.' Moreover, pride in the performance of a national side is by no means incompatible with a genuinely internationalist perspective.[63] The irony is that globalisation not only encouraged white middle class New Zealand to cling tenaciously to familiar and reassuring manifestations of Pakeha culture, but served to strengthen the All Black 'brand'. Chris Laidlaw, the most scholarly skipper of any All Blacks side, has voiced alarm at the speed with which sporting excellence became a 'metaphor for successful enterprise of almost every kind'. Thus the 'silver fern is now jealously protected intellectual property', while Auckland entrepreneurs claim for themselves the 'corporate virtues and values' that bring victory to the nation's yachtsmen and rugby players.[64] Australia has of course ridden a similar rollercoaster of commercialisation and commodification but, as the America's Cup demonstrates, with far less angst and anger.

Clearly any contest between the two countries is no longer a simple case of one side seeking to best the other, while making some implicit statement about the supposed superiority of a vague set of national values. The irony is as the rivalry intensifies, fuelled by television's insatiable appetite for large audiences, the less each sporting fixture has in common with such an outmoded conception of international competition. Increasingly, when rival teams meet the players share a variety of loyalties, and a simple love of one's country competes with a myriad of contractual obligations. Not only do club and sponsor have first call upon a professional sportsperson's loyalty, but he or she may have multiple national and regional identities. An All Black may be a Kiwi first and a Samoan or Tongan second. But what is the real driver – patriotism or ambition? Ignoring any suggestion that the answer could be both, liberals lament that 'the All Blacks no longer play for the rest of us. They play for a corporate enterprise, on the basis of a contract that dictates almost every aspect of their lifestyle'.[65] Conservative critics agree that the pursuit of money is corrosive; witness the paradox of free marketeers complaining that pay TV prevents the whole nation from coming together to watch international rugby. However, they go further, arguing that a more racially diverse All Blacks side lacks the physical and mental strength embodied by previous generations of country-bred 'hard men'. Hence a second Australian victory in the World Cup fuelled a furious assault upon urban multiculturalism and a reaffirmation of the myth that winning All Blacks sides drew their strength from a rural heartland.[66]

A renewed debate about the mythology constructed around New Zealand rugby has formed part of a wider discourse on the profound social changes experienced by the country since the mid-1980s.[67] Labour's embrace of neo-liberalism and assertion of first loyalty to the South Pacific region left a permanent legacy, most visibly in the Polynesian immigrant communities of south Auckland. Limited sporting success, with, prior to 2003, the notable exception of the America's Cup, provided valuable ammunition for those most critical of the 'new' New Zealand. The National Party encouraged such dissatisfaction, albeit without the ferocity with which it had once defended sporting links with apartheid South Africa. In fact, as has been seen, the National Party in office took serious steps to increase rates of participation, while providing modest support for elite athletes. After 1999 the Labour-led coalition maintained the same basic infrastructure until the disappointment of Sydney 2000 forced a radical rethink. A belated commitment to enhancing elite performance drew upon the Australian academy system, looking eastwards for inspiration and collaboration. The readiness of Australian coaches and administrators to advise reflected an all-pervasive view of New Zealand as the poor relation, as well as a further illustration of national confidence. Centenary celebrations of Australian federation prompted serious soul searching, not least with reference to past and present treatment of the aboriginal population, but this was introspection of a different order from the dominant discourse across the Tasman on the eve of a new century.

The novelist Hilary Mantel insists that, 'At the beginning of the century, we want to carry our past with us, without being bowed under its weight'. Australians appear more than capable of doing this, but is the same true for most New Zealanders? Mantel also suggests that behind every nation or state there lies 'the state-that-might-have-been': national mythology reaffirming both individual and collective potential, as in Australia 'the lucky country'.[68] James Belich would argue that in New Zealand's case this meant not just a 'Greater Britain' but a 'Better Britain', with rugby an early demonstration of the latter: 'How better to prove Better Britishness than by being better than Britain at the most British of games?'.[69] Dismissing 'the more independent national history we would like to have happened', Belich identifies a period of 'recolonisation' ('voluntary neo-colonialism') from the 1880s to the 1970s when, in terms of quality of life and standard of living, New Zealand endeavoured to surpass its imperial role model and principal trading partner. The collapse of this multi-faceted economic, ideological, and emotional relationship after 1972 initiated a belated process of 'decolonisation'.[70] New Zealand's economic travails attracted little sympathy in Britain or the United States, with the latter becoming increasingly hostile. Labour's new right agenda of slashing subsidies and public expenditure accelerated the breakdown of 'Better Britain's' largely progressive, populist consensus, embracing as it did an always fragile myth of racial harmony.[71]

Belich asks, 'Has New Zealand emerged at long last from the shadow of recolonisation only to have its nascent cultural maturity and national independence washed away by globalising tides?'.[72] Television's aggressive promotion of Tasman sporting rivalry took place against a backdrop of Australia forging much closer economic and strategic ties with an ever more dependent New Zealand. The timing was more than coincidental. As previously noted, within sport that dependency extended to advice on creating a new infrastructure to increase mass participation, and above all, enhance elite performance. New Zealand coaches and administrators were – and are – receptive, but the system established in the 1990s, and revisited after Sydney 2002, is only a pale shadow of its Australian model. Economic reality dictates that government investment, whether direct or indirect, can not, *even in relative terms*, match the levels of federal, state or local spending maintained across the past quarter century.

Prior to 1987 Australia and New Zealand shared a similar growth pattern, but since then there has been a marked divergence in output, productivity, per capita incomes, and above all, income distribution. The acute level of inequality evident in New Zealand by the mid-1990s seriously undermined any community initiatives to promote sport. Furthermore, it eroded an already narrow tax base, and distorted the distribution of Treasury spending, via the opportunity costs of basic welfare support.[73] By virtue of its size New Zealand could never compete with Australia, but the enthusiasm with which successive governments from the mid-1980s embraced the free market made the task of forging a world-class support system for its elite athletes that much harder. Sydney 2000 highlighted all too harshly just how big a mountain SPARC had to climb, but two years later came an even greater humiliation. Predictably, in a row over sponsorship and broadcasting rights, the International Rugby Board stripped New Zealand of its status as co-host with Australia of the 2003 World Cup. The country that had initiated, staged, and then won the first tournament was unceremoniously dumped because it could not match the commercial nous of its erstwhile partner. New Zealand was taught a brutal lesson in how the power-brokers of global sport penalise even the most resourceful of small nations for their lack of financial muscle – a lesson compounded by the loss of the America's Cup to a Swiss billionaire and his Kiwi 'mercenaries'.[74] In the modern era tradition and history count for very little, and what better illustration than trans-Tasman competition? It was clearly in the interest of cable/satellite TV to stoke up the sibling rivalry, but would this have been possible had a revolution in telecommunications not coincided with the emergence of the first great Wallaby side? For romantics and idealists, it is reassuring to know that the key player in this not so happy story is a Native Australian, Mark Ella, and not Rupert Murdoch, a non-Australian if his current passport is to be believed.

Notes

1 For example, J. Belich, *Paradise Reforged A History of New Zealanders*, London: Penguin, 2002, pp. 440–3. A contrary, Australian perspective can be found in P. McPhee, 'An Australian view of New Zealand' and G. Blainey, 'Two countries: the same but very different' in K. Sinclair (ed.) *Tasman Relations*, Auckland: Auckland University Press, 1988, pp. 277–97 and 315–32. McPhee argued that New Zealanders know far more about Australia than vice versa, and are thus that much more sensitive to any perceived national sleights, particularly in sport; Australians do not have the same inferiority complex, and are more interested in nations on the Pacific rim and beyond.

2 On the Australian belief in innate talent, both individual and collective, and that the 'lucky country' has a unique sporting heritage, see D. Adair and W. Vamplew, *Sport in Australian History*, Melbourne: Oxford University Press, 1997, pp. ix–xiv, 6–14; R. Cashman, *Paradise of Sport The Rise of Organised Sport in Australia*, Melbourne: Oxford University Press, 1995, pp. 205–8; W. Vamplew, 'Australians and sport' in W. Vamplew and B. Stoddart (eds) *Sport in Australia A Social History*, Cambridge: Cambridge University Press, 1994, pp. 11–13; and a more theoretical discussion in B. Stewart and A. Smith, 'Australian sport in a postmodern age', in J.A. Mangan and J. Nauright (eds) *Sport in Australasian Society Past and Present*, London: Frank Cass, 2000, pp. 278–304.

3 The much-publicised visit of Steve Waugh's 2001 touring side to Gallipoli en route to England reinforced a still popular theory that Australia's crushing victories in the early 1920s were motivated by revenge for the disproportionate losses at the Dardanelles and on the Western Front. See *Guardian*, 6 August 2001. For a complementary argument, that Irish immigration and assimilation 'provided much of the intensity and energy that surrounded Australia's primary sporting passion: beating the British', see P.A. Horton, 'The Irish-Australians and Australian sports culture' in Mangan and Nauright (eds) *Sport in Australasian Society*, pp. 66–70. On the importance since 1925 of the ANZAC tradition in motivating All Black touring sides, see C. Laidlaw, 'Sport and national identity: race relations, business, professionalism' in B. Patterson (ed.) *Sport Society and Culture in New Zealand*, Wellington: Stout Research Centre Victoria University, 1999, p. 14.

4 R. Sissons and B. Stoddart, *Cricket and Empire: the 1932–33 Bodyline Tour of Australia*, London: Allen & Unwin, 1984. As with rugby, the then NZ premier Robert Muldoon used the Chappell incident to foster cheap popularity. Despite an imminent election, in January 2002 Labour's Helen Clark remained silent when NZ cricketers were assaulted and abused at the MCG.

5 New Zealand toured in 1905, losing only to Wales, and South Africa in 1906. J. Nauright, 'Colonial manhood and imperial race virility: British responses to post-Boer War colonial rugby tours' in J. Nauright and T.J.L. Chandler (eds) *Making Men: Rugby and Masculine Identity*, London: Frank Cass, 1996, pp. 121–39.

6 32 of Australia's 58 Olympic medallists in 2000 attended the AIS.

7 1948–2000 New Zealand won 7.3 Olympic gold medals per million people and Australia 4.6. Belich, *Paradise Reforged*, p. 369.

8 Not that television offers the only explanation. As shall be seen, the emergence of the Wallabies as a major threat to All Black supremacy owed a lot more to the Ella family than to the Murdoch clan.

9 The aboriginal peoples' contrasting experiences offer important insights in to both the power of national mythology and the sharply differing manifestations of national consciousness. On Maori and sport, see Belich, *Paradise Reforged*,

pp. 212–15; G. Dunstall, 'The social pattern' in W.H. Oliver with B.R.Williams (eds) *The Oxford History of New Zealand*, Oxford: Oxford University Press, 1981, pp. 423–7; and M. MacLean, 'Of warriors and blokes: the problem of Maori rugby for Pakeha masculinity in New Zealand', in T. Chandler and J. Nauright (eds) *Making the Rugby World: Race, Gender, Commerce*, London: Frank Cass, 1999, pp. 1–26. On Native Australians and sport, see Adair and Vamplew, *Sport in Australian History*, pp. 163–70 and 142–3; and Cashman, *Paradise of Sport*, pp. 131–50. On women and sport, see Adair and Vamplew, *Sport in Australian History*, pp. 48–62; Cashman, *Paradise of Sport*, pp. 72–91; and A. Burroughs and J. Nauright, 'Women's sports and embodiment in Australia and New Zealand' in Mangan and Nauright (eds) *Sport in Australasian Society*, pp. 188–205. On Native Australian women, see J. Hargreaves, *Heroines of Sport The Politics of Difference and Identity*, London: Routledge, 2000, pp. 78–106 and 123–8.

10 New Zealanders never acquired the obsession with cricket evident in Australia before and after the First World War. Between 1945 and 2002 Australia have won 18 tests and NZ 7, with 16 drawn; this approximate 2:1 ratio is the same for one-day internationals. Belich, *Paradise Reforged*, pp. 369 and 373–4; F. Andrewes, '"They play in your home": cricket, media and modernity in pre-war Australia' in Mangan and. Nauright (eds) *Sport in Australasian Society*, p. 93; Online. Available HTTP: http://www.CrincInfo.com. (2 August 2002).

11 Cashman, *Paradise of Sport*, p. 106.

12 Australia have beaten New Zealand on all 10 occasions they have met in the Davis Cup.

13 Similarly, New Zealand's medal-winning and record-breaking male/female sprinters ran in the 1920s, and Australia's in the 1950s.

14 J. Nauright and D. Black ' "Hitting them where it hurts": Springbok-All Black rugby, masculine national identity and counter-hegemonic struggle, 1959–1992', in Nauright and Chandler (eds), *Making Men*, pp. 205–26; F. Andrewes, 'Demonstrable virility: images of masculinity in the 1956 Springbok rugby tour of New Zealand', *International Journal of the History of Sport*, 1998, vol. 15 (2), 119–36.

15 The inferior status of the Wallabies for much of their history is reflected in the fact that up to 2002 NZ had won 94 matches and Australia 41, with 5 drawn.

16 S. Smith, *The Union Game A Rugby History*, London: BBC, 1999, pp. 235–40 and 243–58; D. McRae, *Winter Colours Changing Seasons in World Rugby*, London: Mainstream, 1998, pp. 311–18.

17 The next official test series was in 1992. On the 1981 tour and its aftermath see Belich, *Paradise Reforged*, pp. 516–19; Smith, *The Union Game*, pp. 154–67, 170–3, and, from a South African perspective, McRae, *Winter Colours*, pp. 45–51. Literature on this defining moment in the history of modern New Zealand history is extensive. See endnotes and bibliographies acccompanying M. MacLean, 'Football as social critique: Protest movements, rugby and history in Aotearoa, New Zealand' in Mangan and Nauright (eds) *Sport in Australasian Society*, pp. 255–77 and 339; and T. Richards, 'New Zealanders' attitudes to sport as illustrated by debate over rugby contacts with South Africa' and Thompson, 'Legacy of "The Tour"' in Patterson (ed.) *Sport, Society and Culture in New Zealand*, pp. 39–48 and 79–91.

18 The balance of victory is in Australia's favour: 41 to 24, with 2 draws. By 1994 women's sport attracted 20.5 per cent of (often prime time) TV coverage in NZ but secured only 1.2 per cent in Australia where netball was restricted to terrestial ABC. J. Nauright and J. Broomhall, 'The development of netball and a female sporting culture in New Zealand, 1906–70', *International Journal of the History of Sport*, 1994, vol. 11, 387–407; J. Nauright, 'Women and sport in

Australia and New Zealand: Historical and contemporary issues', in K. Hardman (ed.), *Sport For All: Issues and Perspectives in International Context*, Manchester: Centre for Physical Education and Leisure Studies, 1996, pp. 59–64.

19 By 1995 sport occupied 15 per cent of Australian television time, and that proportion was clearly set to rise. Adair and Vamplew, *Sport in Australian History*, p. 27.

20 Smith, *The Union Game*, pp. 263–8; McRae, *Winter Colours*, pp. 82–3 and 240–3.

21 They were proved right about what is now the Viaduct Basin: retaining the America's Cup in 2000 cost NZ$30 million, but generated around NZ$640 million, created 8,000 jobs, and boosted the economy by one per cent. NZ Government economic-impact study, 2000. *Guardian*, 22 August 2001.

22 Adair and Vamplew, *Sport in Australian History*, p. 42. In fact Australia had since 1962 won the previous seven elimination competitions, and a NZ boat had never reached the final seven races.

23 S. and A. Seward, *Top Yacht Races of the World*, London: New Holland, 2000, pp. 146–51.

24 RAYS member quoted, *Guardian*, 7 October 2002. On TV in January 2003 Coutts and Butterworth offered a plausible explanation for their leaving TNZ for Alinghi, but a xenophobic media offered scant sympathy. *Guardian*, 12 February 2003.

25 E. Hobsbawm, 'Mass producing traditions: Europe, 1870–1914' in E. Hobsbawm and T. Ranger (eds) *The Invention of Tradition*, Cambridge: Cambridge University Press, 1983, pp. 263–307. On the application of Hobsbawm, Anderson, and Thompson's ideas to sport, see G. Jarvie, 'Sport, nationalism and cultural identity' in L. Allison (ed.) *The Changing Politics of Sport*, Manchester: Manchester University Press, 1993, pp. 72–76. J. Maguire and J. Tuck, 'Global sports and patriot games: rugby union and national identity in a united sporting kingdom since 1945', *Immigrants and Minorities*, 1998, vol. 17, 110–12.

26 On locations as symbolic of 'the Australian experience', especially with reference to sport, see 'From bush to beach Australia' in D. Denoon and P. Mein-Smith with M. Wyndham, *A History of Australia, New Zealand and the Pacific*, Oxford: Blackwell, 2000, pp. 432–5.

27 Belich, *Paradise Reforged*, p. 212.

28 The haka dates from the 1905 tour, and was briefly replaced in 1924 by George Nepia's more inclusive rugby-oriented haka, acceptable to South as well as North Island Maori. Indifference to Maori concerns resulted in the reinstatement of the *ka mate*. M. MacLean, 'Of warriors and blokes', pp. 1–26.

29 Arguably, sponsorship of the All Blacks and of victorious yachts racing round the world has given the Steinlager brewery a unique national as well as commercial identity. Nauright suggests that the 150th anniversary of the Treaty of Waitangi in 1990 gave renewed focus to national symbols, providing a commercial opportunity. J. Nauright, 'Sustaining masculine hegemony: rugby and the nostalgia of masculinity' in Nauright and Chandler (eds) *Making Men*, p. 233.

30 J. Phillips, 'Sport and future Australasian cult' in Mangan and Nauright (eds) *Sport in Australasian Society*, p. 322. 'Black makes Kiwis proud and heart is the source of our passion. Put them together and it sends out the wrong messages'. Auckland journalist quoted, *Guardian*, 7 October 2002.

31 On a definition of globalisation pertinent to its impact upon rugby union, see B. Hutchins and M. Phillips, 'The global union: globalization and the Rugby World Cup' in Chandler and Nauright (eds.) *Making the Rugby World*, pp. 150–1.

32 B. Keane, '"Ex-pats' and "Poofters" rebuild the nation: 1982, Kiwi culture and the All Whites on the road to Spain' in Patterson (ed.) *Sport, Society and*

Culture in New Zealand, pp. 49–60; G.M. Robinson, R.J. Loughran and P. J. Tranter, *Australia and New Zealand Economy, Society and Environment*, London: Arnold, 2000, pp. 185–6; R. Hay, 'Croatia: community, conflict and culture: the role of soccer clubs in migrant identity', *Immigrants and Minorities*, 1998, vol. 17, 49–66. Re: Sky's two initiatives in Auckland, note the contrast between the public perception and the consequent popularity of the Football Kings (perpetual losers) and the Warriors (potential winners). Interview with John Graham, University of Waikato, 4 April 2002.

33 Nauright, 'Sustaining masculine hegemony: rugby and the nostalgia of masculinity', p. 232.

34 On Freeman as a role model for Native Australian sportswomen, see Hargreaves, *Heroines of Sport*, pp. 123–8.

35 Cashman, *Paradise of Sport*, pp. 106–7. Nor was the flow of innovative elite coaching all one way, witness top Australian squash players relocating to Auckland.

36 Ros Kelly quoted in W. Vamplew, 'Australians and Sport', p. 5. For an expatriate historian's alternative description: 'East Germany *sans* steroids'. R. McKibbin, 'Class, politics, money: British sport since the First World War', *Twentieth Century British History*, 2002, vol. 13 (2), 200.

37 B. Houlihan, *Sport, Policy and Politics A Comparative Analysis*, London: Routledge, 1997, pp. 68–71

38 Cashman, *Paradise of Sport*, pp. 118–20; T. Magdalinski, 'The reinvention of Australia for the Sydney 2000 Olympic Games' in Mangan and Nauright (eds) *Sport in Australasian Society*, pp. 305–22. On popular perception of Melbourne 1956, see P. Cliff (ed.) *A Sporting Nation Celebrating Australia's Sporting Life*, Canberra: National Library of Australia, 1999, pp. 1–8.

39 1956–64 saw Dawn Fraser break 39 individual or team world records, and win four gold and four silver Olympic medals, and six gold and two silver Empire and Commonwealth medals.

40 1950–68 saw Australian men win 32 Grand Slam singles titles and the Davis Cup 15 times (and runners up on four occasions). 1960–73 saw Margaret Court and Evonne Goolagong win Wimbledon on three and two occasions respectively, and the Australian Championships 11 and four.

41 1991 *Australian Sports Directory* data on participation cited in Vamplew, 'Australians and Sport', p. 13; Adair and Vamplew, *Sport in Australian History*, pp. 40–1, 108–10, and 137; Houlihan, *Sport, Policy and Politics*, p. 70.

42 On targeted investment within an overall strategy for Olympic success, see Houlihan, *Sport, Policy and Politics*, pp. 72–6.

43 New Zealand's first Labour Government tried to promote sporting participation pre-war, but the National Council of Sport proved ineffective, increasingly handing the initiative to local authorities after 1945. Not until 1973 was the Council of Recreation and Sport, accountable to a minister, established. The NZ Sports Foundation was incorporated in 1978. The Hillary Commission acquired full statutory authority as a crown agency in 1992.

44 *Report of the Hillary Commission for Recreation and Sport for the year ended 31 March 1988*, Wellington: Government of New Zealand, 1988, pp. 5–16.

45 *Hillary Commission*, 1988, pp. 5–16.

46 *Hillary Commission*, 1989, p. 7.

47 *Hillary Commission*, 1990, pp. 21 and 3.

48 *Hillary Commission*, 1992, p. 10; *Getting Set – For an Active Nation*, Report of the Sport, Fitness & Leisure Ministerial Taskforce, Wellington: Government of New Zealand, January 2001, Part 2. Online.

49 Even in 1984, when no less than eight golds were won, it was thanks to the canoeists and rowers matching a double victory in the yachting.

50 *Hillary Commission*, 1993, pp. 18–19.
51 Given their past record, rowing and canoeing were notable omissions. Equestrianism, since the 1950s one of New Zealand's most successful sports on the world stage, was not surprisingly left to rely on commercial sponsorship. Women's softball became the eighth academy in 1994.
52 The case for funding the All Whites was made that much more difficult by recruiting a former All Black, Wilson Whinary, to chair the Commission.
53 *Hillary Commission*, 1994, pp. 23–7. In 1993–94 the Commission spent approximately $NZ4 million in total on international sport, of which around two-thirds went on direct or indirect support for elite athletes and coaches.
54 *Hillary Commission*, 1995, pp. 24–8.
55 New Zealand Olympic Committee, 'New Zealand's Summer Olympic History in Brief'. Online. Available http://www.olympic.org.nz (18 July 2002).
56 In 1956 67 nations competed in 17 sports, and in 2000 199 nations competed in 28 sports. Australia secured 14 bronze medals in Melbourne and 17 in Sydney, and the ratio of overall male:female medal winners was 22:13 and 36:22 respectively. Australian Sports Commission, 'Sport Information: Australian Olympic Medal Tally'. Online. Available http://www.ausport.gov.au/info/Factsheets/ausolymw (18 July 2002).
57 National anticipated that an All Black triumph in the 1999 World Cup would boost its chances of success in the subsequent general election. At Twickenham *Les Bleus* memorably blew that strategy apart, to Labour's ultimate advantage.
58 *Getting Set – For an Active Nation*, Report of the Sport, Fitness & Leisure Ministerial Taskforce, January 2001, Executive Summary. Online. Available http://www.executive.govt.nz/minister/mallard/sflreview/taskforce/summary; www.sparc.org.nz (31 July 2002).
59 *Getting Set*, Executive Summary.
60 New Zealand Academy of Sport website. Online. Available http://www.nzas. org.nz (5 August 2002). The 2002 Commonwealth Games 'big four': Australia, England, India, and Canada.
61 Jarvie, 'Sport, nationalism and cultural identity', p. 79; J. Hill, *Sport, Leisure and Culture in 20th-century Britain*, Basingstoke: Palgrave, 2002, p. 14.
62 McPhee, 'An Australian view of New Zealand', pp. 289–92.
63 Adair and Vamplew, *Sport in Australian Society*, p. 141; M. Cronin and D. Mayall, 'Sport and ethnicity: some introductory remarks', *Immigrants and Minorities*, 1998, vol. 17, p. 9.
64 C. Laidlaw, 'Sport and national identity', p. 15.
65 Laidlaw, 'Sport and national identity: Race relations, business, professionalism', in Patterson (ed.), *Sport, Society and Culture in New Zealand*, p. 15.
66 G. Ryan, 'Nostalgia, rural mythology and New Zealand rugby in the professional era', British Society of Sports History annual conference, 14 April 2002, and 'Rural myth and urban actuality: the anatomy of All Black and New Zealand rugby 1884–1938', *New Zealand Journal of History*, 2002, vol. 35, 45–69.
67 J. Phillips, 'The hard man: rugby and the formation of male identity in New Zealand', in Nauright and Chandler (eds) *Making Men*, pp. 70–90, and 'Rugby, war and the mythology of the New Zealand male', *New Zealand Journal of History*, 1984, vol. 18, pp. 83–103. Phillips' ideas on the centrality of rugby to a 'rural pioneering mythology' have been challenged by Greg Ryan [see note 66], and M. MacLean, 'Of warriors and blokes', pp. 1–26, and 'Football as social critique', pp. 256–7.
68 *Guardian*, 12 October 2002.
69 Belich, *Paradise Reforged*, pp. 386–8.
70 On the 'recolonisation' thesis, see Belich, *Paradise Reforged*, pp. 543–9, and

H. Richards, 'Dynamic, frenzied, vigorous – it must be the Kiwis', *Times Higher Educational Supplement*, 13 September 2002.

71 On the economic and social consequences of 'Rogernomics' [Roger Douglas: Labour's Treasurer and neo-liberal strategist], and the Australian parallels, see Robinson *et al.*, *Australia and New Zealand Economy, Society and Environment*, pp. 195–207, 251–55.

72 Belich, *Paradise Reforged*, p. 548.

73 For a detailed comparative study with Australia, see P. Dalziel, 'New Zealand's economic reforms: an assessment', *Review of Political Economy*, 2002, vol. 14, 31–46.

74 *Guardian*, 9 March 2002; S. Jones, 'Tug of War', *Rugby World*, October 2002.

Index